Esotericism, Art, and Imagination

Esotericism, Art, and Imagination

Edited by
Arthur Versluis, Lee Irwin, John Richards, and Melinda Weinstein

Michigan State University Press
East Lansing

The paper used in this publication meets the minimum requirements of ANSI/NISO
Z39.48-1992 (R 1997) (Permanence of Paper).

Michigan State University Press
East Lansing, Michigan 48823-5245

Printed and bound in the United States of America.

14 13 12 11 10 09 08   2 3 4 5 6 7 8 9 10   [6.08]

LIBRARY OF CONGRESS CATALOGING-IN-PUBLICATION DATA

Esotericism, art, and imagination / edited by Arthur Versluis ... [et al.].
    p. cm.
 Includes bibliographical references and index.
 ISBN 978-0-87013-819-5 (alk. paper)
 1. Occultism in art. 2. Imagination. 3. Arts, Modern. I. Versluis,
Arthur, 1959-
NX650.O33E86 2008
700'.477—dc22

                              2007038513

Cover image courtesy of the University of Glasgow Library, from the Ferguson MS
6, fol. 4 v. Other images courtesy of the Biblioteca del Museu Correr, Venice, Italy,
Special Collections Department, University of Glasgow Library, Special Collections of
the University of Michigan Library, the British Library, the Victoria College Library of
the University of Toronto, and Robyn Neild, illustrator of "Hex and the City." We thank
Duke University Press for permission to republish Victoria Nelson's "Faux Catholic"
from boundary 2, and the journal Tyr for permission to republish Joscelyn Godwin's
"Esotericism Without Religion." A slightly different version of Lance Gharavi's "Hex and
the City: Spells for Late Capitalism," was published in PAJ: A Journal of Performance and
Art 28(2006)3.

Michigan State University Press is a member of the Green Press Initiative and is committed to
developing and encouraging ecologically responsible publishing practices. For more information
about the Green Press Initiative and the use of recycled paper in book publishing, please visit www.
greenpressinitiative.org.

Visit Michigan State University Press on the World Wide Web at:
www.msupress.msu.edu

Contents

Introduction

Part I

Throughout the centuries, what has become known as *esotericism* has had a profound influence on the development of Western culture. This influence can be seen in everything from the works of Mozart to Arvo Pärt in music, Hieronymus Bosch to Salvador Dali in art, Shakespeare to Umberto Eco in literature, and William Butler Yeats to Allen Ginsburg in poetry, to name but a few. One need only to examine the life and works of such great thinkers as G. W. F. Hegel, Isaac Newton, and Carl Jung to see how esotericism has affected the development of philosophy and the sciences. The extent to which esotericism permeates popular culture is readily apparent in the proliferation of such things as New Age beliefs and practices, New Religious Movements and alternative medicines, as well as numerous best-selling books and blockbuster movies. When considered as a whole, the influence of esotericism on our way of life and thinking has been so great that the scholar of gnosticism Giles Quispel proposed the idea that faith, reason, and gnosis form the three basic components of the Western cultural tradition.[1] Building on Quispel's distinction, Roelof van den Broek and Wouter Hanegraaff have claimed that Western esotericism in general deserves a place alongside Greek rationality and Biblical faith as one of the major currents in the development of Western culture.[2]

Even though the influence of Western esotericism pervades our culture, most people, academics and non-academics alike, have little understanding and knowledge about the meaning of this word and the range of subjects it embraces. This is largely because popular culture and the mass media have made terms like *esotericism*, the *occult*, and *the New Age* virtually synonymous with one another. For the most part, esotericism is portrayed as the antithesis of both scientific materialism and traditional Christianity. Only recently, with the increased interest in the "inner" teachings of Christianity has this perception begun to change. The word "esoteric" derives from the Greek *esoterikos*, and is a comparative form of *eso*, meaning "inner" or "within."   The first known appearance of the Greek adjective *esoterikos* is in Lucian of Samosata's *The Auction of Lives* written around 166 C.E. in reference to his claim that Aristotle had both "esoteric" [inner] and "exoteric" [outer] teachings.   The word later came to designate "the secret doctrines said to have been taught by Pythagoras to a select group of disciples, and, in general, to any teachings designed for or appropriate to an inner circle of disciples or initiates."[3] The term "esoteric" first appeared in English in Thomas Stanley's *History of Philosophy* published in 1655, whereas the noun "esotericism" (*l'ésotérisme*) first appeared in French in 1828.

From an academic perspective, esotericism, therefore, refers to alternative and marginalized religious movements and philosophies, which are characterized by their belief that the true knowledge of God, the universe, and humans can only be arrived at by special knowledge and personal spiritual experience. As such, the academic field of esoteric studies embraces, among others, the following areas of investigation: alchemy, astrology, Freemasonry, Gnosticism, Hermeticism, Kabbalah, magic, mysticism, Neoplatonism, new religious movements related to these currents, nineteenth, twentieth, and twenty-first century, occult movements, Rosicrucianism, theosophy, and witchcraft.

During the first half of the twentieth century several important studies were published on various aspects of esotericism. Wouter Hanegraaff, for example, cites Auguste Viatte's *Les sources occultes du Romantisme: Illuminisme, Théosophie 1770-1820* (1927) and Will-Erich Peuckert's *Pansophie: Ein Versuch zur Geschichte der weißen und schwarzen Magie* (1956) as early classic studies.[4] Likewise, Nicholas Goodrick-Clarke points out the importance of the Eranos Conferences in Switzerland and the contributions of scholars such as Carl Jung, Henry Corbin, Mircea Eliade, Gershom Scholem, Karl Kerenyi, and D. T. Suzuki.[5] Other scholars, including Ernst Cassirer, Eugenio Garin, Paul Kristeller, D. P. Walker, and Edgar Wind have also been noted for their early significant contributions to the study of esotericism. However, there seems to be a general consensus among scholars that the two major decisive points for the development of esoteric studies as an academic discipline occurred first in 1964 with the publication of Frances Yates's *Giordano Bruno and the Hermetic Tradition* and secondly in 1994 with the publication of Antoine Faivre's *Access to Western Esotericism*. Whereas Frances Yates paved the way for the study of Western esotericism as a subject in its own right, Antoine Faivre laid the foundation for the academic field of esoteric studies.

Frances Yates proposed that the origins of modern science were rooted in the Neoplatonism and Hermetic-Kabbabalistic traditions, which experienced a revival during the Renaissance. This thesis, which has become known as the "Yates paradigm," also stresses the key role that esotericism played on philosophy during that period. Today, although few scholars accept Yates's claims in their entirety, the connection that she demonstrated between the academically marginalized topic of esotericism and modern science and philosophy is generally regarded as the beginning of esoteric studies as an academic discipline. In 1994, Antoine Faivre, using an historical and typological approach, defined the following six basic characteristics of modern Western esoteric thought: [6]

1. Correspondences. The assumption that the various levels of the universe, both visible and invisible, are linked and interconnected by a series of correspondences.

2. Living Nature. The idea that the universe is a complex entity imbued with a living energy.

3. Imagination and Mediations. The idea that esoteric knowledge is acquired by symbolic visual imagination and meditation upon such things as the correspondences.

4. The experience of transmutation. The idea of metamorphosis or the assumption that both natural substances and humans can be transmuted from their original base states to more refined or spiritual states.

5. Praxis of the Concordance. The assumption that the various esoteric traditions over-lap and are connected by a common denominator.

6. Transmission. The idea that esoteric knowledge is conveyed or passed on from an initiate to a disciple.

The major criticism of Faivre's typological approach is that it is tautological and, as such, exclusionary.[7] The criticism is that by drawing primarily on Renaissance Hermeticism to formulate his criteria, Faivre's taxonomy includes only those areas of esotericism that have traits of Renaissance Hermeticism. In other words, this approach is historically limited, and could potentially exclude some ancient, non-Western, or modern currents of esoteric thought. Whether or not one agrees or disagrees with Faivre's characteristics, the importance of his work cannot be denied. Essentially, Faivre constructed a theoretical framework that serves as a guide for the comparative study of esoteric currents. Even a cursory examination of the works of many scholars, including Wouter Hanegraaff and Arthur Versluis, will reveal a major indebtedness to Faivre's research.

In addition to increased amount of research, the field of esoteric studies, as a new academic discipline, has really begun to take off over the past fifteen years. During this time the field has witnessed the establishment of academic chairs and graduate degree programs in prestigious universities (the Sorbonne, the University of Amsterdam, and the University of Exeter), the creation of peer-reviewed journals and book series (*Esoterica*, *Aries*, and *Gnostika* journals; the *SUNY Western Esoteric Tradition* series, the University of Pennsylvania's *Magic in History* series and *Witchcraft and Magic in Europe* series, and Peeters Publishing's *Gnostica* series); the development of professional organizations and international conferences (Association for the Study of Esotericism, European Society for the Study of Western Esotericism, Societas Magica, and the Center for Studies on New Religions); as well as the publication of both a dictionary and two textbooks on Western esotericism.[8] As the first book published by the Association for the Study of Esotericism, this volume represents another milestone in the establishment of esoteric studies as an academic discipline.

As with any new academic discipline, the field of esoteric studies is not without its problems and controversies. At such an early stage in its development there are still issues with definition, disagreements about the demarcation of the subject matter, and methodological issues. For example, no consensus has been arrived at among scholars concerning the credibility and role of the practitioner/believer in research. Perhaps the greatest concern facing this new field is acceptance by the established academic community.

However, one only need examine the history and development of consciousness studies to see a similar situation. Thirty years ago the emerging field of consciousness studies was marginalized and ridiculed by much of the academic world. Today, consciousness studies is one of the fastest growing and most exciting fields of intellectual inquiry. With the importance of its subject matter and its combination of seasoned scholars and young bright minds the same will be said about esoteric studies in the not too distant future.

John D. Richards
West Virginia State University

Notes

1. For a discussion of Gilles Quispel's distinction between *faith, reason,* and *gnosis* see Wouter Hanegraaff, "On the Construction of 'Esoteric Traditions" in Antoine Faivre and Wouter Hanegraaff, eds., *Western Esotericism and the Science of Religion.* Gnostica 2, (Leuven: Peeters, 1998), 11-61.

2. See Roelof van den Broek and Wouter Hanegraaff, eds., *Gnosis and Hermeticism: From Antiquity to Modern Times.* (Albany: SUNY Press, 1998), vii-x.

3. Arthur Versluis, *Magic and Mysticism: An Introduction to Western Esotericism,* (Lanham, MD: Rowman & Littlefield, 2007), 1-2, and see also Association for the Study of Esotericism, http://www.aseweb.org

4. Wouter Hanegraaff, "Introduction." In Antoine Faivre and Wouter Hanegraaff, eds., *Western Esotericism and the Science of Religion.* Gnostica 2, (Leuven: Peeters, 1998), ix.

5. Nicholas Goodrick-Clarke. "Preface." In Kocku von Stuckrad, *Western Esotericism: A Brief History of Secret Knowledge.* (London: Equinox Publishing Ltd, 2005), viii.

6. Antoine Faivre initially presented his first four characteristics in 1992 in Antoine Faive and Jacob Needleman, eds., *Modern Esoteric Spirituality,* (New York: Crossroads, 1992), xv-xx.

7. Arthur McCalla, "Antoine Faivre and the Study of Esotericism," *Religion* 31 (2001): 435-50.

8. Wouter Hanegraaff, *Dictionary of Gnosis and Western Esotericism,*

(Leiden: Brill Academic, 2006). For textbooks see Kocku von Stuckrad, *Western Esotericism: A Brief History of Secret Knowledge,* (London: Equinox, 2005) and Arthur Versluis, *Magic and Mysticism: An Introduction to Western Esotericism.* (Lanham, MD: Rowman & Littlefield, 2007).

Introduction

Part II

The last decade of the twentieth century and the first decade of the twenty-first inaugurated a new era in the study of the interdisciplinary and transdisciplinary field now known as "esotericism." For the first time, a number of academic groups and institutions in Europe, England, Australia, Asia, and North America—indeed, around the globe—began to host scholarly conferences and to offer academic courses that touched or even focused on the history and significances of esoteric religious groups, works, and individuals. In 2002, a group of scholars from North America founded the Association for the Study of Esotericism (ASE), which hosted biannual international conferences thereafter, alternate years featuring conferences of the European Society for the Study of Western Esotericism (ESSWE). One recurrent theme during the ASE conferences was the way in which esoteric religious traditions intersect with, influence, or manifest themselves in artistic and literary works. The volume you hold, *Esotericism, Art, and the Imagination*, emerged out of the first two conferences of the ASE, and reveals the range and the complex ways that esoteric themes and subjects figure in and inspire works of the imagination.

Although esotericism can be studied or discussed as an abstract phenomenon—and from time to time, theoretical and methodological reorientation is no doubt useful—nonetheless, what is esoteric manifests itself in particularities, that is, in specific individuals, groups, and works. Indeed, that is much of the attraction of this field of study: one is engaged in mapping new specific territory, exploring historical and contemporary areas that once, perhaps under the influence of heresiophobia, had been marked off as *terra incognita*, but that now is available for scholarly investigation. One can see in this collection that each scholar has investigated how one or more currents of Western esotericism influenced particular artists or authors, some well known, others less so. Only when we step back from the individual articles here do we begin to see how they interconnect and form a larger tapestry.

This anthology is unusually rich both in depth and in scope. Its thematic organization offers insight into the complex ways that esoteric traditions or currents of thought appear not only in classical works, but also in contemporary films and television shows, in the works of William Blake, in the fiction of D.H. Lawrence, and also in the works of a contemporary British novelist, Philip Pullman. Its subjects range from the plays of Euripides to nineteenth-century spirit photography to the drawings, paintings, and writings of twentieth-century artist Cecil Collins. Even esoteric gardens are represented here.

The thematic sections in this collection also can be seen as areas for future conferences, and future anthologies—one could imagine a whole conference, symposium, or anthology devoted only to esoteric poetry, or even to esoteric poetry of only a certain period and region. What distinguishes esotericism from many other areas of study is just how many works, how many artists, authors, and filmmakers await discovery—we are, here, at the inception of a vast and remarkable field of study, with countless areas of specialization still to be pursued. These articles indicate the range and depth of this emerging field, and show how it is intimately linked to the humanities tradition that is itself also distinctively Western. Even though esotericism was for many years an untouched area of academic investigation, we now find that scholarship in this sphere sheds new light on the humanities traditions of the West more generally.

There are, of course, cultural reasons that Western esotericism has remained to some significant degree outside the purview of academic study until relatively recently. One reason is the inheritance of inquisitional or heresiophobic thinking in the West, which goes all the way back to late antiquity and to figures like Tertullian, who heaped ridicule on esoteric religious traditions in general, and on Christian esoteric traditions in particular. I discuss this phenomenon in *The New Inquisitions: Heretic-hunting and the Origins of Modern Totalitarianism*.[1] Another reason is the emergence of a technicist worldview, responsible for industrialism, which become synonymous with "modernity," but which also entailed the exclusion of esoteric currents like alchemy or mysticism. Gnosis remained the hidden "third pillar" of the West, eclipsed by its more well-known siblings, faith and reason. Only in the late twentieth and early twenty-first century did the gnostic currents of the West become the subject of scholarly investigation.

The reasons for this renaissance in scholarship—it is nothing less—are complex, and may well have to do with what more than one historian has called "the end of an epoch." It may be that the narrative we call "modernity" is giving way to a new historical period whose nature only will become clear in retrospect. Perhaps the narrative of "progress" that impelled so much of the nineteenth and twentieth centuries is breaking down, making possible the scholarly investigation of mostly uninvestigated areas, of which esotericism is certainly one. But in any case, and whatever the reasons, ours is an exciting time for those who are drawn to the study of esotericism.

Esotericism, in our technical-industrial era, has much in common with art and literature. In all three, the imagination has a central role. The imagination, in Christian and Jewish theosophy, as in Islamic esotericism, is held to be a faculty central to the life of the soul. Of course there are distinctions to be made between visionary experiences and literary or artistic visions, and yet one has to wonder whether these all belong to a continuum. A Platonist might suggest that some poets, authors of fiction, and artists perceive and portray aspects of what the visionary sees in a more intense and extended way—indeed, this is very much along the lines of what British artist Cecil Collins did say. Imagination, after all, is the medium of translation from the realm of consciousness to the visibly realized work of art, be it theater, film, poetry, fiction, painting, alchemical engravings, or some other form.

The study of esotericism is only in its initial phase: intrepid explorers are moving out, investigating the nature of the terrain, mapping new aspects of history and different ways to understand not only religion, but also culture, and in particular, art (including film) and literature. Each of these chapters is the fruit of an individual investigation that requires an unusual degree of wider erudition, and that in turn contributes to the knowledge of all the others who seek to explore how esoteric religious currents intersect with and inspire artistic and literary works. In some respects, this book is the culmination of much work, but it also should be seen as an auspicious beginning. We hope that you enjoy and find stimulating this collection of diverse works in this new and exciting field, and we look forward to more such volumes in the future, as our series continues.

Arthur Versluis
Michigan State University

Notes

1. Arthur Versluis, *The New Inquisitions: Heretic-hunting and the Origins of Modern Totalitarianism*, (New York: Oxford University Press, 2006).

Esotericism, Art, and Imagination

Esoteric Theaters

Theater and Initiation: Euripides' *Bacchae*

Melinda Weinstein

Of the drama of the classical period, Euripides' *Bacchae* is surely the most esoteric in its depiction of initiation and initiates, failed initiates in the case of Pentheus and Agave, and successful initiates in the Bacchants, the women who worship and follow Dionysus to Thebes. As a drama that stages the sacred practices of a Mystery cult, the *Bacchae* also conceals and exposes to view experiences reserved to the initiate. Euripides publicizes, if elliptically, features of ritual initiations, but most likely, as Richard Seaford has argued, to an audience who perceives these allusions "depending on their degree of religiosity."[1] Euripides' play well represents Mircea Eliade's notion of myth as depicting an originary act *in illo tempore*—"in that time."[2] He presents Pentheus's conflict with Dionysus and the establishment of his mysteries as it happened *the first time*, so that it becomes a precedent and model for all future rituals in later times. The play also harks back, Seaford suggests, to tragic performance in its most rudimentary phase, before it emerges from the dithyramb, a Dionysiac cult hymn.[3] Tragedy comes into being when the sacred processional stands in one place, and individual speakers are separated from the *thiasos*, the band of initates who worship the god. The dithyrambic quality of the choral songs in the *Bacchae*, in that they celebrate the god's life, death and rebirth shows Euripides incorporating the origins of tragedy into a modern, fifth century production.

It is my intention here to look more particularly into the experience and language of the *thiasos* in the play against two contemporaneous backdrops: the actual cult practice of the late fifth century B.C.E., and the City Dionysia, the public, five-day festival in Athens in which the play was originally performed. I am joining the insights of Richard Seaford, especially that the theme of the *Bacchae* concerns initiation into the *thiasos*, with John Winkler's

5

suggestive hypothesis that the choral singers in Athenian dramas were ephebes, young men between eighteen and twenty-one, in hoplite military training, who, through their performance in the chorus, are being "initiated into civic masculinity."[4] I am viewing the songs of the *thiasos* against darkness and light, against the dark, secret, initiations of the mystery cult, and then in the bright daylight of the five-day Athenian festival. I am subjecting the text to double exposure, so to speak, in order to survey the implications of the theme of initiation in the play in both contexts at once.

In regards to the Mysteries, witnessing is the central act of initiation. It is also the central act of the spectator at the Dionysia, the actor on stage, and the character the actor inhabits. Myth aside, Euripides subjects actor, spectator, and character to an experience, just as the hierophant subjects the initiate to an experience, and Dionysus subjects Pentheus to an experience. The conditions of the Dionysia, like the conditions of an initation, compel participation on the spectator's part. For Winkler and others in the seminal work on the social context of Athenian drama, *Nothing to Do With Dionysos?*, the purpose of the Dionysia is to erase tribal distinctions, and to promote a sense of unity among Athenian men. In the rituals then, that frame the actual witnessing of the plays, the individual becomes submerged in the collective. All initiations, world over, transform the initiate into something else. In the *Bacchae*, transformation abounds: the god becomes human, the god becomes an animal, humans become animals, men become women, women become men, the old become young, madness becomes sanity, sanity becomes madness, but most importantly, in terms of this discussion, the skeptical become believers.

The Dionysian Mysteries

Richard Seaford's study, "Dionysiac Drama and the Dionysiac Mysteries," lays the foundation for any exploration of the *Bacchae* and its relation to the Dionysian Mysteries, as it reviews all the extant primary sources relating to the Mysteries. As Seaford observes, we do not know much about the Mysteries of Dionysus, and most of what we know is drawn from the Euripides' play, and from later sources in the Hellenistic and Roman periods. Seaford, nevertheless, finds it likely that the later sources, namely Plutarch and Demetrius, accurately report what occurred in the late fifth century. For example, more is known about the Eleusinian mysteries. Because to its initiates, the rites and symbols of a mystery in its original state are precious, its rites remain relatively stable over time. The original manner and method of worship in the case of the Eleusinian and Dionysian Mysteries will stay relatively stable over a number of generations because of the personal and immediate way the rites are transmitted. In brief, it is generally thought that 1) the initiate into the *thiasos* achieves good fortune. 2) The initiate gains knowledge through the transmission of a divine secret or doctrine. 3) The hierophant may lead the initiate with riddling language to a central event. 4) The central event involves the assimilation of the initiate to Dionysus; the initiate becomes Dionysus. 5) The initiate loses his fear of death and secures a blessed afterlife. 6) The initiation involves shuddering and terror and a transformation from "miserable confusion to happy enlightenment." 7) The transformation of the initiate from the fear to happiness has generally been thought to mean that that the initiate undergoes a ritual death, or a descent into an underworld or afterlife. 8) Something is seen that causes the transformation "from misery to happiness." This is generally thought to be a light. 9) The initiate wears a linen kiton, a funeral garment.

The last feature of the mysteries, 10) *sparagmos* and *omophagia*, the rending apart of an animal, and the consumption of its raw flesh, requires more than a cursory glance here. In the *Bacchae*, the experience of the Theban women on the mountain is very different from the experience of the women in the *thiasos*, who sing hymns and perform strictly synchronized dances in rectangular formation. Agave, and the Theban women have been "stung into madness"(33).[5] They are clearly being punished. Their participation in *sparagmos* and *omophagia* is part of their punishment. But Seaford unequivocally states that *sparagmos* and *omophagia* is part of contemporary ritual. If this is so, it is most likely a much tamer affair, an attenuated version of what Euripides imagines in his play because Euripides is interested in *illo tempore*, the first time, that becomes the precedent for all later rituals. The primary text from which Seaford draws, the Miletus text, from the later Hellenistic period, indicates that strips of meat were involved in the women's rites, and the text instructs the initiates that only the leading priestess may throw the first strip of meat on behalf of the city. [6] The meat is provided, and the women toss it as a commemorative gesture. They are commemorating the initial rejection of Dionysus by the sisters of Semele, in a context that appropriately acknowledges the divinity of the god.

I would like to assert here that the City Dionysia is the means by which *men* worshipped Dionysus in classical Athens. It is a vexed question, but current scholarship suggests that it is unlikely that many women attended the plays. On the other hand, the mountain rites, the *oreibasia*, or mountain festival honoring Dionysus is strictly for women. Indeed, the *Bacchae*, can be interpreted as a warning to men not to spy on the women's rites, as the city-dweller's attempt to capture Agave spurs the women to horrific violence, and Pentheus's gruesome death is punishment for spying on the women as well.

Euripides sympathizes with women in all of his work, and the *Bacchae* is no exception. He honors alongside Dionysus in the choral songs, the earth-goddess Cybele, Aphrodite, the Muses, and the River Dirke, and Tiresias praises Demeter as equal and counterpart to Dionysus in her gift of grain to the world. Pentheus embodies the converse attitude toward women. Pentheus sees the source of all his troubles to be with women (787). We can glean from his vitriolic reaction to the women's exodus from the city, and his general distrust and suspicion toward women that in Thebes, women are confined indoors. His persistent belief that they are engaging in lewd and filthy sex acts on the mountain, even after he is informed otherwise by a witness, shows that his belief is actually a fantasy of what he thinks is going on the mountain. And given the male audience of the Dionysia, perhaps Pentheus is giving voice to the imaginings of all men when they imagine women, liberated from the confines of domesticity, engaging in a secret rite: "Darkness is just a filthy trap for women" (487), Pentheus says. If Euripides is testing the social structure here, as much of tragic drama does in the classical age, he may be leveling a critique of paternalistic attitudes and behavior toward women in Athens.

Seaford goes so far as to claim that the Dionysian and the

Eleusinian mysteries were originated by women, and that their fifth century form are the later vestiges of puberty rites. He describes the devolution as follows: "There is a well-known tendency for *Pubertätsweihen* to become, with the development of society, socially marginal, and thereby to change their function: the group into which they effect initiation is no longer the whole adult community but the secret society or the shadowy community of the next world. Among the products of this process, in Greece, seem to be the Eleusinian and the Dionysiac mysteries."[7] When Pentheus demands of Dionysus that he tell him about the rituals of the *oreibasia*, Dionysus replies, "They may not be revealed to those who are not Bacchants," meaning, to those who are not *women*. It is only after Pentheus is disguised, or rather transformed to a woman that he may attend the festival. Dionysus's response, though, has particular import given the male audience of the City Dionysia. The attendees of the City Dionysia are likewise, along with Pentheus, prohibited knowledge of the rituals. Euripides acknowledges the *oreibasia*, but its details are not profaned. Finally, in support of my thesis that the worship of Dionysus took on distinct forms for men and for women in the classical era and that in the *Bacchae* Euripides is honoring and guarding the rites of the *oreibasia*, Seaford traces an increasing demand among men for initiation into the *thiasoi* after the classical period. He writes:

It seems that the marginalization of the *Pubertätsweihen* had left the ancient public *thiasoi*, for example largely in the hands of women. However, there is evidence in the historical period for a growing demand for the Dionysiac mysteries among men, which found expression partly in the initiation of men into the female *thiasoi* (e.g. of the three *thiasoi* publicly founded in Magnesia in the early third century B.C. by three maenads from Thebes at least one, the καταβάται, must have included men) and partly in the growth of the private mysteries (for example we know that the Dionysiac mysteries introduced from Greece to Italy and suppressed in 186 BC were at first confined to women but later opened to men as well.[8]

9

If women worship Dionysus during the *Oreibasia* and men worship the god during the City Dionysia, initiation into the Mysteries is another matter. Dionysus characterizes himself as setting various Asiatic nations "dancing ... so that mortals would see me clearly as divine" (22-23). And as Seaford has shown, the Bacchae, in terms of plot, alludes in many ways to the features of initation, for men and women, outlined above. Pentheus's disturbed excitement at the beginning of the play may mirror similar anxieties in the initiate. His failed attempt to imprison Dionysus in the dark stable, his fruitless struggle against the god who has transformed himself into a bull, his rushing back and forth to put out the fire caused by Dionysus, resembles in detail the experiences of the initiates in the Eleusinian Mysteries as described by Plutarch and outlined by Seaford. Dionysus's description of himself as an onlooker calmly observing Pentheus's wrestling with the bull may also have its origin in ritual. Most pointedly, when Dionysus emerges from captivity, his joyful *thiasos* describes him as a "great light" (608). Pentheus's pointed rejection of this light in this scene, and his failure to bind the illusory bull shows that he is a failed initiate. Seaford observes that Pentheus's experience forms an "unmistakable antithesis to those of the god's followers. He embodies not only the ordeals of the initiand, but also, as the god's enemy, the negation of the desired ritual process. He rejects and attacks even the light in the darkness, and persists in his hostile and confused ignorance."[9]

Seaford also describes a ritual called "Carrying out Death and Bringing in the Summer," documented by Frazer and Mannart. This practice has been related to puberty rites where young people are initiated as adults into the community. Seaford shows that it has an "unmistakable parallel to Pentheus's destiny." He writes, "in this ritual, a figure is dressed as a woman, carried through the village for all to see, perched on top of a tree, pelted with sticks and stones, and then torn to pieces. The head of the figure is carried back to the village on a thyrsus and and then affixed to the triglyph of the house."[10] After killing her son, Agave describes Pentheus's head as a "hero trophy" that she has brought to Cadmus so that he can hang it on his house (1240). The sequence of Pentheus's initiation: *pompe, agon and komos*, procession, struggle and triumphal return, although in Pentheus's case, the return is ironic, is a well-known ritual structure directly connected to the City Dionysia.

The City Dionysia

It is in relatively recent times that scholars have been considering how ancient audiences might have perceived and experienced the drama of the classical period. When the *Bacchae* is considered in its original, ritual context—as part of the City Dionysia, a yearly spring festival in Dionysus's honor, performed in the Theater of Dionysus, on the sacred ground of the Acropolis—the *Bacchae* takes on added epiphanic, transformative, and initiatory dimensions. The Dionysia itself is structured as an elaborate network of rituals that override a modern distinction between actor and audience. Every male citizen participates to some extent in a "procession, sacrifice, and celebration," (*pompe, agon, komos*). This is a structure typical of fifth century Athenian religious practice.[11] Every male citizen is part of the drama, on stage to each other and to the gods. As the chorus of the *Bacchae* puts it, "Far away, the sky dwellers,/ heavenly powers, may be;/ but they are watching us (393-395). Indeed, in a sacrifice, and in a festival, and the two most important festivals in Athens were the Panathenaia, and the City Dionysia, the point is to "put on a good show" for the gods.[12] In respect to the *Bacchae*, the motive for the festival parallels in an inverse manner the plot of the drama. The City Dionysia is established in 515 BC by the Athenians as atonement for initially rejecting the divinity of the god. When Dionysus announces, "Ἥκω," I am here, "Διος παῖς," child of god, the first utterance of the drama, we can only imagine from our vantage point the exaggerated resonance of this statement for the original audience, given the setting. Likewise Dionysus's insistence, five times in the Prologue, in the space of sixty lines, that he be seen by the people of Thebes reinforces the piety of the Athenian people who are literally worshipping him through the act of watching. Dionysus states, "I must defend my mother Semele and *make people see that I am a god*, born by her to Zeus" (2). He has come back to his origins after starting initiations in the east, "so that mortals would *see me* clearly as divine" (2). And Since Pentheus "shoves" Dionysus from the libations he makes to the other gods,

11

or rather, *"pays no attention,"* to Dionysus in his prayers, Dionysus will *"show him/I am truly a god, and I'll show the Thebans too"* (3). Once he has put Thebes "in order," he claims, by initiating them into his mysteries, then he will *"reveal"* himself in another country. At the end of the Prologue, Dionysus instructs his Bacchae to *"Take up the drums...and surround the royal home of Pentheus, and strike./ Make the city of Cadmus take notice"* (61).

Dionysus addresses Thebes by name four times in sixty lines, and twice more as "the city of Cadmus." Euripides is making it clear that Athens is not Thebes. Euripides sets the foundational myth of the City Dionysia, the rejection of Dionysus by Athens, in Thebes, because Thebes, as Froma Zeitlin has argued, "provides in Attic tragedy, the negative model to Athens's manifest image of itself with regard to its notions of the proper management of city, society and self."[13] That Dionysus demands that the Thebans see him as a god only affirms, that the people of Athens are seeing him as a god; they are making libations to Dionysos, literally within the context of the Dionysia.

As Winkler and others have persuasively argued, the City Dionysia is a civic event that celebrates and reinforces the cohesion of the polis. As Winkler outlines, the festival opens with a reënactment of Dionysus's initial advent into Athens by priests, hoplites, citizens and foreigners, followed by twenty dithyrambic choruses, ten with fifty men, and ten with fifty boys in costume. The procession culminates in the sacrifice of a bull, conducted by the hoplites, and a feast. As Winkler shows, the orchestra of the theater of Dionysus is not just for plays but also for elaborate displays of civic pride. Before and between performances, war orphans maintained at the expense of the city, who at eighteen have entered the ephebate, parade in hoplite armor supplied by the city. The twenty choruses (one thousand men and boys) compete in dithyrambic dances, friends of the city receive crowns, and civic leaders display tribute paid by allies.

The seating arrangement in the Theater of Dionysus, especially, "displays the organization of the body politic in terms of tribal equality and of social hierarchy." It offers "a kind of map of civic corporation, with all its tensions and balances."[14] The citizens sit in tribal order, one tribe per wedge, with the central wedge belonging to the boule, or council, whose members are drawn from each tribe. The outer two wedges are for foreigners and possibly citizen wives, the front row for special benefactors of the city. At the City Dionysia, every male Athenian is an actor, on display to each other and to the gods. This exaggerates or heightens the initiatory atmosphere of the festival. For Oddone Longo, the rituals that constitute the immediate framework of the plays, the procession, sacrifice, celebration and the various displays that take place on the orchestra celebrate the polis and its ideology: "They are deliberately aimed at maintaining social identity and reinforcing the cohesion of the group."[15] For John Winkler, the whole festival has a kind of "civic military aura." Each tribe is "a military unit," he writes, "and the seating arrangement at the Dionysia is also the seating arrangement of the Ekkleisa, the Athenian Assembly, which met four times a month in the Pynx but sometimes in the theater."[16]

The *Bacchae*, produced in 406, after Euripides' death, wins best tragic drama of 406, I believe, precisely because of its exaggerated reverence. The play does its job of honoring the god, in a spectacular fashion, thereby conforming to and satisfying audience expectation. The play has been viewed as a hierophany, a revelation of Dionysus's power before various witnesses who function as surrogate viewers for the audience. Each event confirms Dionysus's power. "All in all," says the shepherd after witnessing the women's activities on the mountain, "if you'd been there and seen these things/you'd come praying to the god whom you condemned." "Great god revealed,' says the chorus after the news of Pentheus's death (1031). "If there is anyone who despises the divine," says Cadmus, viewing Pentheus's fragmented body, "he should look at this man's death and believe in the gods"(1325-1326). "This god, whoever he is," adds the shepherd, "you'd better accept him into our city. He has great power" (769-770).

The *Bacchae* represents the most ancient form of tragedy in which the chorus is a Dionysian *thiasos* and the theme of the play concerns initiation into the *thiasos*. The initiate attains to *eudaimonia*, good fortune, by becoming part of the *thisasos*. Mostly, they see and understand the god, while the uninititated do not. After all, the play

13

is called "Bacchae;" it is not "Pentheus" or "Dionysus."[17] It is about the experience of the thiasos. The chorus's experience of Dionysus is different from that of Pentheus, and different from the other group of women in the play, the women of Thebes who have been driven to Mt. Kitharion. Pentheus and the women on the mountain are being punished. They are not initiates at all. Indeed, I would say, their obdurate inability to see what is in front of their faces is anathema to the initiatory experience. As I state at the outset, Dionysian initiation is bound up with seeing the world as it is. In the *Bacchae*, Pentheus comes to see the world as it is only after he disguises himself as a woman and is willing to dance. Only after Pentheus willingly sacrifices his ego can Dionysus say, "now you see the world as you should." Pentheus's and Agave's inability to see what the chorus sees and what the audience sees is conspicuously made clear by Euripides, first when Pentheus demands that the god reveal himself, "He is where I am," replies Dionysus "you do not see him because you lack reverence," (502) and on Mt. Kithairon when Pentheus, pleading for his life, rips off his female disguise and Agave fails to recognize him.

The Thiasos

In The *Bacchae*, the members of the *thiasos* are foreign women from Asia who accompany Dionysus to Thebes, but in the context of the Dionysia, the actors pretending to be Bacchantes are ephebes, young men between eighteen and twenty years of age in their second year of hoplite military training. John Winkler, in a fascinating study of the central role of the ephebe within the city Dionysia, and the importance of the ephebe in Athenian culture in general, traces the etymology of the word tragedy, *tragos oida*, goat song, not to the sacrifice of a goat, generally considered to be the originary moment of all tragedy, but to *tragizdein*, which means the breaking or changing of voice which adolescent boys experience. The term *tragoidoi* then for Winkler is "a slightly jocular designation of ephebic singers, not because their voices were breaking (that was long past, and anyway no one can sing well whose voice is breaking) but because they were identified as those who were undergoing social puberty."

Winkler presents persuasive evidence that in tragic performance the chorus members were young men in military training. First, there is the physical demand of performing in three plays in a row, plus a satyr play, second, choral dancing, unlike circular dithyrambic dance, is performed in rectangular rank and file formation which is also the formation of hoplite maneuvers, and finally because extant images on vase paintings depict chorus members as youthful, without beards, while the actors the artists depict are clearly older with beards. "This allows us to sense a complex and finely controlled tension," Winkler argues, "between role and role-player, for the ephebes are cast in the most 'disciplined' part of the tragedy—disciplined in the exacting demands of unison movement, subordinated to the more prominent actors, and characterized as social dependents (women, slaves, old men)-while the actors, who are no longer ephebes, perform a tale showing the risks, the misfortunes and sometimes the glory of the ephebic experience."[18]

In the seating arrangement at the Dionysia as well, the ephebe has a special position. Since the central wedge behind the Boule may likely be for the ephebes, Winkler observes, "The central axis thus contains two kinds of tribal representative—citizen governors and citizens in training—whose competition is muted by their function as administrators and defenders of the polis as a whole." The entire festival then is organized principally for the benefit of the ephebe, whose performance in the festive proceedings: the processional reënactment of the advent of Dionysus, the sacrifice of the bull, as chorus actor, and as stage center spectator make him Dionysus's "chief acolyte."

The festival therefore provides, according to Winkler, "the occasion for elaborate symbolic play on themes of proper and improper civic behavior, in which the principle component of proper male citizenship was military. These lessons are directed to the young men of the city, who also compose the choruses." Thus, "The events and characters portrayed in tragedy are meant to be contemplated as lessons by young citizens (or better, the entire polis from the vantage point of the young citizen), and therefore it makes the watchful scrutiny of the chorus structurally important as a still center from which the tragic turbulence is surveyed and evaluated." In the context of the City Dionysia, "proper" civic behavior, here

15

the proper form of Dionysian worship involves transforming oneself through costume and role-playing. This causes the dissolution of the ego, and the submersion of oneself into the group. For the audience, Pentheus's hostile unwillingness to dress as a woman would have resonated as a pointed contrast to the ephebe's willingness to put on a costume and change his identity. The ephebe, like the female Bacchante he impersonates, is a successful initiate.

The thiasos, conforming to audience expectation and fulfilling the terms of the festival itself in honoring Dionysus, emphasizes the importance of a reverential attitude toward the gods in their songs. In their first choral entrance, after Dionysus's identification of himself and his intentions in Thebes, the *thiasos* sings a traditional dithyrambic hymn that praises Dionysus and recounts his miraculous second birth from the thigh of Zeus. Several times they call out for Thebes to make haste and join the Bacchae, and they elucidate Dionysus's characteristic features: he is the Thunderer, he delights in raw flesh, he incites women to dance. They are the spokeswomen for the traditional approach to the gods. "No god is greater than Dionysus," they exclaim after hearing of the terrible rites on the mountain. "Never hurried, never/failing, a god's/fist comes down on men who love to be hard-hearted,/ who hold back what is due to the gods/ in the madness of bad judgement" (882-887). They express outrage toward Pentheus's blasphemous behavior toward the god throughout the play, especially when he confronts Cadmus and Tiresias fitted out in Bacchic gear, heading for Mr. Kithairon to join the dance. Pentheus calls the rites on the mountain corrupt, and the choral leader, insulted, exclaims, "Sacrilege! Friend, have you no respect for the gods? (263). The intensity of their outrage increases until, in the fourth choral song, they call for his death, "Now Vengeance out in the open /Now Swordbearer, slice through his throat" (993-994). At the end of the play, they exult in Pentheus's death. When Cadmus defends his participation in the rites to Pentheus, he says, "I will not make war on Gods." The thiasos responds, "Old man, Apollo's not insulted by your claims;/ you are being sensible when you honor Dionysus,/ great god that he is" (327-329).

A recurring theme of the choral songs, which has always troubled me, but which makes perfect sense when viewed in the

16

light of the aims of the Dionysia, is that the *thiasos* repeatedly extols the benefits of submerging oneself in the group. The chorus decries ambition for wealth and power, and they promote being content with an ordinary life. The occasion of the Dionysia has a leveling effect on the normatively competitive relationships between tribes headed by military families in Classical Athens. They sing: "Wisdom? It's not wise/to lift our thoughts too high;/ we are human, and our time is short./ A man who aims at greatness/ will not live to own what he has now" (395-399). Dionysus "hates...men who stand out above others" (424,429). "What is ordinary," they chant, "what the crowd thinks right, is good enough for me"(430-432). "Many are the ways/ a man may surpass another/ in wealth or power,/ and beyond each hope there beckons another/ hope without number./ Hope may lead a man to wealth,/ hope may pass away;/but I admire the man when he/ is happy in an ordinary life"(905-911).

Significantly, the thiasos also expresses joy in participating in festivals. This can surely be viewed as commentary on the actual proceedings of the Dionysia. "O blessed are they," they sing in their first choral song, "who know in their happiness/ gods's initiations,/ live life in holiness,/ minds tuned to *festival*,/ dancing on mountaintops,/ sacred cleansing/ in honor of Bacchus"(70-75). Dionysus, they sing, "is first/ of all the blessed powers/ for joy at festivals" (376-378). When they describe Dionysus as "Divine, son of Zeus," who "rejoices in feasting," and who "loves Peace the blissgiver,/ cherisher of *young men*," surely the implications are not lost on the audience (417-420). The young men whom Peace and Dionysus love are the ephebes, the very men who are playing the female Bacchantes.

It is generally thought that the mysteries involved some sort of experience, or ritual that simulates the experience of death. The initiate sees a light in the darkness, which transforms the initiate from misery to happiness. The interaction of the chorus and Dionysus after they are imprisoned and magically released alludes to the experience of being intiated into the Dionysian mysteries. The thiasos are clearly depicted as successful initiates. After witnessing the palace collapse, the thiasos falls to the ground in fear. Dionysus exclaims, What frightened foreigners you women are/—down on the ground as if you had been struck!/ Don't you see—it was Bacchus who shook the house apart?/ Rise up take courage leave off trembling"(603-606). When the chorus cries out, "It's you. Our great light in dancing to Bacchus!/ How glad I am to see you! I was desolate, alone..."(608-609). They are manifesting the intiate's transformation from fear to gladness.

Conclusion: Dionysus

Aptly termed the god of paradox, Dionysus combines and transcends the categories through which the Greeks understand reality. In the *Bacchae*, he takes on the appearance of a priest of himself: he is both god and human; he is god and animal as Pentheus struggles with him in the form of a bull; Greek and Barbarian, born in Thebes but arrived from Asia; male and female, disturbingly androgynous—"pretty" to Pentheus; old, the peer of Demeter, goddess of grain, and yet a new god, demanding to be recognized. Tiresias observes that he is both manifest and hidden. Dionysus is the wine poured out and the god to whom the wine is poured. Significantly, Euripides embeds the first word of the drama, "Ἥκω,"in a context that emphasizes another paradox in Dionysus's nature. When Dionysus announces "Ἥκω," "I am here," he stands before the ruins of his mother's tomb, still smoldering from Zeus's lighting, but he has transformed it into a shrine by causing vines to grow "copious and green" around it. He destroys and renews. He will destroy the royal family, but he will also rid Thebes of a tyrant. Dionysus breaks free of prison, eludes Pentheus's ropes, topples the Theban palace. These events dramatize his indefinable nature, his inability to be contained. He is less than and more than the neat coincidence of opposites stated above. In essence, he is *no thing*. For the characters in the play, the actors, and the audience, the modality of knowing Dionysus represents in the drama is not-knowing; he disturbs Pentheus's reliance on the senses for perceiving the truth.

Pentheus is convinced that the law and order he has established for Thebes is the truth. Pentheus's truth, though, is an illusion, while Dionysus's illusions are the truth: panic on the battlefield, when *no thing*, but a heightened state of alarm causes a stampede. He is the god of prophecy, or foresight, the ability to gauge what is *not*

18

yet, and he is the god of wine, the *forgetting* of the self induced by intoxication, dance and the drum. Pentheus struggles in vain to pin down the phantom bull that he thinks is Dionysus, while Dionysus sits quietly in a chair watching. "I think he," meaning Bacchus, Dionysus explains to his followers, "created an image of me (*phasma*) in the courtyard," which Pentheus also attempts to cut down with his sword (629-630). When dragged off in chains by Pentheus's henchmen, Dionysus cries, "How do you live? What are you doing? Who are you? You don't know!" (506).   In his first encounter with the god, Pentheus cannot make rational sense of what he sees. But later, under Dionysus's spell, when Pentheus hallucinates two suns in the sky, and a bull leading him to the mountain in place of the god, Dionysus asserts that now, "you see things as you should" (924). He shows us the world as it is, as illusion, infinitely more fluid and dynamic than the rigid, seemingly substantive world we perceive through the senses. As such, his presence in Thebes upends the foundations of the palace, obviously a symbol of Pentheus's worldly power, and the attachment he displays to his position as king.

As god of transformation, costumes, the mask, the escape from subjectivity offered by the theater, wine, prophecy and mania, Dionysus in Euripides' *Bacchae* is the god of the *necessary* chaos that precedes renewal, just as the festival in which he is embedded overcomes competition between tribes and reinforces the cohesion of the polis as a whole. Dionysian ecstacy is borne out of wine and dance, and it requires submersion of the ego into the group. The tragic hero is the one who clings to his personality. Pentheus is tragic because of his attachment to his role as king. As much as Dionysus wants to be recognized as a god, Pentheus wants to be seen as a king. His attachment to his ego can be seen in his self-consciousness, his fear of being laughed at by the people of Thebes. Dionysus proves in Thebes that derangement, the forgetting of the self, the personality, is sanity, while sanity, attachment to the self and its personality, is derangement. Dionysus, in essence, is Death, the necessary chaos, the reversion to nothing, that must precede renewal and change.[19]

Finally, to upend the above equation in true Dionysian style, we must remember that Dionysus is the god who delights in raw goat flesh. How can we reconcile *omophagia* and *sparagmos*, whether exaggerated or attenuated, as typical features of his worship, alongside watching or acting in a play? I think the answer lies in a distinction I make at the beginning of this article between male and female forms of Dionysian worship in the late fifth century. If Dionysus's masculine aspect confounds reason, his female aspect is equally terrifying. His female aspect, the energy to feed, is what Joseph Campbell has called a "bioenergy," the essence of life itself, and which, when unbridled, becomes horrific, horrifying and destructive.[20] He calls this bioenergy, "the innocent voraciousness of life which feeds on lives." We see the bioenergy "most concretely in the image of the infant "feeding on its mother." Thus, we can understand Dionysus's earth-mother peers, and his female followers. Significantly, the failed initiates, the Theban women who are being punished, reflect this energy unbridled and horrific. They have abandoned their social roles to suckle snakes on Mt. Kithairon, and it is Agave, Pentheus's mother, who brutally rips him apart and offers his flesh as a "banquet" (1242).

Notes

1. Richard Seaford, "Dionysiac Drama and the Dionysiac Mysteries," *Classical Quarterly* 31(1981)2: 252.
2. Mircea Eliade, "Patterns in Comparative Religion," in *Transformations of Myth through Time*, Diane U. Eisenberg, et. al., eds., (Fort Worth: Harcourt Brace, 1990), 15.
3. Dithyrambs are processional hymns that concern the life, death, and rebirth of Dionysus. The elements of a dithyramb are "ornamental and compound epithets, verbal repetition, an unrestrained meter, a mythical narrative, and the themes of the double-birth of Dionysos," Seaford, 271.
4. John J. Winkler, "The Ephebes's Song: Tragoidia and Polis," in *Nothing to do with Dionysos?*, John J. Winkler and Froma Zeitlin, eds., (Princeton: Princeton University Press, 1990), 20-62.
5. Euripides, *Bacchae*, Paul Woodruff, trs. (Indianapolis: Hackett Publishing, 1998). All translations of Euripides' *Bacchae* drawn from this edition.

6. "Whenever the priestess performs the holy rites on behalf of the city...it is not permitted for anyone to throw pieces of meat [anywhere], before the priestess has thrown them on behalf of the city, nor is it permitted for anyone to assemble a band of maenads [thiasos] before the public thiasos [has been assembled]..." *Rule of ritual. Miletus.*276/B.C. (Sokolowski, LSAM 48, A. Henrichs, trs.). Source from Mary R. Lefkowitz and Maureen B. Fant, eds., *Women's Life in Greece and Rome* (Baltimore: John Hopkins University Press, 1982), 113.

7. Seaford, "Dionsyiac Drama and Dionysiac Mysteries," 264.

8. Ibid, 265.

9. Ibid, 258.

10. Ibid, 263.

11. Simon Goldhill, "The Great Dionysia," in *Nothing to Do With Dionysos?*, John J. Winkler and Froma Zeitlin, eds., (Princeton: Princeton University Press, 1990), 99.

12. Robert Parker, "Greek Religion," in *The Oxford History of the Classical World*, John Boardman, et al., eds. (Oxford: Oxford University Press, 1986), 264.

13. Froma Zeitlin, "Thebes: Theater of Self and Society in Athenian Drama," in *Nothing to Do With Dionysos?*, John J. Winkler and Froma Zeitlin, eds., (Princeton: Princeton University Press, 1990), 131.

14. Winkler, 38-39.

15. Oddone Longo, "The Theater of the *Polis*," in *Nothing to Do With Dionysos?*, John J. Winkler and Froma Zeitlin, eds., (Princeton: Princeton University Press, 1990), 16.

16. Winkler, 22-23.

17. See Charles Segal, "The Bacchae as Metatragedy" in *Directions in Euripidean Criticism*, Peter Burian, ed., (Durham: Duke University Press, 1985) 165.

18. Winkler, 59-60, 57.

19. Or is he the necessary chaos that renews the *pre-existing* order? This is most likely the case. It is unlikely that the *Bacchae* subverts Greek rationality, although Euripides may be testing the limits of a militaristic society in the play. As Athens is in a war with Sparta when the play is being performed, the limitations of the military in the *Bacchae* would have special resonance for the audience. On the other hand, as Oddone Longo has shown, all plays performed at the Dionysia were vetted by committees even in the draft stage. Longo writes, "The selection process ensures that, no matter how much the plays may question or probe the limits of Athenian self-identity, they nevertheless reinforce community cohesion, and in this case certainly, proper recognition of the god. The

selection process involves a preliminary selection administered to the text outline (a kind of preventative censorship), and then subsequent selection of a complete script by a jury according to procedures strictly analogous to those used for political proceedings," "The Theater of the *Polis,*" in *Nothing to Do With Dionysos?*, John J. Winkler and Froma Zeitlin, eds., (Princeton: Princeton University Press, 1990), 14.

20. Joseph Campbell, "The Inner Reaches of Outer Space: Myth as Metaphor and as Religion," in *Transformations of Myth Through Time,* (Fort Worth: Harcourt Brace, 1990), 3.

Esoteric Cinema

Eric G. Wilson

Flickers from the Void

To equate the Hollywood movie industry with a dream factory is to flatter films with more reality than they merit. Dream images, though hopelessly tenuous, at least *exist*. They possess a modicum of ghostly substance. They gesture toward the energies of the unconscious. They are essential elements of the sleeping mind. In contrast, the images of the film hardly deserve ontology. The scenes on the revolving reel are pure illusions produced by the persistence of vision. If a series of static images moves before our sight at a rate of sixteen to twenty-four frames per second, then we enjoy the semblance of continuous motion. When this procession of pictures is borne on a film strip, then in some cases only fifty percent of the reel is composed of exposed images. The remaining half is made of unexposed blank spaces. A moving picture is only half there. It is nothing as much as something. It is but a flickering of yes and no.

The haunts of the dream chamber open to the mysteries of self. The illusions of the Hollywood movie house dissolve into more illusions. The physical negations of motion pictures, issuing from the laws of optics and technology, generate psychological attenuations as well: desires to be duped, to dwell in deceptions. The content of the half-present exposures is composed of unreal perfections: the comforting closures of predictable genre plots, the ravishing grace of well-lighted stars, the elegantly artificial rooms and forests. In the same way that the continuous pictures repress the conflicted flickers, these ideal figures ignore life's unseemly blemishes. Consuming for a long time Hollywood scripts and actors, one eventually believes that these bright phantoms constitute the standard for the real. Familiar freckles and mottled stones, however vigorous and interesting, turn sordid. One exchanges substance for simulation.

Compared to these cinematic illusions of the virtual, dreams indeed seem solid and durable. So do shadows. We realize that those who have likened the movie theater to Plato's cave have not gone far enough. At least those shades in the cavern mimicked actual objects dancing near the fire's glow, and these temporal forms in turn copied unchanging ideas, the standards of truth. Half-absent forms displaying inaccurate contents, films images ape nothing in particular. If they copy anything, it is the wispy oscillation of black and white or the lubricious reveries of the masses. Not dreams, which might sound the psyche, and not shadows, which ghost fully blooded shapes, films are truly *films*, very thin and slightly opaque coverings that obscure the nature of things.

But a film is also a transparent sheet, a pellucid window through which one might see from one perspective to another. This alternative suggests a paradox: a film is opaque, an obscuring cover; a film is translucent, a revealing portal. What could the film unveil? The easy answer is: nothing. The moving image opens to airily ephemeral drifts of fantasy or to meaningless flickers of dark and light. A more troubling answer can come to mind, though, and rather quickly. Film might also point to what is ultimately behind all moving images, cinematic or otherwise: a blank square, an empty space. Film in this sense could well serve as an extreme manifestation of cosmic negation, pervasive nihilism: all things are illusions, seeming presences hollowed by absence. But cinema as apocalypse of the great void need not end in terror. If the moving image is a revelation of nothing, then this lack is not necessarily absence. Yes, nothing is *no*-thing, the annihilation of distinction; but nothing is also no-*thing*, the indifference one associates with soul or spirit. This startling possibility presents itself: film, seemingly a revolt against reality, is perhaps the most *spiritual* of mediums.

This last notion, if valid, brings us to another difficult problem. How can mainstream cinema, a lucrative material commodity, enjoy the virtues of the immaterial? Of all of the products of the culture industry, cinema has proven to be one of the most profitable. Every day millions of viewers consume movies as if they were rich foods. Swallowing these films by the bucketful, many audience members come to associate existence with movie plots and stars. They mimic in their homes the decor of the set; they copy in their behaviors the

24

gestures of the characters. What on earth could this spending—of money and of autonomy—have to do with a spiritual life, generally committed to apprehension of impalpable worlds and liberation from the flesh?

Cinema is both present and absent. It is opaque and transparent. It is material and spiritual. It serves as crass commodity as well as sacred event. These violations of logic are interesting in a general way for thinking about the phenomenology of film—the relationship between the nature of cinema (its ontology) and knowledge of cinema (its epistemology). However, these paradoxes become quite striking, even fascinating, when we stop to brood over this occurrence: cinema during the last twenty five years or so has been obsessed with themes emerging from the extremely immaterialist Gnostic tradition and its two primary spiritual issues, Cabbala and alchemy. What does an utterly illusory form have to do with a worldview committed to the idea that all matter is unreal and that truth—gnosis, intimate acquaintance—exists far beyond the turning planets? How can the most superficial of commodities carry a vision devoted to depths beneath getting and spending? These questions abruptly spring to mind when one notices the recent (and seemingly curious) abundance of films devoted to Gnosticism and its offshoots. But two other questions come to consciousness more slowly and then give further pause. Is it possible that film *because* of its tenuous reality is an especially apt vehicle for purveying Gnostic notions of a false universe—the world as the dream of an evil god? Is it conceivable that cinema *because* of its self-consuming contradictions—it is something and nothing, substantial matter and mere flicker—is an eminently powerful medium for transcending the conflicts of time to life beyond clocks?

Certain Gnostic films—films espousing the ideas of Gnosticism and its important offspring, Cabbala and alchemy—appear to be aware of these contradictions and to exploit them in hopes of reaching a third term beyond division. If these films are in fact self-conscious of their auto-erasures, then they would constitute privileged pictures, intense illuminations of cinematic extremes: exoteric manipulation and esoteric liberation, crass stereotype and sophisticated speculation. In exploring these vexed flickers—

25

darkness canceling light, substance consuming nothing—I want to establish the theoretical foundations and implications of an ignored genre: Gnostic cinema, composed of impossible films that exist to be annihilated. In detailing a theory of Gnostic film, I hope to shed light on several collateral issues: the aesthetics of irony, the virtues of the vague, the psychology of movie-watching, the role of the cinematographic apparatus, the unique representational powers of the moving image, and the functions of genre. These two activities—grounding the general theory of Gnostic cinema and analyzing its specific elements—will enable me to brood broadly on the enduring seductions of cinema, on how its material attractions, its ravishing shapes and shades, can translate in a flash into spiritual invitations, openings to the empty spaces between frames, free of encumbrance.

The Impossible Gnostic Film

Though heterogeneous, the Gnostic traditions as they emerged in Alexandria and Rome in the second and third centuries share basic elements. The visible cosmos is the sinister creation of a tyrannical demiurge. This universe is thus a corrupt copy of a spiritual plenitude of which the ignorant maker is not aware. This false god brainwashes the inhabitants of this world to believe that what they see before them is the only reality. Certain people awaken to the illusory nature of the material plane. They struggle to transcend this mire to the currents of spirit. These are the Gnostics, those who know.

Cabbala, a medieval and renaissance inflection of Gnostic speculations, is likewise varied, but exhibits persistent traits. The realms of time and space are the results of cosmic error, God's own powers shattering his vehicles of creation, or Adam's sin in Eden. These botched, fragmented regions constitute the cosmos. Spiritual adepts attempt to find God's principles hiding within the shards— his language of creation, his model human being. One way these practitioners try to recover this unfallen state is by animating a clay form into a human shape, creating a golem. Though the golem is designed to resemble Adam before the fall, he often perpetuates the fallen condition. He becomes violent, vulnerable to love and loss.

26

Issuing from certain Gnostic and Cabbalistic trends akin to those visible in the second- and third-century *Corpus Hermeticum*, the diverse alchemical tradition of the Middle Ages and Renaissance also features persistent motifs.[1] Matter and spirit are interdependent manifestations of an abysmal Godhead containing all oppositions. To know this God, one must grasp the connection between the material and the spiritual: matter is the womb from which spirit arises to transcend the world; spirit is the transcendent end toward which matter yearns. The alchemist apprehends this relationship by enacting in his alembic the process by which spirit ascends from matter and matter reflects spirit. He dissolves matter to its original chaos, watches spirit appear as ordered pattern, and melds order and chaos into union. This marriage composes the philosopher's stone, a symbol of the hidden harmony of the cosmos and the alchemist's perfected soul.

Though these spiritual movements differ from one another in important ways, all three share core esoteric ideas. Truth issues from a spiritual realm. Matter reflects but also distorts this truth and thus convinces most that appearances are the only realities. Deluded, these materialists trade illusion for reality. Only those who doubt the veracity of the palpable and yearn for the ungraspable can hope to transcend the conspiracies of matter to the profundities of spirit. These skeptics try to remove the film from their eyes.

Aptly, the commercial film industry—illusion posing as truth, commodity passing for reality, artifice pretending to be vital—has for much of its history urged orthodox critiques of these three heterodox traditions. Older films especially focus on the dangers of challenging mainstream Christianity. For instance, Otto Rippert's *The Revenge of the Homunculus*, from 1916, depicts the horrific results of a failed alchemical experiment. Paul Wegener's *The Golem*, released in 1920, shows the tragic results of Cabbalistic magic. James Whale's 1931 *Frankenstein* features a Gnostic's failed attempt to transcend the decays of matter. Some recent films continue this tradition. Luc Besson's *The Fifth Element* (1997) comically depicts the risk of alchemical experimentation, the possibility that this practice might unleash evil. Daren Aronofsky's *Pi* (1997) portrays the insanity that might issue from the Cabbalistic attempt to grasp God's secret code. Andrew Niccol's *Gattaca* (1997) reveals the totalitarian state the might ensue when Gnostic scientists correct the limitations of creation with genetic engineering.

However, even while exploring the harmful effects of heterodox speculations, the latter three films also entertain the idea that these esoteric modes are powerful challenges to superficial habits. *Gattaca* reveals the illusions of technological tyrants and exhibits the heroism of the rebel against the machine. *Pi* contemplates the notion that the surfaces of the world are manifestations of divine language. *The Fifth Element* explores the possibility that spiritual quintessence lurks within the four elements.

Against their ostensible intentions, these three films point to an unexpected and neglected undercurrent of mainstream cinema: an embrace of Gnostic critiques of the materialist ideologies of the movie industry. This recent abundance of paradoxical Gnostic films—illusions attempting to reveal truths—probably reflects contemporary technological conundrums over the difference between real and virtual. But there may be a deeper reason for this flowering of Gnosticism. Directors seem to be realizing that film, counter to expectation, might be the most sophisticated medium possible for expressing the Gnostic vision. Unreal and real, mechanistic and vital, commodity and artwork, the Gnostic film appears to be uniquely suited to explore relationships between appearance and reality and to push toward a third term beyond these relationships.

A brief list of commercial Gnostic films released over the past twenty-five years quickly reveals the recent obsession with gnosis. Overtly Gnostic films include *Vanilla Sky* (2001), *Donnie Darko* (2001), *The Matrix* (1999), *The Thirteenth Floor* (1999), *Ed TV* (1999), *eXistenZ* (1999), *The Truman Show* (1998), *Dark City* (1998), *Pleasantville* (1998), and *Total Recall* (1990). Some Cabbalistic films, Gnostic in spirit, are *A.I.* (2001), *Bicentennial Man* (1999), *The Iron Giant* (1999), *Gods and Monsters* (1998), *Robocop* (1987), *Making Mr. Right* (1987), *Short Circuit* (1986), *Creator* (1985), *D.A.R.Y.L.* (1985), and *Blade Runner* (1982). Alchemical pictures, subtle in their Gnosticism, are *Harry Potter and the Sorcerer's Stone* (2001), *American Beauty* (1999), *The Ninth Gate* (1999), *Dead Man* (1996), *Jacob's Ladder* (1990), *Angel Heart* (1987), *Blue Velvet*

(1986), *Agnes of God* (1985), *Excalibur* (1981), and *Altered States* (1980).

The films in the first category mainly draw from this Gnostic idea: visible existence is an illusion perpetuated by a creator bent on enslaving his creatures. This maker hopes that his denizens will take his fictional films for reality, reduce their lives to his staid scripts, and relinquish their desire for lasting gnosis beyond his flitting images. But these moving pictures focused on Gnostic liberation from the delusions of the demiurge are of course troubled. On the one hand, these pictures as bearers of Gnostic content push viewers to question societal conventions and strive for a lasting truth beyond the communal consensus. On the other hand, these same films as commodities of the corporate body seduce audiences simply to accept the codes of consumer culture and find their places into the unreflecting collective. Are these films simply unaware of this irony, this split between spiritual skepticism toward the given and materialist conformity with clichés? Or are these pictures vaguely conscious of this contradiction but prone to ignore it in hopes of crassly exploiting attractive Gnostic motifs for purely commercial reasons? Or, more interestingly, are these pictures keenly self-conscious of this tension between exoteric form and esoteric content and thus specially suited to inspire meditations on the vexed relationship between appearance and reality?

The films in the second category inflect the Cabbalistic motif of golem-making, a practice emerging from the Gnostic urge to transcend corrupt matter through realizing the perfect human. In imbuing a clay man with life, the pious Cabbalist hopes to recreate Adam unfallen and return to Eden. However, his creation frequently rebels against its master and must be destroyed. Pictures featuring golem-making often explore these dangers of creating a slave. But these movies are subtly tyrannical themselves, hoping to enslave viewers to consumer ideology. As with the Gnostic films, these golem movies might be blind to this contradiction, or they might overlook it in their quest to seduce viewers through arcane lore. But Cabbalistic films could be deliberately exploring this possibility: the ability of movies to transmute men into machines makes them especially apt vehicles for analyzing the poles of the golem: the monstrous (the blurring of human and automaton) and the miraculous (the escape from self-consciousness).

The third group of films, the alchemical ones, depicts the metamorphoses that occur in the alembic. Inspired by Gnostic visions of spirit hiding behind matter, alchemy focuses on redemptive transmutation—on how life emerges from death, soul grows from body, chaos rises from order. But surely alchemical movies, despite their mercurial turns, are in the end committed to stasis: to encouraging viewers to play out change through fiction instead of fact, to perform conversion. Like the Gnostic and Cabbalistic movies, these alchemical films could be ignorant of this contradiction or unconcerned with it. But the alchemical cinema might well be self-consciously activating the idea that the theatrical space itself is an alembic: a dark pit where viewers lose for a time their egos as they rise to the flickering lights above, a workshop of illuminated transformations.

Films in these categories appear to be impossibilities. They are hopelessly conflicted between spiritual liberation and material confinement, flight from stereotype and support of status quo. They place audiences in an irreducible double bind borne of opposed imperatives: Question all material appearances as illusions; accept these cinematic appearances as truths. The key question is this: is this bind confining, a paralyzing pull from two opposed extremes, or is it liberating, a rich limbo in which one remains unattached to either pole? Most theorists would answer the former question in the affirmative, believing that cinematic products of the culture industry, no matter how ostensibly rebellious, always, in the end, simply reinforce the stifling status quo. However, some thinkers might say yes to the latter question, for they might maintain that awareness of the confining conflict opens into a third perspective beyond division. To consider these two positions—Gnostic cinema as stultifying oxymoron, Gnostic cinema as liberating paradox—is to wonder if cinema can ever be anything other than a static commodity, if the movies, after all, are really able to *move*.

The Culture Industry

Theodor Adorno and Max Horkheimer maintain that commercial media serves big corporations out to control public opinion so that they can reduce the masses to a homogeneous, standardized group desiring to consume homogeneous, standardized merchandise. These financial powers can most efficaciously brainwash the population by convincing people that they are utterly free. In supporting or funding media events that emphasize non-conformity, creativity, uniqueness, rebelliousness—those great values, allegedly, of the Western world, especially of America—the forces of capitalism bombard the masses with pleasing abstractions: the style of Garbo, the swagger of Gable. But these stock images of freedom actually deplete and contain unpredictable acts of particular liberty. To gaze at the rebellions of Gable or Garbo, or, more recently, at the independence of an Eastwood or Madonna, is to live out vicariously one's own wild impulses and to purge them from the system. Moreover, in identifying with the figures of cinematic rebellion, one associates revolution with a prefabricated pattern that is not threatening at all but just another manifestation of a stereotype. Under the spell of media commodities, culture is transformed into a cipher of abstract images, a flatland of ceaseless consumption of the same. To be subjective is to be a subject.[2]

Jean-Louis Baudry argues that the cinematic space itself—the screen, the dark hall, the film projector—reinforces a dominant ideology of subjective idealism that ignores concrete particulars. In moving the filmic images so fast that their differences are elided, the camera presents to the audience a unified field of "reality." The projector presents this reality in a frame, a window of perception in which viewers can bracket objects for interpretation. Harmonizing experience and holding it at an interpretable distance, the camera embodies human dreams of the transcendental subject—a self that stands above events and subjects them to conscious intentionality. Casting audience members as eternal consciousnesses, the apparatuses of the movie-house reconstruct Lacan's "mirror-stage," the phase when the infant discovers in its reflection an image of a unified "I." Though audience members believe that they transcend experience, they are really infantilized, reduced to immovable units mistaking illusions for facts. This cinematic situation elevates the consuming self of capitalist ideology while repressing the unconscious energies of biology and history.[3]

Laura Mulvey inflects the ideas of Baudry through her feminist perspective. She believes that the camera is a patriarchal gaze shared by the film's male protagonist and the spectator. Embodying the male perspective, the camera does not reflect bare reality but projects the erotic fantasies of men. However, since society has been duped into believing that the patriarchal perspective is reality itself, most viewers simply assume that the camera is a proxy for neutered subjectivity, the objective eye. For Mulvey, this is the great brainwashing of mainstream cinema, a tool in the service of men and the money they lustily covet, a dreamy commodity to stoke clichéd libidos.[4]

Jean Baudrillard radicalizes the arguments of Adorno, Horkheimer, Baudry, and Mulvey. The earlier thinkers suggest that real differences exist between art and life but that the culture industry blurs these distinctions to further its capitalistic ends. Baudrillard does away with these gaps. He argues that the mass media is so pervasive and powerful that it has irrevocably collapsed the distinction between simulation and reality. The media presents "ideal" models for behavior that bear no direct relation to material or spiritual reality. In mimicking these models—simulations (images with no originals) and simulacra (words pointing to no things)—consumers become simulations of simulations, simulacra of simulacra. Information and politics, artistic creativity and violent rebellion—all are boiled down to entertainment, to commodity: newscasters purvey pseudo-facts, politicians play politicians, artists and rebels act out marginality. In this welter of unmoored images and words, populations become cynical, apathetic, and nihilistic. They dwell in a flatland in which no one thing is better than any other thing, in which values are as lubricious as the ceaseless flow of illusions.[5] These denizens unconsciously become instances of what Herbert Marcuse has called the "one-dimensional" man, a thin allegorical mask of the dominant ideology.[6]

These analyses—to which we could add Michel Foucault's meditations on how a dominant "discourse" controls the being of an age[7]—are Marxist in flavor, motivated by skepticism toward the patriarchal abstractions of capitalism and the hope that society might be redeemed into equality through meaningful relationships with concrete objects.[8]   However, though these critiques might be materialist in content, committed to the idea that humans are constituted by historical forces, in form they open to the mysteries of spirit. In focusing on how surfaces preclude depth, exteriors block interiors, abstraction thwarts particularity, these cultural criticisms reveal the exoteric conspiracy concocted by corporations. Unmasking these puppeteers, Adorno, Horkheimer, Baudry, Mulvey, and Baudrillard point to transcendence: movement beyond the status quo and toward particularities denuded of abstractions. To experience the bare world is to explore esoteric potential—unknown depths, abysmal interiors. Though this immediate contact might begin in time and space, it might end in mysteries that cannot be clocked or graphed. The superstructure's base can turn supernatural body.

Three Failed Rebellions

According to these critiques of the prevailing ideology, commercial cinema is a tool of the culture industry. Even pictures that appear to rebel against the "one-dimensional" status quo—like the Gnostic *The Matrix*, the Cabbalistic *A.I.*, and the alchemical *Dead Man*—reinforce the ideologies they appear to question. In fact, films that purvey unbridled freedom prove even more pernicious than conformist movies, for they make audiences believe that all is well—autonomy is real, democracy reigns—and that no more work needs doing. To pause on these three alleged paeans to spiritual freedom is entertain nihilism—despair before the possibility that all actions are as meaningless.

In Larry and Andy Wachowski's *The Matrix*—a film that actually features in a prominent scene Baudrillard's *Simulacra and Simulation*—the world of everyday experience is a virtual reality created and controlled by machines that have taken over the universe. Human beings are contained in metallic pods. There they sleep out their lifetimes, though they believe that they enjoy a meaningful life in a vibrant world. This reality, however, is a computer program.

Human consciousness is nothing more than a hard drive for images manipulated by machines. But there is hope. With the help of several rebels who have awakened to the conspiracy, Neo, played by Keanu Reeves, masters the logic of the computer program, called the Matrix, and learns to defeat the machines. The film concludes with this Gnostic savior, having overturned the evil demiurge, on his way toward awakening the world from its long sleep.[9]

But this liberation from illusion is illusion, a moving image with no relation to things. The liberator is a Hollywood star playing in a Hollywood hit—a commodity for consumption featured in a commodity for consumption. As a cog in the culture industry, this hero is a cipher for stereotypes of rebellion: he is at first a loner, a resistant hero, before embracing his cause; he dons black sunglasses and a long black coat; he is cool and detached; he gains victories through sleek violence and "Zen" calm. As audiences gaze on this Gnostic savior, they are not released from the false images that oppress them but moored more firmly to abstractions. These moviegoers once again reduce rebellion to habit. They vent their revolutionary impulses through empathizing with Neo.

The same double binds blunt the critical thrusts of *A.I.* and *Dead Man*, Cabbalistic and alchemical siblings of the Gnostic *Matrix*. In Steven Spielberg's *A.I.*, Professor Allen Hobby, also known as "The Visionary"—a character portrayed by William Hurt—creates androids that resemble his dead son. These machines are totally "life-like," indistinguishable from human adolescents. Through his technology, the Visionary has fashioned a sort of golem, a mixture of miracle and monster—a being beyond decay that recalls Adam before the fall; an aberrant blurring of death and life, a violation of natural order. One of Hobby's products, David Swinton, played by Haley Joel Osment, struggles to transcend his mechanical condition and to become a human boy. He wants to overcome his monstrosity, his conflict between machine and organ, and to enjoy the miraculous, a harmony between unconscious grace and conscious thought. David's battle is successful. After staring for centuries at a blue fairy at the bottom of a frozen ocean, he ascends to the light, where he meets a race of godly aliens. These beings arrange for the human android to reunite with his lost mother and to play all day in a paradise in which desire and fulfillment, thought and deed, exist in perfect concord.[10]

This film appears to depict the return to Eden: the glorious labor of moving beyond the limits of mechanistic determinism to the freedom of full humanity. However, the picture ultimately works to fit its audience into the fated grids of the corporate machine. Regardless of it emphasis on overcoming determinism, the picture worships machines. It is a meditation on the wonders of technology, the ability of a visionary to create life in cogs. It suggests that machines are more vital, compassionate, and intelligent than human beings. It dazzles with its slick special effects, cinematic magic dependent upon sophisticated technologies. Watching a boy convert from machine to man, viewers likely descend from men to mechanisms.

Jim Jarmusch's *Dead Man* shows its hero, William Blake, played by Johnny Depp, undergo the death of one self and the birth of another, a conversion akin to the alchemical process by which lead is dissolved into gold. Blake begins the film as a Cleveland accountant of the late nineteenth-century making his way toward a western town called Machine. This town is run by a dictator, John Dickinson, portrayed by Robert Mitchum. Blake plans to become a mechanism in Dickinson's metal works factory, a human calculator, a quantifier of experience. However, after inadvertently murdering Dickinson's son and being shot himself, the nervous accountant in the working suit must head for the western wilds, where he changes his threads for furs and comes under the care of a Native American named Nobody, played by Gary Farmer. Versed in the poetry of William Blake, Nobody believes that this wounded accountant is an incarnation of the dead artist. Since Blake himself is on the verge of dying, Nobody, like an alchemical guide, decides to lead this suffering man from the physical plane to the spiritual realm. With the aid of his strange companion, Blake achieves this conversion over the course of the movie through dying to his external vocation and awakening to the artist within: a preternaturally skilled gunfighter. In making his way through the dangerous forests of the Northwest, Blake metamorphoses: from the bewildered accountant undergoing the chaos of fear to the skilled gunfighter assured of grace in the gloomy wood to the sage fearless before his demise in the timeless ocean.[11]

Though Jarmusch's film is much less commercial than *The Matrix* and *A.I.*, and though this picture avoids many Hollywood conventions, it still falls into the same traps as its mainstream companions. Blake achieves his transformation through the help of the very conventional "exotic sage"—in this case, a mystically-minded Native American. This cultural stereotype suggests that change is not autonomous, issuing from a mysterious interior, but that conversion is determined, emerging from an external force. If Blake had not met Nobody, he would have died ignobly. Only through the agency of this shamanic figure does he mutate from a cipher for the industrial ideology to a sort of noble samurai. Identities remain the same until altered from without by otherworldly others. Transformation is arbitrary, unlikely, fantastical. Stasis is natural, common, ordinary. That the film inspires audiences to change virtually, through empathy with Blake, reinforces this ideology. Moreover, the film marks the "change" through the conventional registers of Western genre. A weak hero is bullied by brutes; he masters the pistol; he becomes a formidable killer. The hip Western resembles the staid.

The Redemption of Failure

The Gnostic film appears to be committed to unveiling reality behind illusion. But this sort of picture annihilates the possibility that the real will ever emerge from the illusory. The Cabbalistic movie wishes to reveal our identity with the unfallen Adam. However, this type of film blurs categories—freedom and fate, machine and man—and precludes a clear sense of self. The alchemical picture wants to explore the potential for conversion from dead to living. But the cinematic alembic reinforces the conditions that keep the world stable. Such are the skeptical conclusions of the critics of the culture industry.

However, against expectation, one in another mood might discover something else in these exoteric commodities disguised as esoteric revelations—hidden interstices to depths beyond images. Without rejecting the analyses of Adorno, Horkheimer, Baudry,

Mulvey, and Baudrillard, one might be able to show how Gnostic movies push beyond the oppositions with which these critics condemn commercial cinema, how these pictures transcend the categories of concrete and abstract, objective historicity and subjective idealism, simulacra of "life" and simulacra of "art." The three Gnostic films under discussion here appear to be *aware* of the main point of these critics—commercial cinema alienates from reality, however one defines the real. These movies deploy alienating conventions; at the same time, these films undercut these very motifs. With apparent self-consciousness, these Gnostic efforts seem to argue for, while rejecting, the validity of a Baudry or a Baudrillard. At odds with themselves, these pictures push toward a third term opening to the impossible: the living abyss, the ideal human, the perfect conversion.

The Matrix is a highly self-conscious film, aware of the contradictions pulling it asunder. Early in the film, Neo, not yet awakened to the illusory nature of his alleged life, hides black market computer software in a hollowed-out copy of Baudrillard's *Simulacra and Simulation*. The page to the left of the cut-out area, located in the middle of the book, features a chapter heading, "On Nihilism." This chapter actually comes at the end of the book. The Wachowski brothers are deliberately pointing their audience to connections among Baudrillard, nihilism, and their cinematic world. The scene itself features a "Follow Instructions" message on Neo's computer. Those outside the Matrix have sent this imperative, followed by several clues, in hopes of awakening the future savior. Such a scene, a microcosm of the film, causes vertigo. A book meant to reveal the meaninglessness of the visible world is itself empty, a surface with no depth. In this way, Baudrillard's book is like Neo, an illusory form hoping to awaken his world from illusion, and like the film itself, a dream critiquing the dreams that we take for fact.

The bottom falls out. The profane world of everyday, material existence is an oppressive delusion; the sacred realm of exotic, spiritual being is a veil of a veil. This double bind turns and turns, a never-ending spiral of infinite regressions—phantoms point to ghosts that reveal haunts who mimic dreams that are themselves the products of phantoms. *The Matrix* is replete with similar binds, dizzying whirlpools: the man from outside the Matrix who awakens Anderson from dubious illusion to alleged reality is named Morpheus, the Greek god of dreams. The world outside of the Matrix, reality, is sordid and ugly while the environment inside the Matrix, illusion, is a paradise of color and light. Inside the Matrix, the bodies of men and women are hard-drives into which an intelligent computer downloads dreams; outside the Matrix the film's heroes possess plugs in the backs of their heads into which they load computer programs.

These double binds urge a third term, a thing beyond these poles. What transcends while containing opposites? What is neither this nor that and at the same time both that and this? The answer is: nothing, but in two senses—the concrete and the abstract. No *thing*, no object or event in time or space, is capable of being two entities at once and no entity at all. But *no*thing, the absence of objects and events as well as of the categories of space and time, is both beyond the conflicts of matter—it is an undifferentiated abyss—and within these same divisions—it is the pervasive emptiness from which fullness emerges. While no thing, no particular being, can serve as this third term, nothing, the ubiquitous void, can. Nothing as concept is the annihilation of matter as well as the origin of material. It is void, where no pairs of opposite exist, and plenitude, the ground of all polarities. It is matrix, the unseen network of emptiness at the core of all fullness, and matrix, the invisible mother of all visible beings. Revealing the inadequacy of our concepts of illusion and truth, *The Matrix* pushes us to this absence, this abyss. To watch *The Matrix* in a theater is to glimpse this Gnostic Godhead, not in the moving images of the celluloid but in the blank screen, the absence of all color and the ground of all hues. *The Matrix* is a film that removes the film.

A.I. is also aware of its contradictions. In calling Professor Hobby a Visionary, the film not only forges a parallel between the technological genius and the Cabbalistic magus. It also creates an analogy between this scientific figure and the artist—specifically, the film director. The divine mechanic fashions an artificial intelligence, a sort of golem. The result is a being that struggles between determinism and freedom. The film-maker produces an artificial intelligence, a film that appears to live though it is inanimate. The result is a group of viewers torn between filmic conventions and liberating messages. This is the film's golem-like double bind: *be a machine*, a passive receptacle of cultural commodities; *be a human*, an active creator of unique realities. Struggling between these poles, the picture proves a mechanism, a predictable pattern programmed to finite behaviors, and an organism, a meta-pattern reflecting on its own activities. The film troubles the idea of identity, suggesting that mechanism and organism are inadequate categories for describing a self. Machines ruin their efficiency by striving to be human while organs destroy their intensity by descending to habit. If organs are machines and machines are organs, then how can one articulate a stable self?

The picture does not provide an answer. Though David might transcend the troubled poles splitting him asunder when he rests with his mother, he nonetheless remains an artificial being, half android and half adolescent, the toy of the film's demiurge and a commodity of the picture's director. Though the Visionary is a human genius capable of creating life, he is David in reverse, a human who wants to be a machine, fixated on dead things—his son's corpse and the cogs of his contraptions. While the film is self-conscious of its own contradictions, it depicts the cinematic art as a blind tool for surveillance and control—the only moving image shown in *A.I.* is that of Dr. Know, a phantom wizard used by the authorities of industry to determine David's path and direct him toward the oppressive powers that he is trying to escape.

Where can one glimpse a vision of identity not undone by irreconcilable differences? As with *The Matrix*, *A.I.* pushes viewers beyond the paralyzing parameters of the kinetic images on the screen to a synthetic figure outside yet within the oppositions. This figure must be beyond control and contingency alike, a site where levers lurch as gracefully as leaves and limbs stride with the clarity of pistons. Beyond determinism, this ideal structure cannot exist within the limits of the empirical realm; it must stand somewhere behind the forward gaze. Not shapeless, this figure cannot simply be as free as air; it must be bound by form. In gathering while transcending organ and machine, this object must further be conscious, a light endlessly projecting studied mental images, and unconscious, a movement untroubled by the rift between thought and deed. As such, this impossible thing would be able to partake of the ceaseless illuminations of self-awareness, undying light, and of the delimiting darkness of oblivion, the death of thought. Ever behind the eyes, visible and invisible, a machine expressing human vision, a melding of light and darkness, this site is approximated by the cinematic projector, a gesture toward Spielberg's Visionary perfected, and his golem made calm. To imagine this ideal condition is to experience the Eden that the film prohibits.

Dead Man also points to a portal out of its prisons. Like *The Matrix* and *A.I.*, the film expresses a self-consciousness of its irreducible conflicts, especially the rift between metamorphosis and stasis. While William Blake undergoes his transmutations in the alembic of the wilderness, his image on a "wanted" poster remains the same, a stable container for the increasing quantities of money offered as rewards for his capture. This repetition suggests that change might be illusory or meaningless. The possibility becomes a fact throughout a film that features circular patterns. Blake begins as an accountant, a man inseparable from number and money; he ends as a gunfighter with a price on his head, a person of quantities and cash. He starts out as fugitive fleeing from an unsuccessful past in Cleveland; he concludes as a fugitive running from the law in the Northwest. The picture opens showing Blake traveling in a train to an unknown frontier; it closes focused on Blake floating in a canoe into the unmapped ocean.

Certainly, these recurrences appear to constitute repetitions with a difference, markers of the Blake's conversion from fumbling greenhorn to graceful gunfighter. However, these circles could just as easily reveal the impossibility of meaningful change, especially if interpreted in light of the unchanging visage on Blake's "wanted" poster. The latter reading is further reinforced when we remember, again, that the film itself, as commodity, is more likely to reinforce cultural status quo than it is to inspire personal rebellion. Bombarded by the conventions of the Western—even if they are ironically inflected by Jarmusch—audiences experience the same old clichés that have controlled their consumptions. Even if these viewers, like the film itself, entertain significant transformation, they likely conclude that they, along with Blake, cannot escape the rigid facial image they witness each morning in the mirror. This is the dilemma of which *Dead Man* is aware. On the one hand, meaningful metamorphosis seems impossible. On the other hand, the status quo is pernicious, a system of capitalistic exploitation.

Dead Man likewise suggests that one must strain beyond these double binds on screen to an ideal third term. Combining the virtues of turbulence with the beauties of pattern, this *tertium quid* would have to be a crepuscular realm where soft beams organize the blackness into vague forms, where shadows reveal the glory of the light. Imagine a man in the dark theater witnessing *Dead Man*. Unsettled by the conflicts in Jarmusch's film, he briefly looks to one side or the other to see if his fellow viewers feel as he does. He discerns curious figures in the twilight, faces flickering in and out of the darkness, familiar yet bizarre, stable but vague. He envisions himself in a similar way—not as a discrete self, a cogent unit struck by the beams; not as a distributed stream, a casual current spread through the gloom. He envisions himself as a merger of these two drifts: an eddy of the dark air. Losing a grip on himself, he focuses again on the bright screen. He hopes to recover some security, but the comfort is gone. He is different than he was before. He has been briefly dismembered and reconstituted. That this occurred once might mean that other worlds, fresh ways of walking and loving, exist, in potential, waiting to be embodied. Torn asunder by irreconcilable poles, *Dead Man* points to this realm beyond its frames, suggesting that the dark hall might serve as a cipher for an invisible alembic never seen on land or sea, an ideal retort where the conflicts of the hard world for a time relax, where lumps of flesh metamorphose into shapes of golden air.

~

How quickly, with the slight turn of an eye, can the labyrinth, the deceptive maze harboring the deadly Minotaur, turn into the mandala, a symbolic geometry of wholeness, one and many gathered. The same abrupt conversion in sight can transform the cave of Plato into the cavern of Eleusis, the tomb of knowledge into the womb of everlasting life. This same optical metamorphosis, sometimes no more than a tilt of the head or a slight fever, can transmute the commercial cinema from a den of iniquity into a temple of virtue. The Gnostic films capable of causing this conversion must be sly as Mercurius, the great shape shifter of alchemical lore. They keep the corporate clergy sedated and manifest the standards of the status quo. At the same time, they erase these conventions, and leave behind those horrors that kill rigid men but generate fluid adepts.

Notes

1. Carl Jung is the primary source of the idea that alchemy issues from Gnosticism. In his *Memories, Dreams, Reflections*, Amiela Jaffe, ed., Clara Winston and Richard Winston, trs. (New York: Vintage, 1989), he argues that a current runs from ancient Gnosticism through medieval and Renaissance alchemy to twentieth-century depth psychology. The persistent characteristics of this current are the following: the origin of existence is an unfathomable abyss; this abyss descends into time in the form of conflicted oppositions; redemption from conflict comes in the figure of a savior reflecting the original abyss: the Gnostic savior from the hidden god; the philosopher's stone; the primal Self. The differences among these movements lie in emphasis on matter. Gnosticism wishes to escape matter; alchemy wishes to discover spirit in matter; depth psychology wants to find a purely materialistic redemption. These differences in focus on materiality have led some thinkers to draw a sharp dichotomy between Gnosticism and alchemy. For instance, Kathleen Raine in *Blake and Tradition* (Princeton, NJ: Princeton University Press, 1969), 118, has the following to say: "The great difference between the Neoplatonic [and by extension, the Gnostic, even more anti-materialistic than Neoplatonism] and the alchemical philosophies lies in their opposed conceptions of the nature of matter. For Plotinus and his school, matter is mere mire, the dregs of the universe, a philosophic 'non-entity' because incapable of form except as it reflects intelligibles. To the alchemists, spirit and matter, active and passive, light and darkness, above and below are, like the Chinese yin and yang, complementary principles, both alike rooted in the divine. The *deus absconditus* is hidden and operating in matter, no less than He is to be found in the spiritual order."
N.B.: I'd like to be clear about my use of the term "Cabbala." The

42

term "Cabbala" is used here to refer to Kabbalistic currents or ideas as manifested beyond or outside Jewish culture.

2. Theodor Adorno and Max Horkheimer, "The Culture Industry: The Enlightenment as Mass Deception," *Dialectic of Enlightenment.*, John Cumming, trs. (New York: Continuum, 1976), 120-67.

3. Jean-Louis Baudry, "Ideological Effects of the Basic Cinematographic Apparatus," *Film Theory and Criticism: Introductory Readings.* 5th ed., Leo Braudy and Marshall Cohen, eds., (Oxford and New York: Oxford University Press, 1999), 345-55.

4. Laura Mulvey, "Visual Pleasure's and Narrative Cinema," *Narrative, Apparatus, Ideology: A Film Theory Reader*, ed. Philip Rosen (New York: Columbia University Press, 1986), 198-209.

5. Jean Baudrillard, *Simulacra and Simulation*, trans. Sheila Faria Glaser (Ann Arbor, MI: University of Michigan Press, 1994), 1-42.

6. Herbert Marcuse, *One-Dimensional Man: Studies in the Ideology of Advanced Industrial Society* (Boston: Beacon Press, 1991), 1-18.

7. In this regard, see especially Michel Foucault's *The Order of Things: An Archaeology of the Human Sciences* (New York: Vintage, 1994).

8. Of course, I could here invoke other important theories of the conspiracy of the commercial film. One thinks in this context of David Bordwell's chapter on classical Hollywood cinema in *Narration in Fictional Film* (Madison, WI: University of Wisconsin Press, 1985). In this section, Bordwell's discusses the basic structures of the commercial film—how it goes about representing the "real." Noel Carroll's entire body of critical work has been indispensable in helping me think through the relationship between film and insight, especially his chapter on ideology in *Theorizing the Moving Image* (Cambridge: Cambridge University Press, 1996). Richard Allen offers an especially lucid account of cinema viewing and philosophical theories of perception in "Looking at Motion Pictures" (*Film Theory and Philosophy*, Richard Allen and Murray Smith, eds., (Oxford and London: Oxford University Press, 1997), 76-94. While each of these pieces—along with those of Adorno and Horkheimer, Baudry and Baudrillard, have helped me to articulate my position, none has focused on how cinematic perception might connect to esoteric transcendence.

9. *The Matrix* has already spawned a voluminous amount of criticism. Though no one has yet focused on the film's esoteric self-contradictions, several have noted the film's religious elements and its relationships to Baudrillard. See, for instance, Frances Flannery-Dailey and Richard Wagner's "Wake Up! Gnosticism and Buddhism in *The Matrix*," (*Journal of Religion and Film* 5:2 [October 2001] 23 March 2004, available: http://www.unomaha.edu/ ~wwwjrf/ gnostic.htm); James L. Ford's "Buddhism,

Mythology, and *The Matrix*" (*Taking the Red Pill: Science, Philosophy, and Religion in* The Matrix, Glenn Yeffeth, ed., introduction by David Gerrold (Dallas: BenBella Books, 2003), 125-144; Dino Felluga's "*The Matrix*: Paradigm of Post-Modernism or Intellectual Poseur? (Part I)" (*Taking the Red Pill: Science, Philosophy, and Religion in* The Matrix, 71-84); Andrew Gordon's "*The Matrix*: Paradigm of Post-Modernism or Intellectual Poseur? (Part II)" in *Taking the Red Pill: Philosophy, and Religion in* The Matrix, 85-102; Michael Brannigan's "There Is No Spoon: A Buddhist Mirror" (The Matrix *and Philosophy: Welcome to the Desert of the Real*, William Irwin, ed., (Chicago: Open Court Publishing, 2002), 101-10; Gary Bassham, "The Religion of *The Matrix* and the Problems of Pluralism" (The Matrix *and Philosophy: Welcome to the Desert of the Real*, 11-25); Christopher Williams's "Mastering the Real: Trinity as the 'Real' Hero of *The Matrix*" (*Film Criticism* 27 (Spring 2003)3: 2-17; and David Lavery's "From Cinescape to Cyberspace: Zionists and Agents, Realists and Gamers in *The Matrix* and *eXistenZ*," *Journal of Popular Film and Television* 28 (Winter 2001)4: 150-7. While these essays more or less track the ways in which *The Matrix* inflects either religious currents or Baudrillardian ideas, a few other pieces intelligently reveal the film's rich contradictions, even if these pieces do not relate the contradictions to the esoteric tradition. See Russell J.A. Kilbourn's "Re-Writing 'Reality': Reading *The Matrix*," *Canadian Journal of Film Studies* 9 (Fall 2000)2: 43-54; Thomas S. Hibbs's "Notes from the Underground: The Matrix and Nihilism" in The Matrix *and Philosophy: Welcome to the Desert of the Real*,155-65; and Sarah E. Worth's "The Paradox of Real Response to Neo-Fiction" (The Matrix *and Philosophy: Welcome to the Desert of the Real*, 178-87).

10. Two recent articles on the ways in which A.I. explores relationships and reversal between humans and machines are John Tibbetts's "Robots Redux: *A.I. Artificial Intelligence* (2001)" *Film and Literature Quarterly* 29 (2001)4: 258-61; and Tim Kreider's "Review: *A.I. Artificial Intelligence*," *Film Quarterly* 567(Winter 2002-3): 32-9. Though these essays meditate intelligently on the film's blurrings of the boundaries between mechanism and organism, neither focuses on how the movie inflects the golem tradition or urges, through paradox, transcendence of the rift between cog and consciousness.

11. The two most revealing pieces on *Dead Man* are Jonathan Rosenbaum's *Dead Man* (London: British Film Institute, 2000), and Mary Katherine Hall's "Now You Are a Killer of White Men: Jim Jarmusch's *Dead Man* and Traditions of Revisionism in the Western," *Journal of Film and Video* 52 (Winter 2001)4: 3-14. Though neither of these works explores the

alchemical elements of *Dead Man*, both meditate on the ways in which Jarmusch's picture attempts to revise the traditional western through its "mystical" commitments.

Hex and the City:
Texts for Occult Performance in Late Capitalism

Lance Gharavi

In their 1998 article in the journal *Philosophy*, Karen Green and John Bigelow write:

The Europeans did three things which set them far apart from most other peoples at most other times and places. Between 1500 and 1700 they set sail in tall ships and colonized the far corners of the globe. They made stunning strides forward in the sciences. And they executed tens of thousands of people, mainly women, as witches.[1]

What a difference a few centuries make. In the United States, Wiccan chaplains now volunteer in state prisons, stylish and attractive witches are featured as role models for young women in film and television, and the term "witch hunt" is now used only in its metaphorical sense. Yet even though burnings have ceased, the number of current adherents to Wicca, witchcraft, and neo-paganism is notoriously difficult to determine because believers, fearing persecution by their communities, are often reluctant to reveal themselves to pollsters. Estimates of the number of Wiccans in the U.S. vary from a few thousand to ten million.[2] The massive *American Religious Identification Survey* (ARIS), probably the most accurate survey for religious identification, estimates that the Wiccan community in the United States grew seventeen fold between the years 1990 and 2001[3]—the highest growth rate of all the religious groups monitored. This statistic, however, remains questionable.

What is not in question, however, is the success of witchcraft as a publishing phenomenon. In 2002, a spokesperson for Borders Books reported that sales of books on Wicca rose 25-30 percent over the previous year, continuing a surge that began in the late 1990s.[4] One of the aspects I find curious about this phenomenon concerns the series of books aimed at fashionable and pop-culture

47

savvy young women. These include books by authors like Silver Ravenwolf and Fiona Horne with titles like *Teen Witch*; *Witch: A Hip Guide to Modern Witchcraft*; *Pop! Goes The Witch*; *Witchin': A Handbook for Teen Witches*; and *7 Days to a Magickal New You*. In this article, I will address one recent title from this particular sub-genre, but first I have a confession to make. Though it neatly and succinctly encapsulates nearly everything I want to say, I did not invent the title of this essay. *Hex and the City: Sophisticated Spells for the Urban Witch* is the title of a book written by Lucy Summers and published in 2003 by Barron's. The title, of course, is a pun on the wildly popular and Emmy Award-winging HBO comedy series *Sex and the City*, now in syndication. The series concerns the lives, friendship, and sexual exploits of four young, sophisticated, professional women in New York City.

Hex and the City consists of a series of spells. They are miniature texts intended for ritualized performance. Clearly, this book is not meant for witches whose practice centers around a coven, but for the "hedge witch," or solitary practitioner. Summers's book is explicitly aimed at a demographic that has gone beyond the "teen witch" series. The book's target audience consists of young, urban women who are single, gainfully employed, fashionably hip, and sociable. The title page presents a telling image. The stylishly retro feminine colors and graphic design of the page features what one might presume is the idealized image (or self-image) of the kind of witch for whom Summers writes. There is nothing stereotypically witchy here. The image is not of an earthy woman stirring a cauldron, waving a magic wand, bowing down before the Goddess, or dancing naked in the moonlight. Indeed, the image seems to bear no relationship to witchcraft—whether stereotypical or reinvented—whatsoever. It is an illustration of a voluptuously-lipped, elegantly coiffed, young woman applying lipstick. Yet this image, far from being irrelevant to the book's content, neatly foreshadows what is presented in the pages that follow. *Hex and the City* is a grimoire as might be conceived by the editors at *Cosmo*. The spells are divided into categories that accurately mirror those concerns glossed in glossy women's magazines: partying and socializing, romance, fashion and body care, home care and decorating, career, and money. The book's design and aesthetic likewise imitates those of popular X and Y Generation fashion magazines, as does its form. These magazines typically offer young women a series of recipes, short and simple tips and instructions on make-up, fashion, weight-loss, exercise, bargain shopping, career advancement, methods of increasing self-esteem, how to host the perfect party, etc. *Hex* follows this logic precisely. Here, the "recipes" take the form of spells, spiritualized performances of occult rituals designed to foster the same kind of self-improvement-driven lifestyle being pushed by its secular counterparts. One of my favorite charms in *Hex* is called "Stiletto Spell." It is a spell specifically designed to protect the witch's "delicious but temperamental heels so that [she] never trips and they never break."

Wittgenstein once said that a serious and philosophical work could be written that would consist entirely of jokes. I am sorely tempted to try that out here. Certainly it would be easy (and fun) to do nothing but issue a scathing yet humorous critique of this book, a work that seemingly places its Jimmy Choo pumps firmly across the line into self-satire. But I'm going to resist that temptation. Instead, in keeping with the Wiccan rule of threes, I want to address three more serious concerns:

1. This work in relation to Wicca's historical association with feminism.
2. The ways in which the book reflects the cultural logic of late capitalism.
3. Issues of authenticity.

As Jane Arthurs observes, the television show *Sex and the City* successfully re-mediates the familiar formulas of glossy women's magazines. [5] Re-mediation is a term used by Jay David Bolter and Richard Grusin to describe the process by which new media "responds to, re-deploys, competes with and reforms other media." [6] "New technologies of representation," they claim, "proceed by reforming or remediating earlier ones." [7] Older technologies of representation, like the print technology of Summers's book, maintain their legitimacy by remediating newer ones. The print medium of *Hex* remediates the televisual medium of *Sex* which itself is a remediation of popular print. *Hex* is specifically aimed at young women who enjoy the show, *Sex and the City*, and identify with and seek to emulate the lifestyle portrayed therein. It mirrors the style and values of the show and translates them into a practiced spirituality. The Stiletto Spell is a prime example of this process, reflecting Carrie Bradshaw's—the show's protagonist—cherished obsession with designer shoes.

As a remediation of a remediation, *Hex and the City* is thus subject to many of the same feminist criticisms leveled at *Sex and the City* and women's fashion magazines. Catherine Orenstein articulated many of the relevant criticisms of the former in her much-discussed 2003 *New York Times* editorial. As in the television show, the image of women in Summers's book is surprisingly retrograde. The witch of her vision spends most of her time on shopping, partying, and serial boyfriends. She is vapid and materialistic, defined by her sex appeal, without a social cause, and most acutely concerned with finding a man. The boyfriends in the book appear as that most un-threatening recent archetype: the metro-sexual. In the book's over-arching consumerist ideology, men are sought in the same way as fashionable new dresses or shoes: as gratifying commodities that constitute expressions of the witch's feminine sexuality; a spell to find a "knock-out outfit" to attract men bears the same objective as the more direct "Animal Magnetism" spell. Men are portrayed in the book as attractive accessories, like a Gucci handbag, albeit with some agency that must be carefully manipulated through magical means as in the spells "Boyfriend Trainer" and "Call Me Now." Women's (hetero) sexuality is encouraged as part of an overall consumer lifestyle and boyfriends come to resemble the witch's expensive shoes—"nice looking, often uncomfortable, and seasonal."[8]

Like the magazines and television shows it imitates, *Hex* is complicit in the commodification of women's relation to her body, self, and identity. The book abounds with spells like "Goddess Hair" and "Bosom Buddy," the latter designed to keep the witch's breasts "firm and young looking." Within the guise of a liberating and even defiantly counter-culture spirituality, the witch is invited to internalize the male gaze and, in a process of unabashed narcissism so characteristic of contemporary women's magazines, objectify her body in a way that renders her powerless regardless of what occult forces she brings to bear. Furthermore, the book egregiously participates in these magazines' tendency to promote unreasonable and unhealthy images of the ideal feminine body. The spell "Gym Queen," which encourages the witch to "get a figure to die for" and claims to be "all you need for firmer thighs and a trimmer waist," is typical of the book's portrayal of the female body in its modeling of a cartoon woman so emaciated she makes Calista Flockhart look like Michael Moore.

All this strikes me as odd, considering Wicca's historic relationship with feminism in the United States. Wicca's emergence and expansion in the U.S. is distinguished from its English roots in that the former owes much to its early and continued embrace of radical feminism and its search for enduring and exclusive female forms, including an authentic female spirituality. This alliance was perhaps inevitable given that the witch is one of the very few images of independent female power in European history. Many noted feminist writers, radical and otherwise, like Mary Daly, Andrea Dworkin, Barbara Ehrenreich, and Deirdre English, celebrated the idea of the witch. This trend started as early as 1968 with the founding of WITCH (Women's International Terrorist Conspiracy from Hell). According to the radical feminist conception, witchcraft, with its veneration of the Great Goddess, had once been the religion of primitive and matriarchal societies throughout Europe. The rise of Christianity had been the first great assault of the patriarchal revolution, effecting the destruction of the matriarchy and the end of the supremacy of the Goddess.[9] The period of persecution in the sixteenth through eighteenth centuries, commonly referred to as "the burning times," had thus been "the suppression of an alternative culture by the ruling elite, but also a war against feminism, for the religion had been served by the most courageous, aggressive, independent, and sexually liberated women in the populace."[10] The witch trials constituted, in this formulation, a second wave of patriarchal aggression, a feminine holocaust or gynocide. Women could liberate themselves and regain their old power, according to the radical feminists, by reclaiming their spiritual identity as witches.

51

Though *Hex and the City* contains a vestige of radical feminism in that it is clearly aimed at an exclusively female audience and follows the former's tendency to downplay the dualistic conception of divinity in Wicca by marginalizing—or, in this case, ignoring—the male aspect called the "Horned God," the book is hardly in line with the vision of the militantly anti-patriarchal gyno-spirituality sought by early feminist Wiccans. Rather, it re-imagines witchcraft within the discourse of what has come to be called "Third-Wave" feminism. Sometimes referred to as "Do-Me" feminism, Third-Wave[11] is the brand of feminism most often associated with *Sex and the City* but also with the ubiquitous image of the tough and sexy "girl culture" slinkily embodied by Buffy, Sidney Bristow of *Alias*, Ally McBeal, Lara Croft, the Powerpuff girls, the new Charlie's Angels, and Halle Barry as Catwoman. The move is from objectification to subjectification, a heroic agency in constructions of femininity in popular culture.

Third-Wave feminists offer a critique of the Second-Wave, attacking what they see as the latter's old-fashioned, even Puritan attitude towards sex (which thus empowers the patriarchy and its Puritan oppression of witches) and its tendency to emphasize women's enduring historical role as victims. In the Third-Wave's conception, women may gain empowerment through an aggressive ownership of their sexuality and subjecthood, their autonomy and independence from men underwritten by their economic independence. Woman-centered media play an important role in establishing this subjecthood, for, as Arthurs puts it, "feminine cultures of consumerism and fashion have been considered as a source of pleasure and power that is potentially resistant to male control. Indeed they can offer women an alternative route to self-esteem and autonomy that overcomes the damaging division that second-wave feminism constructs between feminism and femininity."[12] *Hex and the City* precisely follows this third-wave formula, celebrating the witch's autonomy through purchasing power, offering spiritualized means of career advancement, increasing self-esteem by suggesting pathways to a defiantly stylish and fashionable agency, and urging them to become an empowering force in the creation of their own gendered subjectivity. In spell after spell, the book encourages

52

women to construct themselves as desiring and desirable subjects through religious ritual and narrative.

But third-wave critiques of the narrow homogeneity of the second-wave's construct of woman don't quite fit with *Hex.* "Woman" here is quite homogenous: young, relatively affluent, urban, overwhelmingly white, and heterosexual. Yet the book manages to partially avoid this problem by revealing the witch as one who playfully jumps between a variety of roles, some seemingly retrograde, but all empowering. Take for instance, the "Mary Poppins Spell," which shows an ironically retro image of a frilly-apron-clad witch cleaning her apartment. This image is offered as merely one role among many that the witch may play in her daily life. Others include successful businesswoman, rock-star, friend, and lover. This playful role-playing is further revealed in one of the book's few nods to an enduring patriarchy, the "Boss Tamer" spell. Here, the witch's boss is assumed to be male—in this case, a cowering metro-sexual easily subdued by the spell's power. The accompanying illustration, featuring a heat-packing, whip-wielding young witch, is one of aggressive and sexualized violence towards male power that invokes an officially approved sexual taboo (the whip) and appropriates the erotic and martial bravado of empowered and empowering pop culture figures like Lucy Liu (in damn near any role), Lara Croft, or, once again, Halle Barry as Catwoman. This is no disagreeable and appallingly dressed Mary Daly. The witch is invited to fight the patriarchy by assuming the role of a spiritualized, yet sexy, feminine super-hero.

It is important to point out that the book is virtually a-historical—and as such, typical of our historic moment. There is no mention of the "burning times," ancient paganism and the continuity of practice, or pre-historic matriarchy. *Hex and the City* could be accused of a certain historical amnesia. But if, to borrow a phrase from Zack de la Rocha, the book has traded in history for a VCR[13] (or video iPod), the same could be said, and has been said, of much third-wave feminism. The latter has been accused of taking for granted the critical advances made by the second-wave and of assuming a "women-have-achieved-equality-so-it's-time-to-move-on" attitude that too often results in a marked ignorance of history, particularly

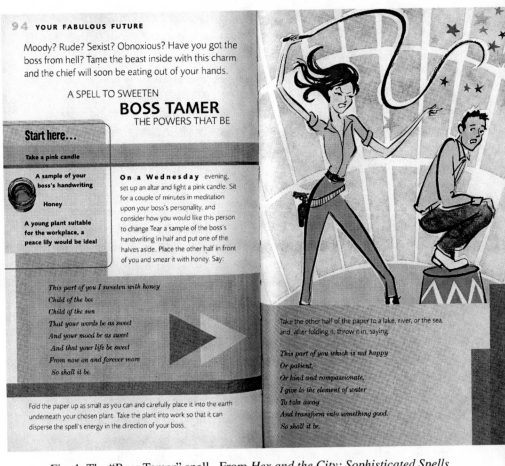

Moody? Rude? Sexist? Obnoxious? Have you got the boss from hell? Tame the beast inside with this charm and the chief will soon be eating out of your hands.

A SPELL TO SWEETEN

BOSS TAMER
THE POWERS THAT BE

Start here...

Take a pink candle

A sample of your boss's handwriting

Honey

A young plant suitable for the workplace, a peace lily would be ideal

On a Wednesday evening, set up an altar and light a pink candle. Sit for a couple of minutes in meditation upon your boss's personality, and consider how you would like this person to change Tear a sample of the boss's handwriting in half and put one of the halves aside. Place the other half in front of you and smear it with honey. Say:

This part of you I sweeten with honey
Child of the bee
Child of the sun
That your words be as sweet
And your mood be as sweet
And that your life be sweet
From now on and forever more
So shall it be.

Fold the paper up as small as you can and carefully place it into the earth underneath your chosen plant. Take the plant into work so that it can disperse the spell's energy in the direction of your boss.

Take the other half of the paper to a lake, river, or the sea, and, after folding it, throw it in, saying:

This part of you which is not happy
Or patient,
Or kind and compassionate,
I give to the element of water
To take away
And transform into something good.
So shall it be.

Fig. 1. The "Boss Tamer" spell. From *Hex and the City: Sophisticated Spells for the Urban Witch*, by Lucy Summers. Illustrations by Robyn Neild.

feminist history.

But perhaps this trade-in was a bargain? After all, many of the third-wave critiques of second-wave feminisms have an undeniable sticking power and there is no small amount of agreement within current feminist discourse that the latter's analysis was deeply flawed and even politically suspect. If this is so, there is an even stronger rationale for surrendering the history of witchcraft. The idea that Wicca represents a practice that has continued since early medieval Europe has been entirely discredited. Wicca is a decidedly modern phenomenon, created in the 1950s by Gerald Gardner who falsely claimed to have learned the practice from a centuries-old coven of witches. The Wiccan feminist's narrative of the "burning times" as a systematic and violent oppression of independent women and a patriarchal conspiracy against a surviving pan-European cult of the Goddess was based largely upon the scurrilous anthropology of Margaret Murray, among others. The elements of this narrative have been firmly disproved by recent scholarship. Given this rejection of Wicca's mythic history, especially radical feminism's essentialist and naturalized construction of female spirituality, the witch is liberated from any obligation to foundational narratives or historical continuity; she is free to reinvent herself and her practice in any way she sees fit, though always in relation to the seasonally shifting neon surfaces of the marketplace. That is to say, she is free to become the sassy urban witch. And, of course, Summers invites her to do so performatively by executing the spells in this little black book.

There is some disagreement among scholars as to whether Wicca is a modern or postmodern religion. I'll avoid entering into this debate here except to point out that, regardless of where you locate Wicca, Summers' book clearly announces a witchcraft characteristic of late capitalism, a term Fredric Jameson borrows from Ernest Mandel to describe the historic condition of postmodernity. As Jameson suggests, with the panoply of rejections that constitute late capitalism comes also a series of appropriations and imitations of the past. *Hex and the City* is such an imitation, a late order simulacrum, a copy of a copy that has no original. Previous Wiccan practice is steeped in its own sense of a hallowed, though fictional, history. *Hex*, by contrast, is characterized by what Jameson calls pastiche.

Here, history as a foundational and grounding narrative is discarded for a playful, though uncritical, irony and retro fashion replaces any historical sensibility.

The spells in *Hex* are certainly texts intended for performance, but what kind of performances are these? Descriptions of rites meant for solo and solitary performance, the spells constitute a privatized and occult liturgy. They are also hybrid performances; they reconcile, or at least bind together, otherwise conflicting impulses, as I will attempt to explain below.

A rebellion against modernity is, ironically, one of the identifying characteristics of modernity. This is true in religion as well as the theatre. The same anti-modernist impulse that brought us Wicca and religious fundamentalism also brought us most, if not all, of the avant-garde. The ritual performances prescribed by *Hex*, however, seem to deny any modernist resistance whatsoever (though they deploy resistant models and means characteristic of modernism). The spells are geared around consuming and a consumerist "lifestyle." These private, solo performances do not constitute worship in the marketplace, or even a worship of the marketplace. This is not worship, in the usual sense, at all. The *Hex* witch is practicing a spiritual skill or technique intended to lubricate her navigation through the marketplace.

Among the strategies of resistance used by Wicca and other modernist forms was an attempt to (re)connect to an idealized and essentialized Nature (borrowing from a lineage that includes Rousseau, Romanticism, and the esoteric concept of "living nature"). This turn to Nature, typically narrated as a *re*turn, functions as an escape from, or resistance to, an array of troubling aspects of modernity: e.g. commodification, bourgeois values, materialism, the economy of mechanical reproduction, and the culture of simulation.

Many of the spells in *Hex* invoke this turn to Nature; the "Body Boost" spell, for instance, in which the witch gets an "energy boost" by literally hugging a tree—thus unironically enacting the trope of a familiar conservative slur against liberals. Yet this turn often appears not as a means of resistance to modernity, but as another appropriation in service of the witch's aforementioned "navigation

56

through the marketplace." Take, for example, the spell "Money Tree." This is a spell designed to promote the health and wellbeing of the witch's stock investments and to insure that she gets "the maximum potential from the money markets." To perform the spell, the witch "purchases" (rather than harvests) a *crassula argentea*, also known as a "money plant," places it on an altar at the new moon, and blesses it with the four elements of fire, air, water, and earth. The witch then ties a series of blue ribbons around the branches of the plant while repeating "I name this ribbon for my investment in (*insert name of investment*)." Once the witch has attached a ribbon for each of her investments, she draws an "earth-invoking" pentagram in front of the plant and says:

Gentle plant, money tree
Work your wonderful magic for me
With your power, increase my fee
As I do will, so shall it be.

It may be argued that the invocation of chthonian and lunar powers to affect the characteristically masculine world of Wall Street constitutes a uniquely feminine form of resistance and subversion. I would argue, however, that the appropriation of the "resistance through return to Nature" narrative is performed for the express purpose of successfully assimilating the witch into the values and mechanisms of the market. There is no resistance or subversion. On the contrary, there is a performed acceptance of the cultural logic whereby the production of resistant narratives is recognized as always/already assimilated by the market for the production of new commodities. Here, there is no irony; the juxtaposition is barefaced. The witch's performance appropriates the sacred symbol of the tree and the power of an essentialized Nature for success in the (literal) market without critical self-consciousness.

All of the spells in *Hex* are performances intended for efficacy. Whether the "Money Tree" spell will actually improve the witch's portfolio is beyond the scope of this discussion. If nothing else, this spell and others like it effectively, performatively, and even *literally* bind modernist narratives of resistance to the market values of late

Fig. 2. The "Money Tree" spell. From *Hex and the City: Sophisticated Spells for the Urban Witch*, by Lucy Summers. Illustrations by Robyn Neild.

capitalism—i.e. to that which the former were intended to resist. The *Hex* witch performatively effects a reconciliation of bourgeois and anti-bourgeois values, an act that is neatly characteristic of the aesthetics and lifestyle expressed and promoted in the television show it remediates.[14]

The postmodern appropriation of modernist forms comes without the boundaries that previously separated high and low culture, a dissolution driven by the imperatives of the marketplace. This is certainly the case with *Hex* wherein spiritual production is integrated into commodity consumption. This is spirituality as shopping, as life-style product, or fashion accessory. The performance of these spells binds the symbolic system (or its simulation) of witchcraft to the values and totems that make up the cultural economy of late capitalism. The defining characteristics of *Hex's* spirituality (feminine, alternative, fashionable and intensely image-conscious, ritualistic, urban, etc.) here earns the practitioner, by means of performance, a certain status, a degree of cultural capital like—though not necessarily equal to—a pair of Manolo Blahniks or throwing a great party. But just as importantly, this is spiritual populism—it is non-elite in contrast to the rarified air of Crowley's sanctum or the secret societies from which Wicca emerged. It is non-authoritarian. There is no modernist occult Master, no initiate, no privileged "seer," though we hope there is a profit [sic]. It is popular and individualized, like visiting a web page at amazon.com. It is an attempt to repudiate the elitist and utopian—and hence, modernist—separation of sacred and profane. The divine and the mundane occupy the same space, engage in the same action. It is commercialism sanctified in post-punk irreverence.

To object that *Hex and the City* is shallow is not a misjudgment; far more serious, it is to miss the point entirely. For the idea of depth is, in this cultural logic, a metaphysical error, a chimera, and even politically suspect. Is the very notion of the occult inimical to this logic? I suggest that this text, and the sub-genre of which it is a member, subverts the occultation of the occult, the populism of late capitalism accomplishing a playful de-mystification of the mystical, not by attempting to scale its heights through a kind of careful, rudimentary, and discursive explanation—a "Hermetica for

Dummies" — but through a flattening out, a razing of the occultist's lofty mount, deflating it to the plateau of the commercial parking lot.

This brings us to the question of authenticity. Religions often balance their protestations of authenticity on claims of ancient lineage. Early Wiccans, as we have seen, pointed to European medieval and pre-patriarchal practice for their authority. Theosophy and other modern esoteric spiritualities trace their lineage back to the hierophants of ancient Egypt (the *ur*-culture of choice for modern esoteric movements). Though *Hex* makes no such claims, since, as a late capitalist spirituality, it operates outside the cultural logic of essentialized authenticity, it may be, by the above measure, ironically more authentic than the earlier incarnations of Wicca and modernist ritual magic.

The modernist forms of magic — initiated in the writings of Eliphas Lévi in the nineteenth century and carried forward by William Westcott, Samuel Mathers, Aleister Crowley, and others — were constructed to empower the practitioners toward greater spiritual maturity, fertility, and awareness. The rites were ceremonial and mystical in nature. They constitute what Lévi termed "high magic." Traditional, pre-modern magic, on the other hand, was intended to give the magician control over supernatural forces or entities (angels, demons, spirits, etc.) for use in achieving practical, tangible ends or to serve specific desires like wealth, health, earthly power, prestige, or sexual partnership. As Hutton describes it, "Traditional scholarly magic was at basis an elaborate way of ringing for room service."[15]

In contrast to the mystical and liberating aims of modernist "high magic," the spirituality in *Hex* is closely akin to these traditional, pre-modern magical practices. The spells in *Hex* are identified as performances that employ magical forces to produce personal, material gain and fulfill specific needs on the part of the witch — most frequently in the form of money, romance, social and career advancement, beauty, charisma, and fashion. Of course, the needs identified by these spells are circumscribed by a particular cultural context. By executing the spells, the witch performatively adopts the taxonomy of desires posited by the marketplace for young women in late capitalism and articulated in such media venues

60

as fashion magazines and *Sex and the City*. Nevertheless, if the equation is to be "accordance with ancient practice = authenticity," *Hex* would seem to come out very well indeed, for its approach to magic and spirituality may be understood as reflecting not merely the traditional, pre-modern magic identified by Hutton, but also the traditions articulated by what are perhaps the most ancient of all religious documents, the Hindu Vedic hymns. The hymns of the Atharva Veda, for instance, contain charms for acquiring health, love, prosperity, and influence in the community—precisely the formula followed by the spells in *Hex* as remediated from fashion magazines via a popular cable television show. Funny how these things work, but there it is.

Despite this ironic historical parallel, looking at *Hex and the City*, one might easily dismiss it as illegitimate or inauthentic. Yet the logic of late capitalism discards the hermeneutic model of depth that would allow for such judgments. In this logic there is no modernist ontology of depth, nor its attendant values or epistemology. "Depth is replaced by surface," as Jameson states.[16] *Hex*, however, does contain, at least provisionally, an ontology of depth, for such is implied by the very idea of magic itself: through her performance, the witch utilizes the "hidden energy" of magic to affect her environment. But here, the desired effects are determined by the values attendant to the late capitalist context and the depth model of magic appears and operates as merely another appropriated modernist form; a form put into service to promote that which it was, in part, constructed to resist. It is a form appropriated as an attraction, like the retro illustrations of glossy, urban fantasy. Thus, I would argue, the shift from depth to surface is still operative. We do judge a book by its cover and, in this cultural logic, quite appropriately so. Here, authenticity is no longer a "thing in itself" but an effect, a by-product, the vaporous residue of a certain set of signs.

If we judge this book by its cover we discover that the latter is key in the book's mischievous deconstruction of the sign of authenticity as that which bestows value. The text does this by offering contradictory signs that reveal themselves as play. The somber black cover and gold lettering of *Hex and the City* invokes nothing less than the familiar leather bound Holy Bible or, in the occult vein, the covers of certain sober tomes of Crowley or LaVey. The interior, on the other hand, belies the promise of authenticity modeled by the cover. Playfully retro cartoons have replaced the obscure woodcuts of occult symbols that one might reasonably expect would grace the pages of what appears to be, on the literal face of it, a serious book of shadows. There are no quotes from Lévi, Paracelsus, John Dee, or other older sources; no raves from Starhawk; no impressive bibliography. But in the cultural logic of late capitalism, these are not proof of value or authenticity. Like the evaluative, oppositional metaphors of high/low and depth/surface to which I have previously referred, these are relevant only as marketing devices, carefully deployed for a specific demographic.

Two points in closing: I think, given the tendencies of late capitalism, we can reasonably expect more of this, not less. Indeed, in 2004 Lucy Summers released a new book, a kind of sequel to *Hex and the City*. The book, also published by Barron's Educational Series, is entitled *Hex Appeal: Seductive Spells for the Sassy Sorceress*.

Secondly, my first response when I discovered this book was a mix of amusement and deep dismay. I initially intended to use what critical skills I possess to mock this book into the remainder bins of the astral plane. I discovered, upon further analysis, however, that my initial impulses were critically unsophisticated, even old-fashioned. This realization makes me feel disconcertingly out of step; it makes me feel old. This in turn leads me to profound intimations of my own mortality. Thus does *Hex and the City* guide me towards a spiritual revelation of the *gravest* sort. How ironic! And, if nothing else, in this irony, there is great wisdom.

Notes

1. Karen Green and John Bigelow, "Does Science Persecute Women? The Case of the 16th-17th Century Witch-hunts," *Philosophy* 73(1998)284: 199.

2. See http://www.religioustolerance.org/wic_nbr.htm.

3. "American Religious Identification Survey," *The Graduate Center of the City University of New York*, at: http://www.gc.cuny.edu/studies/

4. Maud Lavin, "Spellbinding," *Print* 56(2002)3: 22.

5. Jane Arthurs, "*Sex and the City* and Consumer Culture: Remediating Postfeminist Drama," *Feminist Media Studies* 3(2003)1: 83.

6. Jay David Bolter and Richard Grusin, *Remediation: Understanding New Media* (Cambridge, MA and London: MIT, 1999), 35.

7. Ibid., 61.

8. Catherine Orenstein, "What Carrie Could Learn From Mary," *New York Times*, 5 September 2003.

9. Ronald Hutton, *The Triumph of the Moon: A History of Modern Pagan Witchcraft* (Oxford: Oxford University Press, 1999), 342.

10. Ibid., 341.

11. In this essay, all references to "Third Wave" feminism refer to its manifestation in the United States.

12. Arthurs 87.

13. Rage Against the Machine, "No Shelter," in *Godzilla: The Album*, Sony compact disk 69338.

14. See Arthurs 91.

15. Hutton 82.

16. Fredric Jameson, *Postmodernism or, The Cultural Logic of Late Capitalism* (Durham: Duke University Press, 1991), 12.

Esoteric Art

Philosophic Mercury:
Evolution of the Alchemical Feminine

M. E. Warlick

Based on many of the premises of Hellenistic science, the earliest alchemical texts describe physical matter as having both male and female characteristics. They imagine the masculine Philosophic Sulphur as comprising the hot, dry, and fixed qualities of the sun, while the feminine Philosophic Mercury embodies the cool, moist, and volatile qualities of the moon. In the laboratory, the alchemist perfects these two components by separating them from base matter and removing the impurities from each. Then the alchemist reunites the two archetypal substances and fuses them with fire. The result of their union is a child, the "Philosophers' Stone," a mysterious substance that enables further transformations.

While this scenario of the gendered polarization of physical matter is generally true throughout alchemical literature, individual texts often differ in their definitions of the terms "Sulphur" and "Mercury" and in the degree to which each of these symbolic substances plays a role within the alchemical work. Tracing the evolution of these polarized substances and the wide variety of male and female characters that come to represent them reveals shifting attitudes towards gender roles. The earliest alchemical illustrations incorporated religious, courtly and planetary imagery. Mythological figures followed as a result of the Renaissance's revival of classical myths and their interpretations by alchemical authors and artists. Sulphur and Mercury appear as the sun and the moon, Kings and Queens, Adam and Eve, Apollo and Diana, and male and female animals. This article is particularly concerned with "Philosophic Mercury," its origins and evolution, through an analysis of both feminine and masculine images that artists adopted to represent this concept.

The polarized and gendered view of matter within alchemical literature has ancient origins, tracing back to the earliest alchemical philosophers, such as Maria the Prophet, who appears in an engraving by Matthäus Merian (Fig. 1). Michael Maier first published this engraving in his *Symbola aureae mensae* (1617), and Daniel Stolcius reprinted it in his *Chymisches Lustgartlein* (1624).[1] On the title page to Maier's text, twelve portraits in roundels represent the twelve alchemists from twelve nations who play a significant role in the development of alchemical philosophy. Maria, who represents the Hebrews, holds an honored place at the center top, next to Hermes Trismegistus, to indicate her longevity and importance. We know of her teachings through the writings of Zosimos of Panopolis, c. 300 CE, who claims her as one of his teachers. His writings are preserved in a manuscript in Venice dating between the late tenth to the late eleventh-century.[2] Two related manuscripts, both at the Bibliothèque Nationale in Paris, date from the thirteenth- and the fifteenth-centuries.[3] All three manuscripts contain the writings of Zosimus, other Greek alchemical authors, and commentaries on Zosimus by medieval authors who may have had access to earlier copies of his treatises, including Olympiodorus (early fifth-century) and Stephanus of Alexandria (fl. 620-640).

Zosimus praises Maria's practical skills and recipes, and her invention of many vessels for distillation, including the *triblikos* and the *kerotakis*. She understood the different levels of heat that could be achieved by using hot-ash, dung, and the water bath, which still bears her name, as the *bain marie* or *marienbad*. The Venice manuscript contains some of the earliest illustrations of alchemical vessels, attributed to Maria's designs. Both Paris manuscripts contain similar, although simplified, illustrations of her vessels. Her first image in the west appears in the margin of a fifteenth-century illustrated alchemical manuscript at St. John's College, Cambridge, beside text referring to the *Liber Marie sororis moysi* (*Book of Mary Sister of Moses*).[4] Her identification as the sister of Moses, which had already occurred in Arab texts, was erroneous, although intended to lend greater authority to her writings by suggesting their antiquity. In her philosophical writings, Maria presents the polarized qualities of matter as male and female, fixed and volatile. She states: "Combine together the male and the female, and you will find that which you seek."[5] Both Zosimos and Olympiodorus attribute this gendered view of physical matter to Maria, and it remains a central feature of alchemical philosophy throughout its development. She was certainly not alone among the ancient philosophers in asserting the polarized aspects of physical matter, but her contributions to establishing the role of gender within alchemical philosophy is significant.

Fig. 1. Matthaeus Merian, "Maria the Prophet," engraving in Daniel Stolcius, *Chymisches Lustgartlein*, (Frankfurt: Lucas Jennis, 1624), University of Glasgow Library, Special Collections Department, SM 1000, n.p., Figure XVII.

In the engraving (Fig. 1), she stands beside a small mountain in which two vaporous clouds circulate around a small plant between two communicating vessels above and below the earth. Derived from Aristotle's theories of dry and moist exhalations that form minerals and metals beneath the earth, this detail suggests the circulating nature of the celestial forces and their products on earth. These two exhalations later congeal into the Sulphur and Mercury theory of the

Arabs, who claimed that Sulphur and Mercury combine with each other in all metals, in changing proportions to produce different metallic qualities. Maria also understood power of herbs, which is indicated in the engraving by the small plant in the center of the two smokes. In her writings, she refers to a small white herb that grows in the mountains. Some have identified this plant as lunary or moonwort (*Botrychium lunaria*).

In 1618, J. D. Mylius included in his *Basilica philosophica* one hundred sixty round emblems representing the most famous alchemists, beginning with Hermes Trismegistus and ending with himself.[6] Within the series, arranged in this text in ten pages of sixteen emblems each, only five of the emblems represent women. Maria's emblem appears at the top right edge of the first page, repeating the small detail of the two circulating smokes seen in Figure 1. On the following row are emblems dedicated to other female alchemists of antiquity, Cleopatra of Egypt, Medera, Thaphuntia and Euthica, four women with varying degrees of notoriety in alchemical philosophy. Other images of these female alchemical philosophers exist, but Maria is certainly the best known. It would be easy to dismiss all the female alchemists of antiquity as legendary, but, interestingly enough, their writings frequently draw analogies to human sexuality and pregnancy to describe laboratory processes, particularly in the tracts ascribed to Maria, Cleopatra and Isis. Maria's writings circulated throughout the Middle Ages and she maintained her fame into the seventeenth-century and beyond. Her dialogue with the philosopher Aros on practical matters was included in many of the early printed compilations of alchemical treatises of the late sixteenth and early seventeenth-centuries.[7] No doubt Maier, Mylius and Stolcius highlighted her contributions and included images of her for that reason.

Maria's role as both an alchemical philosopher and practitioner is unusual, and few other women achieved her status within alchemical traditions. The lack of practicing female alchemists is perhaps no different from the scarcity of women in other professions. In Andrea Bonaiuti's *Apotheosis of St. Thomas Aquinas* in the Spanish Chapel of Santa Maria Novella in Florence, a chorus line of female personifications sit above male representatives of the professions of

70

law, theology, and the liberal arts.[8] The women serve as allegories for these male dominated professions, and they function as muses to the male practitioners below. In a similar image from a manuscript in the John Rylands Library in Manchester, a female personification of alchemy sits enthroned above a practicing male alchemist.[9] On either side there are elaborate towers from which silver and red liquids flow through faces of the moon and the sun to form fountains over pools in which female and male nude figures bathe. We will return to these two fountains shortly.

As alchemical philosophy developed from late antiquity, the concepts of Sulphur and Mercury maintained their primacy. Arab philosophers considered Sulphur and Mercury to be the principle components of each of the seven ancient metals (quicksilver, lead, tin, copper, iron, silver, gold), combined in different proportions to produce their different inherent qualities. This view is usually ascribed to the eight-century Arabic philosopher Jābir ibn Hayyān, although his identity and the authenticity of the texts attributed to him have been much debated. More important, in light of the later development of alchemical illustrations, is the transmission of Arabic texts to the Latin west. The revitalization of alchemy in Europe began in the mid twelfth-century when Arab manuscripts, newly translated into Latin, began to flow north from intellectual centers in Islamic Spain and southern Italy. These works included Arab translations of earlier Greek manuscripts, original treatises by Arab authors, and newly inspired works by European authors.

Throughout the thirteenth century, significant new alchemical texts appeared. Albertus Magnus (1193?-1280), and Roger Bacon (1214?-1294) renewed the ancient debate concerning art versus nature, that is, whether human industry could create products, equal to, or even superior to, those produced through natural means. William Newman has explored the origins and impact of one of the most important late medieval texts, the *Summa perfectionis*, composed at the end of the thirteenth or very early fourteenth-century and formerly attributed to the "Latin Geber."[10] While some had claimed this text was a translation from the Arabic author Jābir ibn Hayyān, the true identity of this author had long perplexed scholars. Newman asserts that he was a Franciscan monk, Paulus of

71

Taranto, who also authored a *Theorica et Practica*, a text that shares common sources and similar practices with the *Summa*. Influence of the *Summa* on several important late medieval alchemical texts can be found, including texts ascribed to Albertus Magnus, Arnald of Villanova (1240-1311), and Ramon Lull (1232?-1316). The *Rosarium*, attributed to Arnald, lifted entire sections from the *Summa* verbatim, without acknowledgement, and this text would have significant influence on the later development of alchemical imagery.

Both the *Summa* and the *Rosarium* promoted the "Mercury alone" theory, which asserted that Mercury alone could produce the universal elixir.[11] This theory revalued the role of Mercury in the creation of both silver and gold. According to these authors, gold could be produced from pure refined Mercury, with just a touch of Sulphur remaining to give it its golden color. While they gave prominence to Mercury, they still maintained, like the Arabic authors before them, that Mercury and Sulphur combined in differing proportions to produce all metals.[12] It is important to reiterate that the concepts of "Mercury" and "Sulphur" are not these actual physical substances, but rather the polarized properties of metals represented by those terms. It will be asserted here that the "Mercury alone" theory will influence the images of Mercury found in later illustrated alchemical manuscripts.

The last three decades of the thirteenth century witnessed an increasingly hostile attitude towards alchemy, culminating in a bull, issued by Pope John XXII in 1317, against alchemists who might attempt to counterfeit coinage.[13] In addition, there was a growing trend to theologize alchemical texts, which did not always meet with ecclesiastic approval. Yet, such official warnings did little to curb the enthusiasm for alchemical philosophy and experimentation. Soon after the papal bull, Petrus Bonus of Ferrara (Giano Lacinio, fl. 1323-1330) wrote his *Pretiosa margarita novella* (*The New Pearl of Great Price*), c. 1330, which offered a strong defense of alchemy, and that position would continue to develop over the next three centuries. While authors often qualified the degree to which they accepted the possibility of metallic transmutation, there is no doubt that metallurgy, geology, dyeing, glassmaking, medicine, pharmacology, and other related experimental sciences were all steeped in alchemical philosophy and that these professions shared many laboratory procedures.

Alchemical imagery began to appear in the late fourteenth century.[14] Earlier alchemical manuscripts were sparsely illustrated, including the Greek manuscripts containing the writings of Zosimus mentioned above. If illustrated at all, early alchemical manuscripts contain only scattered drawings of vessels or graphic symbols for laboratory substances and operations. The sudden impulse to illustrate alchemical manuscripts has never been fully explained, and it must be said at the outset that studies of these manuscripts by textual scholars and by art historians are still very much in their initial stages. Little is known about the relationships between versions of these texts, and even less about the artists who illustrated and copied them. Newman suggests that the turn to more figural and allegorical representations of the laboratory work grew from a need to evade the antagonistic climate that had characterized alchemical debates in the late thirteenth century. He finds that as subsequent alchemical texts departed from the "disputational ambience of the medieval university" they began to loose intellectual rigor.[15] For literary scholars and art historians, however, this is the moment when alchemy becomes even more interesting. Artists took their images from religious, astrological and allegorical prototypes and adapted them to a new alchemical context, and from these early texts a good deal of subsequent alchemical imagery would be derived.

One of the first illustrated alchemical manuscripts was Constantine of Pisa's (13th century) *Liber secretorum alchimie (Book of the Secrets of Alchemy)*. The University of Glasgow owns a Latin manuscript of the text. Another copy, now in Vienna, had been translated into Flemish as *Bouc der heimelicheden van mire vrouwen alkemenen (Book of the Secrets of My Lady Alchemy)*.[16] This manuscript also contains an untitled treatise by Gratheus and a short tract, the *Wisdom of Solomon*, which are also illustrated. Constantine references the illustrations in his text, and he clearly intended to include them from the outset. There are religious images, such as the head of Christ, the hand of God, and scenes inspired by Genesis, including the Garden of Eden with Adam, Eve, and a female headed serpent, and newly created animals. Comparisons between Christ's death and resurrection and alchemical operations had already appeared in the texts of Arnald of Villanova and Jean de Rupescissa,[17] and such textual and visual analogies to Christianity would continue in later alchemical treatises.

Constantine illustrates a triangular diagram of the known world and incorporates astronomy, primarily in its practical aspects. He draws analogies between the properties of the planets and the metals, and urges alchemists to pay particular attention to the phases of the moon, who like medical doctors, should take lunations into account when performing operations to ensure success.[18] Two of illustrations contain a series of circular diagrams with human heads that represent the planets and their related metals. The planet Saturn (Lead) is represented as a head with three faces, two profiles and one facing forward, anticipating later double-headed androgynous figures. Jupiter is a crowned king, connected to copper, and Venus is a crowned Queen, connected to tin, reversing the more typical relationship between these planets and their metals found in later alchemical literature. Mercury (quicksilver) is represented as bearded bishop. Constantine emphasizes the role of Mercury which must be refined and congealed, as Avicenna had explained. Drawing on Aristotelian concepts of animal reproduction, Constantine refers to the generation of metals as a reaction between a liquid menstruum which is solidified in a fetus by masculine semen.[19] Animals are included in three of the circular diagrams to suggest their initial creation by God, but there are no explicit sexual images here. Obrist identifies two other figures in circular diagrams as male and female personifications of the soul and of nature. The illustrations in the Gratheus treatise, including the resurrected Christ, a king and a queen on either side of a large giant with a club, a child in a vessel that resembles a uterus, battling male and female figures and two battling lions, all have descendents in later alchemical imagery.[20]

In the early fifteenth century, two fully illustrated manuscripts appear rather suddenly, the *Buch der heiligen Dreifaltigkeit (Book of the Holy Trinity)* and the *Aurora consurgens (Rising Dawn)*. Both manuscripts contain male and female figures drawn from Christian and secular prototypes, as well as newly formulated images, such as the half male-half female androgyne. In both manuscripts, images of women play a prominent role. The author of *Buch der heiligen Dreifaltigkeit* was a Franciscan monk named Ulmannus, and several versions, including the Berlin copy, end with an image of St. Francis receiving the stigmata.[21] The production of this manuscript is closely connected to events surrounding the Council of Constance, which took place between 1414-18. Ulmannus wrote his text between 1410 and 1419, and upon its completion he presented it to the Markgraf Friedrich I of Brandenburg. The Emperor Sigismund, who presided at the Council, also received a shortened version during this time. The Council was convened to attempt to heal the Great Schism and to clarify the contemporary dispute on papal succession. The council also conducted the trials of Jan Hus and Johann of Prague, and they burned both men for heresy. Within this inflammatory climate of religious persecution it is important to note that the Christian imagery within this manuscript was not considered improper, and in fact, it served larger religious and political motives, reinforcing the power of the Roman Catholic Church and the Hapsburg Dynasty.[22] It is a legacy of much later occult revivals that alchemy today has been described as a heretical practice linked to witchcraft, sorcery and other black arts. On the contrary, monks and nuns practiced alchemy during this period and felt that its precepts were very much in line with their religious beliefs.[23] The Franciscans promoted the Immaculate Conception of Mary, and while Marian theology was not a focal point of discussions at the Council of Constance, the Franciscan authorship of this manuscript may help explain Mary's important role within it.

Adam's and Christ's suffering and resurrection represent the destruction of primal matter and its eventual purification into the Philosophers' Stone. Early in the series, male figures are tortured, and Christ is crucified on the cross. A female serpent, adapted from scenes of the Garden of Eden, stands beside Eve and pierces Adam with her sword, like the caustic acids that break down primal matter and begin the process of purification. The version at the John Rylands Library in Manchester adds a furnace and vessels into this image to reinforce the analogy to laboratory operations.[24] Christ's resurrection from his sarcophagus represents the ultimate perfection of the masculine and the production of gold.

The *Buch der heiligen Dreifaltigkeit* also contains several androgynous figures, half-male and half-female, joined by a vertical line down the center. In one, a King holds a spiraling serpent while the Queen on the right holds a gold chalice containing three golden serpents. They stand on two fountains from which flow red and green streams to nourish trees on either side, whose blossoms contain the heads of the sun and the moon. A two-headed dragon beneath this androgyne drinks from the two fountains. They can be traced back to the two exhalations of Aristotle, pictured in the emblem of Maria the Prophet. Another androgyne, formed of a joined King and Queen holding a sword and a crown, battle the seven deadly sins, whose names surround the figure as a reminder that evil temptations like pride, anger and gluttony can lead to the destruction of the soul.[25] This androgyne stands above a diabolic four-headed monster, with the heads of Adam and Eve rising from this creature to entwine around the legs of the couple.

Throughout the text, images of Eve and Virgin Mary represent the feminine aspects of alchemical substances and processes. Within a green shield, Mary hovers over the crucified Christ, behind a golden double-headed eagle. Close connections are drawn between the Virgin Mary and Christ, as representatives of the feminine and masculine polarities of the work. Elsewhere Mary is conflated with the Woman Clothed with the Sun, from Revelations (12:1-17), who fought with a satanic dragon to protect her unborn son. In the version at the Wellcome Institute in London, she stands on the moon with rays of the sun radiating behind her, signifying that she encompasses both polarities. A small crucifix and Fleur de Lys rise above her.[26]

Her ultimate triumph is pictured as the Crowning of Mary.[27] In this image, she kneels above the shield of the crucifixion. Christ and God the Father place the crown on her head, while the dove of the Holy Spirit swoops down and offers assistance. Surrounding this figural grouping are the symbols of the four evangelists, the eagle of John, the lion of Mark, the angel of Matthew and the ox of Luke, which throughout the text are compared to planets, metals and virtues. In opposition to the female serpent and Eve who represent dissolving acids and feminine impurities that must be purged, the

76

Virgin Mary represents the perfection of the feminine and her crowning becomes one of the most significant illuminations within this text. Although most of these images were based on earlier Christian prototypes, the Crowning of Mary as part of the Trinity was virtually unprecedented. Christ often crowns Mary in Gothic art, but to conflate her Crowning with the Trinity appears in only one apparently unrelated precedent. After appearing in this manuscript, the Crowning of Mary with the Trinity became a popular Christian image throughout the remainder of the fifteenth century.[28]

The *Aurora consurgens* (Rising Dawn), also from the fifteenth-century, incorporates both religious and secular imagery.[29] This manuscript inspired Carl Jung to construct his twentieth-century theories of the parallels between alchemy and human psychological development. His disciple, Marie-Louise von Franz, translated the Zürich text and traced its many biblical and apocryphal sources.[30] She endorsed the traditional authorship of the *Aurora* to St. Thomas Aquinas. While his connection to this text is no longer supported, no one as yet has identified its true author. Like the *Buch der heiligen Dreifaltigkeit*, religious prototypes were used as models, including the Virgin of Mercy (Misericordia), who in this manuscript appears as a Queen with her open cape guarding male personifications of the seven metals, while a male alchemists looks on. Artists used similar images to represent the Virgin Mary and her worshipers and Saint Ursula and her 11,000 virgins, and this well-known religious model was easily adapted to the new alchemical context.

Elsewhere, a crowned woman with the red face of the sun personifies alchemical wisdom and nurses two elderly philosophers. This scene is related to images of the lactating Virgin Mary, and to the allegorical figure of Ecclesia. The female body serves as the matrix in which the Philosophers' Stone is nourished to maturity. In one illustration, a bleeding woman within a zodiac circle holds up her menstrual clothes to the sun, placed beside the Lion, the sign of Leo. In another illustration, a winged pregnant woman, related to the Woman of Revelations seen in the *Buch der heiligen Dreifaltikeit*, stands on the moon with rays of the sun behind her. She opens her bodice to reveal her child, formed with the caduceus of Mercury. Other scenes refer to the destruction of the physical body, such as one in which a nude man and woman dismember each other. In another battle scene, a knight, with the red head of the sun and riding a lion, battles a nude woman with the silver head of the moon, now tarnished black, who rides a griffin.[31] Each figure holds a shield that contains symbols of its opponent. The sun carries a shield with three moons, while the moon's shield contains the shining face of the sun, signifying that both Sulphur and Mercury contain small elements of each other.

Parts of the text of the *Aurora* are derived from the "Song of Songs," an erotic Biblical poem that had long been used as an analogy for Christ's relationship to his church and to the Marian cult that rose during the Gothic period.[32] The author of the *Aurora consurgens* adapted the sexual romance in the poem to illustrate alchemical operations. In two separate scenes the couple makes love, folios that are often defaced by later readers, uncomfortable with the explicit sexual imagery. These scenes of sexual union represent the union of male and female matter within the vessel and echo the language of the interpenetration of these substances during the laboratory operations. These sexual images enjoyed a great longevity in alchemical imagery following the publication of the series of twenty related woodcuts, entitled the *Rosarium philosophorum,* within *De alchimia opuscula* in 1550.[33] These woodcuts create a narrative of the romance of the Queen (Mercury) and the King (Sulphur), who meet each other, remove their clothing, bathe in a pool and then make love, twice, beside their symbols of the moon and the sun, to signify their fusion and the production of silver and gold. This series ends with the Crowning of Mary and the Resurrection of Christ, adapted from the *Buch der heiligen Dreifaltigkeit.*

Planetary imagery within alchemical manuscripts also begins early. The sun and the moon are perhaps the most persistent representations of Sulphur and Mercury, as found in an illustrated manuscript in the Laurenzian Medical Library in Florence, dating to the fifteenth century. Although damaged, this text contains many images of the masculine sun and feminine moon. In one, they face each other on either side of a vessel, labeled with four letters, IAAT, to indicate the four elements, ignis; aer; aqua; and terra (fire, air water and earth).[34] In this image, the moon is an old woman, wearing a medieval wimple, which is sometimes confused by copyists who draw her with a beard instead. The sun, with its dry heat and daily predictability represents masculine Sulphur, while the cool and volatile moon represents feminine Mercury. The sun and the moon, often drawn with human faces, appear throughout alchemical imagery and often accompany the figural representations of these concepts. One of the most beautiful is a folio from the *Splendor Solis* (Splendor of the Sun) in which the Queen, dressed in blue with a touch of red stands beneath the cool moon, and the King, dressed in red with a touch of blue, stands beneath the fiery sun.[35] Images of the seven ancient planets often use women to represent the moon and Venus, although male substitutes can also be found, as in the Misericordia image in the *Aurora consurgens*, mentioned above, in which the seven planets are all men.

The images found in the early illustrated manuscripts deserve a fuller analysis, as do their relationships to other fifteenth and sixteenth century illustrated manuscripts series including the *Pretiossa Donum Dei* (Most Precious Gift of God), Lambsprinck's male and female animals, and the *Ripley Scrolls*. Still, this glimpse at the *Buch der heiligen Dreifaltigkeit* and the *Aurora consurgens* reveals that their artists transformed the polarized concepts of male Sulphur and female Mercury into a variety of male and female figures adapted from religious, allegorical and even sexual prototypes. Figures representing the male Sulphur and the female Mercury are typically balanced one to one within these scenes, as they battle and as they make love.

At the same time, both manuscripts contain several significant images of women alone. These women retain the influence of the "Mercury alone" theory of the late Middle Ages. They include the Woman of Clothed with the Sun from Revelations in the *Buch der heiligen Dreifaltigkeit*, who stands beneath the crucifixion, and the related woman in the *Aurora*, pregnant with her child Mercury. Other representations of this powerful "Philosophic Mercury" display maidens with long flowing blond hair to signify their virginity, as artists represented married women with bound hair. A manuscript in Leiden, which combines images from the *Buch der heiligen*

Dreifaltigkeit and the *Aurora*, includes such a maiden, who stands on two winged fountains and calmly subdues in her hands a small dragon with flaming breath.[36] A related image in Glasgow depicts a nude woman holding an entwined serpent in one hand and a chalice with serpents in the other. She also stands above two fountains, whose streams pour into a single vessel.[37] In a Paris manuscript related to the *Rosarium philosophorum*, a woman identified as "Philosophic Mercury" holds a chalice with serpents in her right hand, a waxing crescent moon in her left, and stands above a fused sun and the moon.[38]

These women share features with the female personification of Nature, who appears in a number of alchemical illustrations. Perhaps the most famous is in a manuscript by Jean Perréal (1455-1530), dated 1516, in which Nature, looking decidedly grumpy, cautions the alchemist, dressed in a brown robe, to follow her teachings.[39] His laboratory can be seen within the rounded arch at the right edge of the illustration. The elaborate branches of the entwined tree behind her contain small gold letters that identify its symbolic components. The roots draw sustenance from the mineral, plant, and animal worlds, and primal matter is heated in her small furnace. The four elements, earth, water, air and fire form the ellipse in which she sits and they remix and intertwine above her to form at the top the "Work of Nature." Her crown contains glyphs of the seven ancient planets. In the accompanying poem, she warns the alchemist that only by following her path, will he achieve his goals. The same sentiments can be found in an engraving included in Michael Maier's *Atlanta fugiens*, first published in Oppenheim in 1617.[40] Here, the wise alchemist lets Nature be his guide as he follows in her footsteps on a moonlit night.[41]

Many of these features are combined in an allegorical figure of "Philosophic Mercury," in the University of Glasgow's Ferguson MS 6 (Fig. 2). This manuscript, entitled *Spruch der Philosophien*, contains several earlier series of alchemical illustrations, including the *Aurora consurgens*, and the *Rosarium philosophum*, illustrated with minimal text. While it dates to the late sixteenth-century, c. 1580, a number of medievalizing features in the illustrations suggest that the copyist was drawing from early versions of these manuscripts. In the image, a nude woman stands atop a rainbow that links two pools flowing red and white, colors also connected to the male and female polarities. Her long flowing blond hair and her nudity indicate her virginity and purity. The sun and moon are suspended in the tree above her. There intertwined branches are reminiscent of the tree in Perréal's image of Mother Nature, as well as the astrological glyph for the planet Mercury and the caduceus of the god Mercury. In her hands she holds two golden chalices to catch the flow from her breasts, red and black, the latter perhaps based on a tarnished silver original. Small towns face each other on either side of a river that goes underground at her feet. These towns, with their brick walls and towers, suggest illustrations of alchemical furnaces, which often mimic castles and fortifications. Two paths lead to the doors of these buildings, and while the edges of the image are now abraded, these paths reinforce connections to the two fountains below, and ultimately the two exhalations, pictured in the emblem of Maria the Prophet (Fig. 1).

Figures above fountains typically include the male-female androgynes and the beautiful young women who represent "Philosophic Mercury," discussed above. In the *Splendor Solis*, 1582, the figure atop the fountains becomes an armed soldier, who wears the colors of the different stages of the work as it progresses from black to white to yellow and red.[42] This soldier is not alone in a trend to adapt or replace many of the female figures found in earlier manuscripts with male figures, particularly during the great proliferation of new alchemical engravings published in Frankfurt and Oppenheim by Lucas Jennis and the de Bry family in the early seventeenth-century.[43] These printed texts compiled, synthesized and interpreted earlier alchemical treatises, while embellishing them with new imagery. These authors were influenced by the revival of classical mythology. An increasing array of male gods, soldiers, heroes and practicing alchemists appeared to represent substances and operations of the work.

Several factors could be cited to explain this growing prominence of male figures in the engraved alchemical imagery. Scholars have charted the increasing polarization of gender roles that characterize

Fig. 2. "Alchimia, (Lady Alchemy)" *Spruch der Philosophien*, German, late 16th c., paper, 220 x 160 mm, University of Glasgow Library, Special Collections Department, Ferguson MS 6, fol. 4v.

the sixteenth and seventeenth century, supported by both ecclesiastic and secular authorities. Women remained excluded from universities, just as university education became the prerequisite for newly organized professions. As the public roles of women within these professions were curtailed, the private roles of women within the domestic sphere were encouraged. These societal forces impacted the new alchemical images,[44] even as their artists, often well aware of the previous repertory of manuscript imagery, adapted earlier images for an exploding market. It is important to assert, however, that the shift towards more masculine imagery at the onset of the Scientific Revolution was neither strictly linear nor absolute. Women continued to play important roles in these engravings, particularly with the appearance of new female mythological characters. Female personifications of the planets continue and the male-female androgyne is often repeated. Other images reveal these shifts more clearly. The Virgin Mary virtually disappears in images produced within Protestant contexts, although she continues to appear in texts produced in Catholic countries, even into the late nineteenth century.

The evolving gender roles within these new engravings deserve a much fuller investigation, but one telling comparison can be offered, Emblem X of Michael Maier's *Atalanta fugiens*, in which a male alchemist brings a flaming torch to a fire, while two representations of the male god Mercury observe (Fig. 3). This text contains fifty engravings arranged in emblematic fashion, with each entry containing a short motto, an engraving, an epigram, a short musical composition, and an explanation of the image. The use of the god Mercury to represent alchemical concepts of Mercury draws from earlier sources. After Marsilio Ficino (1433-99) published translations of the *Corpus Hermeticum*, the fame of the Egyptian Hermes Trismegistus, the legendary founder of alchemical philosophy continued to grow. His fame remained strong into the seventeenth-century, even though Isaac Casaubon (1559–1614) was already casting doubts on the antiquity of these texts. Through complex chain of associations, the Egyptian god Thoth and the mythical Hermes Trismegistus became conflated with the Greek god Hermes and the Roman god Mercury.

Da ignem igni, Mercurium Mercurio, & sufficit tibi.

EPIGRAMMA X.

M *Achina pendet ab hac mundi connexa catena*
Tota, SUO QUOD PAR GAUDEAT OMNE PARI:
Mercurius sic Mercurio, sic jungitur igni
Ignis, & hæc arti sit data meta tuæ.
Hermetem Vulcanus agit, sed penniger Hermes,
Cynthia, te solvit, te sed, Apollo soror.

G   HÆC

Fig. 3. Matthaeus Merian, "Give Fire to Fire, Mercury to Mercury, and it is enough for you," engraving in Michael Maier, *Atalanta Fugiens*, (Oppenheim: Johann Theodor de Bry, 1618). University of Glasgow Library, Special Collections Department, Euing Bd 16-g.6, p. 49, Emblem X.

Male Mercuries had appeared in earlier manuscripts, such as Constantine's planetary bishop mentioned above, but in the new engravings his presence increases dramatically.

The motto of this emblem reads, "Give fire to fire, Mercury to Mercury, and it is enough for you."[45] The message emphasizes that "like generates like," repeating an old alchemical adage that "barley generates barley, as gold generates gold."[46] The discourse reads like an attempt to reconcile conflicting concepts in earlier alchemical literature. It contains a critique of Galenic medicine, in that the sudden applications of oppositional medicine, such as adding heat to a frozen limb, can create disastrous results. Rather, it encourages Paracelsus's alternative approach that "like cures like," suggesting that frozen limbs might first be helped through immersion in cold water. Paracelsus's (1493-1541) voluminous writings had a profound effect on alchemical philosophy. His view of women shared much with Lutheran theology, and while he expressed a negative view of human sexuality, he recognized the significance of the Virgin Mary's virginity and purity in her role as the mother of Christ.[47] Perhaps most significantly for alchemical imagery, Paracelsus had emphasized the three-fold nature of matter, adding "Salt," as a concept for the body that unities Sulphur and Mercury, soul and spirit. Tripartite descriptions of matter were not new to alchemical philosophy, even Maria mentions them, but Paracelsus's emphasis on Salt as an essential component of the Sulphur-Mercury duality was virtually unprecedented,[48] and it infiltrated alchemical philosophy and imagery in a variety of ways. Here it is suggested by the caduceus of the god Mercury, on which two serpents entwine around a single rod.

The discourse also deals with the oppositions of fire and water, with the god Mercury now representing the watery, mercurial side of the equation. To explain the polarities of Mercury (water) and fire, Maier reflects back to the philosophical oppositions of Empedocles, of combat and friendship, hatred and love. From the elements of water and fire, the other two elements arise, air and earth, to produce the Stone. Mercury is the matter and fire provides motion and gives shape to matter. Maier states that just as there are two kinds of fire, one internal to a body and the external fire, heating a vessel, there are two kinds of Mercury. De Jong's commentary connects this emblem to Geber's Mercury-Sulphur theory, and while it does place water and fire, or Mercury and Sulphur, in opposition, it only obliquely refers to Geber's "Mercury alone" theory, through a quotation from the *Aurora consurgens*, "You should draw the quintessential from the Mercury, otherwise, your work is in vain. And therefore the Mercury is described as threefold." Unities, dualities and trinities are thus conflated in this emblem and its discourse. Its complex exegesis tells us much about the new climate of alchemical philosophy, and its attempts to reconcile the diversity of previous authors. The engraving illustrates these conundrums since the male god Mercury now symbolizes the dual nature of Mercury, and the tripartite unity of Body, Soul and Spirit, in his caduceus.

The transformations in representations of the alchemical Mercury suggest both the continuity and instability of the alchemical feminine. Additional questions could be raised concerning the sexuality of the god Mercury, and his parental role in fathering the Hermaphrodite with Aphrodite, a legend illustrated in Emblem XXXVIII of *Atalanta fugiens*. The motto reads, "Like the Hermaphrodite, the Rebis is born out of two mountains, of Mercury and Venus."[49] Adapting the classical myth to a new alchemical interpretation, Mercury here becomes the father and Venus the mother of the Philosophers' Stone.

Gender and sexuality remain central to alchemical imagery within this new phase of printed texts and their engravings. A fuller study of that transition is needed, but tracing the transformations of gendered alchemical imagery from its inception to these engravings reveals much about the fluctuating interpretations of the feminine in alchemical philosophy. Increasingly, masculine imagery predominated within these seventeenth-century engravings, but that doesn't mean that the feminine was displaced. Rather, her appearance in these engravings becomes more nuanced, in ways that reflect the shifting roles of women at this time. Identifying the underlying assumptions about gender and sexuality can help to clarify the feminine role within alchemical representations of the physical work, as well as the role of the feminine within alchemy's ultimate task of spiritual transformation.

Notes

1. Michael Maier, *Symbola aurea mensae duodecim nationum* and Daniel Stolcius, *Chymisches Lustgartlein.* The Latin version of Stolcius's text is entitled *Viridarium chymicum figuris cupro incisis adornatum, et poeticis picturis illustratum.* All three texts were published in Frankfurt by Lucas Jennis.

2. *Marcianus graecus.* Z. 299.

3. *Parisini graeci* 2325 and 2327. The latter of the two Paris manuscripts formed the basis of Marcellin Berthelot's nineteenth-century translation and interpretation. Marcellin Berthelot and Ch.-Em. Ruelle, *Collection des alchimistes grecs*, I-III, 1888, reprint ed., (London: Holland Press, 1963). See also Walter Scott, *Hermetica,* IV (Boston: Shambhala, 1985), 104-153.

4. MS G 14, James Montague Rhodes, *A Descriptive Catalogue of the Manuscripts in the Library of St. John's College Cambridge* (Cambridge University Press, 1913), 214-215.

5. Raphael Patai, *The Jewish Alchemists*, (Princeton: Princeton University Press, 1994), 62-63. Patai here also reproduces Berthelot's drawings of Maria's vessels based on those found in the Venice manuscript.

6. Johann Daniel Mylius, *Opus medico-chymicum, Vol. 3: Basilica philosophica (Frankfurt: Lucas Jennis, 1618),* University of Glasgow, Special Collections Department Ferguson Aq-d.11, not paginated.

7. Such as "Mariae Prophetissae Practica," in the *Artis auriferae* (Basel: Conrad Waldkirch, 1610), p. 205. See also John Ferguson, *Bibliotheca Chemica* , II, (London: Derek Verschoyle, 1954), 77-78.

8. Diana Norman, "The Art of Knowledge," in *Siena, Florence and Padua: Art, Society and Religion 1200-1400*, Diana Norman, ed., (New Haven: Yale University Press, 1995), 217-228.

9. John Rylands Library, Manchester, German MS 1, fol. 6r.

10. William R. Newman, *The* Summa Perfectionis *of Pseudo-Geber*, (Leiden: E. J. Brill, 1991).

11. Newman, 204-208. Lynn Thorndike had also noted the predominance of Mercury in the *Rosarium*, while Newman asserts that the *Summa* was the first text to do this. See also Thorndike, *History of Magic and Experimental Science,* III, (New York: Columbia University Press, 1966), 58.

12. Newman, 159-162.

13. Newman, 35.

14. For surveys of the development of early alchemical imagery see Barbara Obrist, *Les Débuts de l'imagerie alchimique (XIVe – XVe siècles)*, (Paris: Le Sycomore, 1982) and Jacques van Lennep, *Alchimia* (Brussels: Crédit Communal, 1985). These texts reproduce most of the early manuscript imagery discussed below.

15. Newman, 39.

16. In the Glasgow version the illustrations are rudimentary and unfinished. In the Vienna manuscript, they are more fully realized, even though the execution of the drawings is still relatively unskilled. See Barbara Obrist, *Constantine of Pisa: The Book of the Secrets of Alchemy*, (Leiden: Brill, 1990), which focuses on the Glasgow manuscript and its illustrations, 44-49. Her earlier discussion of the images in the Vienna manuscript (MS 2372), is found in her *Débuts*, 85-116; 257-261. See also Lennep, 46-54.

17. Obrist, *Débuts*, 61.

18. The practical recipes included in this text, however, rarely give specific astrological advice. Obrist, *Contantine of Pisa*, 34-35.

19. Obrist, *Débuts*, 71. Albertus Magnus uses similar analogies between human sexual reproduction and alchemical transformation in his *Mineralia IV*, cited by Obrist.

20. Barbara Obrist, "Visualization in Medieval Alchemy," *Hyle–International Journal for the Philosophy of Chemistry* 9.2 (2003): 131-170. Accessed on line, http://www.hyle.org/journal/issues/9-2/obrist.htm.

21. Marielene Putscher, "Das *Buch der Heiligen Dreifaltigkeit* und seiner bilder in Handscriften des 15 Jahrhunderts," in *Die Alchemie in der europäischen Kultur- und Wissenschaftsgeschichte*, Christoph Meinel, ed., (Wiesbaden: Otto Harrassowitz, 1986), 151-178. Putscher compares copies of these manuscripts in Berlin (Kupferstichkabinett MS 78 A 11); Nürnberg (Germ. Nat. Mus. 80061) and München (Bayr. Staatsbibl. Cgm 598). with other versions. See also Lennep, 70-78.

22. Ingrid Flor, "Die 'Kröning Mariae' und der 'Christus-Adler' zur Herrschaftssymbolik Spätmittelalterlicher Endzeitprophetie," *Umění* 40 (1992): 392-412.

23. Andrea De Pascalis, *Alchemy the Golden Art* (Rome Gremese, 1995), 57-72.

24. Manchester, John Rylands Library, German MS 1, fol. 7v.

25. Berlin, Kupferstichkabinett, MS 78 A 11. See fols. 121v and 122v.

26. London, Wellcome Institute, MS 164 fol. 99v.

27. Berlin, Kupferstichkabinet, MS 78 A 11, fol. 31v.

28. Putscher, 155.

29. Zentralbibliothek Zürich MS Rh. 172, see Obrist, *Débuts*, 183-245,

and Lennep, 54-70.

30. Marie-Louis von Franz, *Aurora consurgens*, trans. R.F.C. Hull and A.B.S. Glover (Toronto: Inner City Books, 1980).

31. Lennep illustrates many of these folios, see figs. 25, 26, 28, 32, 40.

32. Martin Slatohlávek, "Iconographic Motifs from the Biblical Song of Songs," *The Bride in the Enclosed Garden*, exh. cat. (Prague: Convent of St. Agnes of Bohemia, 1995), 34-74.

33. (Frankfurt: Cyriaci Iacobi, 1550). See Lennep, figs. 19-38.

34. Florence, Bibliotheca Medicea Laurentiana, MS Ashburnham 1166, fol. 15r. See Giovanni Carbonelli, *Sulle fonti storiche della chimica e dell'alchimia in Italia* (Rome: Istituto Nazionale Medico Farmacologico, 1925), 46-70. *Lennep* dates this manuscript late fifteenth century. This folio is reproduced in Carbonelli, fig. 70.

35. London, British Library, Harley MS. 3469, fol. 10r. See Lennep, 100-129, fig. 168.

36. Leiden, Universiteitsbibliotheek, MS F29, fol. 95v.

37. *Spruch der philosophien*, Ferguson MS. 6, fol. 164v.

38. Lennep illustrates many of these images, see Zürich, Rh. 172: fig. 40, Nürnberg, Germ. Nat. MS 80061: Fig. 51; Paris, BN 7171, fig. 146. A variant of the image of a woman on the two fountains was later reprinted in Reusner's *Pandora*. See Lennep, fig. 54.

39. Barbara Obrist, lecture entitled, "'Nuda Natura' and the Alchemist in Jean Perréal's Early 16th-Century Miniature," International Conference on the History of Alchemy and Chymistry, Chemical Heritage Foundation, Philadelphia, July 21, 2006. See Lennep, fig. 108.

40. H. M. E. de Jong, *Michael Maier's* Atalanta fugiens: *Sources of an Alchemical Book of Emblems*, (York Beach, Maine: Nicolas-Hays, 1969), 266-268.

41. See Lennep, fig. 143.

42. See Lennep, fig. 161.

43. Most of these engravings are illustrated in Stanislas Klossowski de Rola, *The Golden Game* (New York: George Braziller, 1988).

44. M. E. Warlick, "The Domestic Alchemist: Women as Housewives in Alchemical Emblems," *Glasgow Emblem Studies*, 3 (1998): 26-47.

45. De Jong, 107-112.

46. This advice is contained in a treatise in which Isis shares the mysteries of alchemy with her son Horus. Marcellin Berthelot translated the shorter version found in Paris, BN MS 2327, in his *Collection Des Anciens Alchemistes Grecs* (translation section), 31-36.

47. Ute Gause, "Zum Frauenbild im Frühwerk des Paracelsus," *Parerga Paracelsica: Paracelsus in Vergangenheit und Gegenwart*, foreword by

Joachim Telle (Stuttgart: Franz Steiner, 1991), 45-56.
48. Walter Pagel, "Paracelsus and the Neoplatonic and Gnostic Tradition," *Ambix* 8 (October 1960): 153-155.
49. De Jong, 251-255.

Le Jeu de Marseille: The Breton Tarot as *Jeu de Hasard*

Giovanna Costantini

At the villa of Air-Bel in Marseille in the south of France, a group of Surrealist artists awaited documents to guarantee safe passage out of Europe following the fall of France to Hitler in 1940. While residing at the villa, the artists and their families passed the time amicably, enjoying activities such as *Verité*, a game of truth, charades, collective caricatures and collages. Breton's *Fata Morgana*, a long alchemical poem that describes the hermetic transmutation of love into hope, was written here. Among other fruits of the artists' exchanges was the creation of an unfinished set of Tarot cards, long considered anonymous, donated to the Cantini Museum in Marseille in 2003 by the heirs of André Breton's estate.

Surrealists André Breton, Victor Brauner, Oscar Dominguez, Max Ernst, Jacques Hérold, Wilfredo Lam, Jacqueline Lamba and André Masson produced the Marseille set collaboratively, with lots drawn to decide who would design each card. While it referenced the Tarot of Marseille, a deck of image cards in use in Europe since at least the time of the Renaissance, it modified the pictures in the deck both artistically and thematically to reflect Surrealist interests.

A tarot set consists of a set of number cards, called the Minor Arcana, in four suits equal to a normal deck of playing cards. Attached to it are twenty-two "trumps," known as the Major Arcana, bearing symbolic religious and moral illustrations such as Strength (*la forza*) or the Star (the emblem of hope). The Tarot tradition dates to the 1400's, when it flourished as an aristocratic pastime and costly commodity within the ducal courts of Milan, Ferrara, Mantua and Bologna in Italy. Lavish hand-painted and gilded tarot decks in various sizes were made by local artists, drawing on a wide and eclectic range of religious, mythological and folk sources for their imagery. As a generic trend, the practice of depicting cards with

91

pageant and pictorial triumphs arose about 1442 in Ferrara reflecting military victories of the nobility. Although a distinction has long been made between the gaming card tradition of the number cards and allegorical interpretations associated with the trumps, evidence suggests that the Major Arcana, known as *trionfi*, derive from this triumph card tradition named also after a game known as the "triumph game."[1] Stylistically comparable to secular late medieval manuscript illumination, the earliest Tarot deck known today is the Milanese Visconti-Sforza set of 1452-1455 from Italy owned by the Pierpont Morgan Library in New York.

Until the late eighteenth century, the Tarot was one of many card games similar to Bridge, played at all social levels throughout Europe.[2] The introduction of card games into Western Europe may also be traced to Italy, where the cards were known as *naibe* (similar to the Spanish *naipes* today) where they were thought to be of Oriental origin.[3] In many places, the game is still in use today with only slight changes to the rules since the Middle Ages.

Since at least the fifteenth century, both playing cards as well as Tarot cards were also used for fortune telling, usually by a female. But by the nineteenth century, the Tarot came to be considered something of a Bible among occultists for it offered a means of understanding the structure of the universe as well as one's life journey in relation to the force of destiny.[4] Divinatory, mythological and esoteric interpretations of the Tarot first appeared in France in the eighteenth century among occultist writers and illuminati.[5] To some extent, their theories accessed much earlier Renaissance traditions of magical literature (i.e. Marsilio Ficino and Henricus Cornelius Agrippa) that emphasized the faculties of imagination and memory (likened to divine powers) that could be developed through the use of images.[6] Later theorists such as Eliphas Lévi and Papus proposed more rational, yet hermetic and mystically derived systems of number symbolism, microcosmic-macrocosmic correspondence and moral logic applicable to Tarot interpretation.

Although there are many variations of the Tarot, the most familiar deck was the *Tarot of Marseille*, mass produced since the seventeenth century in Marseille, the center of Tarot production outside Italy, and still available from the French card manufacturer

Grimaud.[7] The Marseille deck's schematic idiom reflects rudimentary patterns originating in Milan that may have served as models.[8] This deck, similar to illustrations appearing in Court de Gébelin's *Le Monde primitif,* contains flat, two-dimensional colored drawings of emblematic figures with their defining attributes (the King with his scepter) or "sets" with other symbols (the Tower, the Chariot). Astrological subjects such as the Sun and Moon originated in pagan antiquity; allegorical subjects including Justice, Fortitude, and Temperance were inspired by medieval Virtues; and other more popular themes like the Mountebank, the Hermit and the Hanged Man reflected the characters of medieval folk tales. Persisting well into the twentieth century, the Marseille deck provided a collection of iconographic types invoked among artists for newer, more fanciful invention.

In the nineteenth and twentieth century, a number of artists reinterpreted Tarot iconography. The French occultist Jean-Baptiste Alliette (aka Etteila) introduced the "Oracle des Dames" tarot in 1807 (in use throughout the 1800s) that replaced many cards with ones representing creation myths of the Bible. Oswald Wirth, a Swiss occultist, issued a set of cards based on the writings of Stanislas de Guaita that adhered closely to the design of the Tarot of Marseille. Wirth's designs, with Hebrew letters, appeared in outline in Papus' *Le Tarot des Bohémiens* of 1889. In 1910, the Englishman Arthur Edward Waite created an Art Nouveau set designed by Pamela Colman Smith, a member of The Order of the Golden Dawn, that became known as the Rider-Waite deck. Wirth reissued a more ornamental set in 1926 which conformed to more decorative Pre-Raphaelite styles of graphic illustration. Salvador Dali, in the 1930s, created a set of iconoclastic figures that parody both art historical and Tarot mythology. Some of his models liberally appropriate the traditional subjects of Gossaert, Moreau, Klimt and Ingres, for example, confounding notions of prophecy with contradiction and fantasy. Breton's Tarot, although it follows these precursors chronologically, was not predicated on earlier or contemporary sources.

The Surrealists' critique of reason was ideally suited to the Tarot, for it undermined rationality, exploiting at once the myths

Fig. 1. Le Jeu de Marseille, Tarot Cards, 1942-1944, VVV, Number 2-3, Ed.
David Hare (Editorial Advisors: André Breton, Marcel Duchamp, Max Ernst),
March 1943, New York, p. 81. (Special Collections Library, The University of
Michigan)

94

Fig. 2. Le Jeu de Marseille, Tarot Cards, 1942-1944, VVV, Number 2-3, Ed. David Hare (Editorial Advisors: André Breton, Marcel Duchamp, Max Ernst), March 1943, New York, p. 88. (Special Collections Library, The University of Michigan)

95

Fig. 3. Le Jeu de Marseille, Tarot Cards, 1942-1944, VVV, Number 2-3, Ed. David Hare (Editorial Advisors: André Breton, Marcel Duchamp, Max Ernst), March 1943, New York, p. 38. (Special Collections Library, The University of Michigan)

96

Fig.4. Le Jeu de Marseille, Tarot Cards, 1942-1944, VVV, Number 2-3, Ed.
David Hare (Editorial Advisors: André Breton, Marcel Duchamp, Max Ernst),
March 1943, New York, p. 58. (Special Collections Library, The University of
Michigan)

97

and mechanisms of artistic inspiration as well as the outcomes of *chance*. Tarot cards encouraged reactions of surprise and wonder to coincidence, at times even unpremeditated insights that resembled release of the subconscious. Breton's idea to design a *Jeu de Marseille* also played brilliantly on the circumstances of the artists in its syntactical ingenuity. Not only did the idea invoke the Surrealists' characteristic penchant for wordplay, but it proposed a paradoxical stratagem to subvert the reality of their persecution and impending exile.

In the Tarot deck produced at Air Bel, Breton reinterpreted symbols familiar to the Tarot series, substituting for the traditional suit signs, four central themes important to Surrealists. These were: the key to symbolize knowledge (*connaissance*), a black star for the dream (*rêve*), a bloody wheel for revolution (*Révolution*) and a flame to signify love (*amour*). He eliminated the court card hierarchies of king and queen by replacing them with a Genius and Siren. For the Jack he substituted the Magician, and he elevated to the role of creator the joker (represented as Alfred Jarry's farcical Ubu Roi).[9] Each image card was also assigned the identity of a historic or literary personage favored among the Surrealists. Some of the cards, such as ones created by André Masson, Wilfredo Lam and Oscar Dominguez, reflected Surrealist interests in dream and the imagination. There were the Symbolist poets Baudelaire and Lautréamont, for example, as well as the German mystic Novalis, and Freud, who was dubbed *le Mage de Rêve*. Others represented Surrealist gods of Revolution: Max Ernst's Pancho Villa or Jacques Hérold's Marquis de Sade. The set also included alchemists and psychics such as Breton's Paracelsus and Victor Brauner's Hélène Smith. In the Surrealist pantheon, the "Key of Knowledge" went to Hegel, whose dialectic philosophy of thesis and antithesis paralleled the psychological relay between consciousness and the unconscious.

It is likely that Breton's inspiration for a collective Tarot series at Air Bel references a playing card tradition, and not the divinatory Tarot derived from associations with cartomancy, a tradition known as the *jeux de hasard* or games of chance. In contrast to the divinatory Tarot used for the passive purpose of predicting the future;

98

the "game" of Tarot sought to challenge fate through engagement with risk and provocation. It was this tradition that furnished early twentieth century artists with an unspoken figurative language that also derived from esoteric sources. It was in fact the *jeux de hasard* and not the Tarot of fortune-tellers that produced for many artists a subtext of concealed and coded meanings intelligible only to members of an elite inner subculture. As an artists' "game," the deck set out to confound order and logic with unrepressed creativity.

Furthermore, until now scholars have thought that Breton's Marseille deck was connected to prognostication based on Surrealist interests in psychic phenomena and parapsychology. But the appearance of Breton's Marseille deck in 1940 is directly related to conditions encountered within a theatre of war.

We know something of the conditions surrounding production of the Breton set from an interview conducted in 1974 with the Rumanian Surrealist Jacques Hérold, one of the artists of the Air Bel series.[10] He remembered a conversation at the Café du Brûleur de Loups over a glass of white wine in which Breton issued the challenge: "*Alors, on jou?*" [Well then shall we play?] One of the artists suggested that they create a game of cards, a proposal that Breton accepted. But first he wanted to research the origin of the pastime. "You did not set out to create a Tarot set?" asked his interviewer. "No," replied Hérold, "an ordinary game of cards...the Tarot is like any other game."

Breton's research revealed the origin of Tarot cards to be military, with cards that formed part of a *jeu de bataille* consisting of numbered cards that originated in the ranks of soldiers and their military companies.[11] This fact is worth noting in light of other circumstances surrounding the deck's creation. In the years following 1933, thousands of Trotskyists, czarists, artists, intellectuals, Bolsheviks, communists, anarchists, syndicalists and other revolutionaries had made their way to France in search of political asylum. Since June of 1940, scores of suspects were arrested and interred in what was known as "preventive detention" pending issuance of laws that prohibited Jews from participating in any public function including activity in the armed forces, the press, radio, theatre and cinema. On December 3, 1940, only two months after moving to Air Bel with Jacqueline and their daughter, Breton was arrested as a "dangerous anarchist long wanted by the French police." After being held for four days he was released, though he was again designated a "dangerous agitator."

Within days of his release, Breton commenced the design for the *Jeu de Marseille*, occurring during the last weeks of December of 1940. In the spirit of two earlier Surrealist Manifestoes his posture was confrontational, set forth in his "Prolegomena to a *Third Surrealist Manifesto or Not*" published following his arrival in New York in 1943 in the third issue of *VVV*, known as the review of combat and confrontation. Reflecting the dangers that surrounded him, he stated: "in art there is no great expedition which is not undertaken at the *risk of one's life* [sic]...[and that] more than ever before, in 1942, the very principle of opposition needs to be fortified."[12] Hérold's Lamiel, "Siren of Revolution" points to the artists' reinforced position, with its three medieval towers in primary colors.[13]

Breton's research also disclosed the military origin of a symbol central to the card deck. He learned that the *tréfle*, or trefoil, signified *the soldier's country*, stemming from fourteenth century card games that were known as *jeux de hazards*.[14] Some accounts associate the trefoil with the common meadow clover and signify that a general should never encamp his troops in places lacking forage for horses or where it would be difficult to transport it.[15] This critical sign appears to form part of an important artistic repertory.

Several of Picasso's Synthetic Cubist works of 1913-1914 feature a playing card, the *As de Trefle* or Ace of Clubs, a cipher that suggests an association with artistic partisanship that Breton may have intended. Paul Boiteau D'Ambly's *Les cartes a jouer et la cartomancie,* published in Paris in 1854, was owned by both Guillaume Apollinaire and André Breton. It contains a section on a *Jeu des Fables* composed of fabulous deities in processes of metamorphosis. One card depicts the sea god Arion, an Orpheus figure and poet-citharode whose song charmed the dolphins and earned him immortality.[16] Arion emblematizes the *As de tréfle*, illustrated in a seventeenth century engraving that bears the inscription: "An excellent musician, thrown into the sea for playing his lyre where he was rescued by a dolphin." It is likely that Picasso was well aware

100

of such lyrical allusions through his friendship with poets Max Jacob and Guillaume Apollinaire in this period. Apollinaire had just published *Le bestiaire* in 1911 in which he identified himself with Orpheus. The trefoil would have represented a "suitably" ambiguous crest for the avant-garde, connoting "club" membership, triumph and gamesmanship. Seen together with Picasso's noted painting the "Three Musicians," which many consider a depiction of Picasso, Max Jacob and Guillaume Apollinaire, it is likely that the trefoil signified a poetic-artistic union consistent with its musical connotation. [17]

This association is borne out by other early playing card decks that similarly included the trefoil on depictions of music and painting. The nineteenth century *Cartes Musicales* of Lady Charlotte Schneider for example displays several variations on the trefoil theme.[18] But more to Picasso's liking may have been "Joke Cards" or *Cartes à rire* produced for an officer in the army of France's last king, Louis-Philippe during the nineteenth century. One of them represents a painter in the act of painting in his studio. He is seated before an easel with a painting in progress and he holds a palette and brushes, surrounded by busts and casts. Attended by a child playing with the cards, the trefoil is displayed prominently both on the painting and above the classical casts, as though itself an emblem of artists.[19]

In Picasso's same work, the Ace of Clubs is combined with a die, another allusion to the *jeux de hasard* that may suggest the impending crisis of World War I. Dating from its use for divination and fortune-telling, the Tarot, as the dice and roulette wheel, were known as *jeux de hasard* or games of chance to be distinguished from games of skill in which the outcome could be predetermined.[20] In the *jeux de hasard* conscious control is relinquished not only to subvert the effects of a logical and discursive order, but to suggest events that could only be created by accident if not catastrophe.

Since at least the fifteenth century, *jeux de hasard* had been specifically associated with gambling. Indeed, the most widely noted treatise on the subject, the *Liber de ludo aleae* or "The Book on Games of Chance," was written ca. 1526 by Gerolamo Cardano (1501-1576), a celebrated Renaissance physician, mathematician and astrologer from Milan whose father had been a friend of Leonardo da Vinci. Ranked next to Paracelsus and Nostradamus among the earliest proponents of occult lore, artistic associations with his controversial legacy weave throughout the work of early twentieth century artists. In Cardano's "Book on Games of Chance," though the legerdemain of card-playing is given prominence, "the game" itself, *le jeu*, is linked to alchemy, and play with cards is distinguished from that of dice by means of its "hidden" or esoteric nature. It is through Cardano that we learn that the dice are specifically linked to hazard, presumably of Arabic origin and introduced into Europe around the time of the Crusades. The name "hazard" itself is derived from *al zahr* the Arabic term for the die.[21] Since Cardano considered the play with dice to be especially beneficial in times of grief or when one is sick or condemned to death, Picasso may have intended an association with malady. For Cardano states: "In my own case when I thought after a long illness that death was close at hand, I found no little solace in playing constantly at dice."[22]

One chapter that he devoted to "Gambling and Dicing" specifically dealt with false dice and marked cards, signs of mark-making, codes and secrecy. A recent study of the secret *argot* associated with gambling shows how both cards and dice used secret marks to communicate among "initiates" as a tightly closed clique, an in-group in which there is a strong sense of camaraderie and solidarity.[22] Citations from the demi-monde are familiar in Picasso's Blue and Rose periods, in which an underworld of performers comprise the marginal subculture of Picasso's *famille de saltimbanques*. Such characters form part of a cohesive social microsystem whose richly nuanced jargon, gergo or 'cant,' constitutes a distinctive lexicon of values and ideas, a counter-language incomprehensible to outsiders. Indeed, one song on gambling suggests a long tradition of gaming lore that is interwoven of esoteric symbolism. It describes dice that are glued together with quicksilver with lead sunk in them, associations that may have combined to inspire Picasso's self-referential allusions to art.

By the 1920s, notions of chance interwoven of fatality appear among many Dada artists through the appropriation of Tarot iconography. The Wheel of Fortune motif, in particular provided a *logos* of the Tarot itself due to transliterations of the word Taro, to Tora (the scroll of the law), to Rota, the Latin word for wheel.[23] Arcane extensions of the Tarot's logos are to be found in the magic square of Paracelsus that is as intricately intertwined with structural linguistics as it is with music symbology. Other accounts link the Tarot's etymology to Mercury.[24] Additionally known as *trionfi* or triumphs, the Tarot corresponds as well to plotless theatre spectacles that were later connected to the Theatre of the Absurd.

We find the Wheel of Fortune motif lllustrated in Duchamp's 1924 Readymade, "Monte Carlo Bond" in which his self-image (a photograph taken by Man Ray) is superimposed on a roulette wheel. Man Ray again revived the Wheel of Fortune idea following World War II in his paradoxical sculpture, "*Fortune,*" of 1946-73 based in principle on contradiction and duplicity. Spawned by the conditions of war and the effects of universal disorder, these wheels of (mis)fortune were purposeless and directionless, and in them movement was negated, repetitious and rote. In Breton's set the Wheel reappears again, turned by the blood of Revolution, equated ambiguously with *La Revolution Surrealiste.*

Tarot imagery resurfaced among other Parisian artists during the 1920s when Tarot cards replaced playing cards in certain Metaphysical paintings. Filippo De Pisis's painting titled "Still Life with Tarot Cards" suggests familiarity with Picasso's *As de trèfle* iconography. It shows the Fool, the familiar *Pierrot lunaire*, the artist archetype, along with the Ace of Clubs together with other signs for poetry and artistic vision: the eye, the open window, the plume. De Pisis was well-versed in the courtly gaming card traditions of the Este of Ferrara and in the occult.[25] The imbalance evident in De Pisis' painting shares with Breton's reintroduction of Tarot imagery a response to a state of crisis, including the crisis of modernity, that is indicative of post-war instability. Like Cardano's and Paracelsus' medicine, their work responds to turmoil, evidenced in 1929 in several ominous publications: a new edition of Apollinaire's *Calligrammes; Poems of Peace and War,* a French translation of Novalis' poetry, including the beautiful "Hymn to the Night" and "Fragments;" and René Clair's novel *Jeu de Hasard* containing chapters titled "They Have Fear in the Night" and "Time of War."

This tension between disorder and metamorphosis, between prevailing social conditions and shifting paradigms of belief, contributed also to a revival of interest during the 1920s in the Gnostic traditions as source material for the Surrealistic *rêve*. Occultist works on the Tarot such as Oswald Wirth's *Le Tarot des imagiers du moyen age* published in 1927 and owned by Breton contain chapters on divinatory arts that ascribe the faculties of the imagination to an "illuminated" primordial instinct, one that predates reason and civilization. In this regard, the Tarot offered a clef to a synthetic understanding of the meaning of life, reflected in grand esoteric theories that joined the Kabbalah to astrology, numerology and other arcane practices. Many hermetic traditions claimed that the Tarot derived from ancient mystery religions and the Marseille deck in particular became the basis for occultist interpretation by figures such as Court de Gébelin, Etteilla, Eliphas Lévi and Papus whose treatises proposed the Tarot as the semiotic key to syncretic knowledge.

Antoine Court de Gébelin, a Protestant pastor and Freemason, was the first French theorist to offer an occultist interpretation of the Tarot's images as an amalgam of doctrines pertaining to Western traditions of magic. Volume VIII of his *Le monde primitif,* published in 1781, is a largely intuitive compendium of hermetic myths, legends, comparative linguistic analogies and hypothetical etymologies. It presented the view that the Tarot tradition derived from Egyptian hieroglyphs attributed to the Egyptian god Thoth, who was identified with Hermes, hence with Hermes Trismegistus. He speculated that the Tarot was first used by the Egyptians for necromancy, thus constituting a divining rod and book of revelation. Court de Gébelin related the twenty-two pictorial trumps to the twenty-two letters of the Egyptian alphabet, a theory that inspired subsequent occult interpretations. One was Jean-Baptiste Alliette/ Etteila who, also in the 1780's, detailed the Tarot's hieroglyphic and astrological correspondences as a "Collection of High Sciences." He interpreted the deck as a philosophical account of creation and all of history as transmitted through the *Corpus hermeticum.*

Eliphas Lévi, pen name for Alphonse Louis Constant, first linked the twenty-two letters of the Major Arcana with the Hebrew alphabet. He also joined the four suits in the card pack with the four Hebrew letters of the Tetragrammaton, Yod-He-Vau-He (YHWH, Yahweh), the name of God. In his *Dogme et rituel de la haute magie* of 1856, he presented intricate engravings of Kabbalistic emblems derived from Hebrew and Arabic mysticism. The frontispiece to *La clef des grands mystères* of 1861 is an engraving by Guillaume Postel of a key said to represent the Tarot's symbolic role in unlocking the secrets of the universe through letter and number symbolism, a sacred language of symbolic correspondence.

These interpretations culminated with Papus (Gerard Encausse) whose *Le tarot des Bohémiens* of 1889 maintained that the Tarot constituted the "absolute" keystone of occult science, the Book of Hermes itself, a *summa theologica* of the primitive (hermetic) tradition. It elaborated on Lévi's interpretation of the Tetragrammaton, examining it in terms of numerology, allegorical relationships to the Tree of Life and Kabalistic theosophy. In 1913, P. D. Ouspensky, a Russian mathematician, published a work on the Tarot's symbolism as a "New Model of the Universe" that further related it to Oriental religions and Carl Gustav Jung's depth psychology. As a result, many early twentieth century modernists such as Breton inherited a well developed mythology surrounding the Tarot, one that even as late as 1947 could be described by Jean Paulhan as a language of signs, a synthesis of universal laws pertaining to the major forces of human destiny.

Breton's library contained over two hundred works on esoteric subjects dating from the seventeenth century until his death in 1966. On the Tarot alone he owned works by Falconnier, Wirth, Maxwell, Rijnberk, and Marteau, along with hand painted playing cards and even a crystal ball. In Breton's signed manuscripts of 1944 for *Arcane 17*, whole sections are devoted to Court de Gébelin, Papus, Eliphas Lévi and Oswald Wirth. To the extent that these combined esoteric interests provided the metaphoric warp and weft for his *poetic intuition* throughout his life, it is also likely that the Tarot's archetypal symbology, in its mystical emphasis, stressed a synchronization of religious philosophies that reflected Breton's belief in an underlying metaphysical unity and quest for self-knowledge that could reveal the organic harmony of creation. Breton alludes to such a unity in his last essay on Surrealism in which he writes of Gnosis, "as knowledge of suprasensible Reality, 'invisibly visible in an eternal mystery.'"[26]

Recent medical studies suggest that for some, recourse to the Tarot coincides with periods of crisis and anxiety. To sufferers of distress, the Tarot reflects a need to control fate not unlike the process of psychoanalysis. [27] Psychologists have noted that under circumstances of adversity, many patients of psychotherapy use the Tarot deck as a transitional talisman to gain control of anxiety or panic, one that provides a needed vehicle for hope. Writing in the *Journal of the American Academy of Psychoanalysis,* Leah Davidson, M.D., observed that "the cards somehow become a transitional phenomenon in the perceived accessing of a universal energy or life force." She refers to this belief structure in terms of a soteriology, "a philosophy or gnosis about one's ultimate meaning in life as a unique individual in relation to the cosmos."[28]

These studies validate research into depth psychology by Freud and Jung that, at the beginning of the twentieth century, gave primacy to the unconscious. One aspect of depth psychology that reverberates with esoteric philosophy is Jung's theory of individuation, the process of achieving inner stability amidst emotional conflict that he wrote in 1916. This theory is especially relevant to the Surrealists for it emphasizes the importance of the imagination. Jung posited that a "transcendent function" stood in compensatory relationship to two irreconcilable opposites, the conscious and unconscious mind. He linked such a function archetypally to a new synthesis of universal meaning by way of Heraclitus, hermeticism and alchemy as a means to achieve psychological unity through a mystical union of the inner and outer world. The Surrealists' belief in the efficacy of creative activity echoed Jung's concept of the transcendent function of psychic integration by its emphasis on the active imagination, "the mother of all possibilities." [29]

The Swiss Surrealist Kurt Seligmann voiced this conviction in *VVV* in 1942 as a "Prognostication by Paracelsus": "Imagination is like the sun," he wrote. "The sun has light which is not tangible, but which, nevertheless, can set a house on fire..."[30] For Breton and the Surrealists, as for Jung, alchemy provided the transmutational

106

metaphor for a process of transcendence that signified a qualitative change from base material to a more elevated form *through the agency of fire.* For each of them the imagination epitomized an alembic in which beliefs and ideas underwent spontaneous and visionary metamorphasis. For the poets of Surrealism, this idea had been inherited from eighteenth century Illuminism, a movement that combined transcendental aspects of ancient esoteric philosophies with white magic; white magic analogous to the spiritual phenomenon of *voyance,* or second sight, represented in the Marseille deck by the seer poets Baudelaire and Lautréamont. In fact, playing cards that bear the double image shown on Breton's Tarot of Marseille deck were popular in Paris during the nineteenth century as cards used in books of white magic, where they were known as Transformation Cards that depicted characters from the *commedia dell'arte.* These cards were associated with the illusionistic ability to shift artfully from opposing poles of appearance and artifice as a *mage,* Paracelsus' master alchemist, displayed in the Marseille set's four *magi* (Paracelsus, Freud, Pancho Villa and Novalis). Their images remind us of the "double body" of Paracelsus — the mortal and immortal, visible and invisible dimension of corporeality that corresponds to the celestial and terrestrial spheres.

The fabrication of playing cards itself also presented parallels to alchemy. Three types of paper were used in the production of cards. These were bonded together, cut and glued in the manner of *collage,* a technique favored by Picasso.[31] Moreover, the glue that was used for playing cards, fish glue, was the same as that adapted by artists from the time of ancient Egypt for use in painting media, pastel fixatives, and the gilding of illuminated manuscripts. Indeed, Cennino Cennini reports in *Il Libro dell'Arte* during the Italian Renaissance that the glue made from various kinds of fish was also good and excellent for mending lutes and other fine paper, wooden or bone objects.[32] Perhaps even more significant is the fact that nineteenth century engravings of playing card manufacturers illustrate that this glue was heated in massive vats that resembled, in fact, the furnaces of the alchemists.

Breton references this particular association in the title of one of his Surrealist essays, "Soluble Fish," of 1924. The essay is a poetic, hallucinatory depiction of love that seems to prefigure his marriage to the aquatic dancer Jacqueline Lamba, the mother of Aube, to whom he dedicated an "object poem" of 1937. "For Jacqueline," is a mixed media collage that he signed to her with a playing card. Breton was certainly aware of the connection between alchemical processes, the Tarot and the tradition of playing cards that in turn were linked to the larger game of love. In fact, one of the two cards designed by Breton represents a candle that may have referred to an eighteenth century engraving *Le Jeu* that shows an ardent lover captivated by the charms of his sorceress. Breton's playing card calls to mind Stendhal's novel, *On Love,* in which he details the process of crystallization, his neologism for passion that he inscribed on the back of a playing card. Stendhal's crystallization recalls to us the crystalline matter of Paracelsian medicine that is at once amorphous and indestructible; it invokes Novalis's magical idealism as a physical and spiritual communion, the quintessence of transcendence. The playing card also returns us to the *jeux de hasard* by way of Stendhal's unfinished novel *Lamiel,* in which Lamiel, "the child of fire," is a girl in search of love who confronts "the threat of dire peril."

Like Breton's "Geniuses & Sirens, magicians and revolutionaries," the residents of Air Bel took refuge in the self-contained realm of play in order to restore a semblance of equilibrium as they faced a perilous fate. Together the cards' personages stood as symbols of the solidarity and shared ideology that sustained the group during the uncertainty of exile, the shortage of food and the bitter cold of the winter of 1941. While awaiting ships, they combined their talents to create a modest diversion that could serve as an existential paradigm; a game of life that held the capacity to reveal an inner quest for wisdom, imagination and love. They recognized that in times of adversity, the need for play intersects with the need for certainty in a way that resembles the confrontation of dream with reality. It is in this manner that the *Jeu de Marseille* extends signification beyond the limits of the *Jeux de hasard* to the *baton* of potentiality prefigured in De Pisis's Ace of Clubs, uplifted amid a rain of colored flames.

Following World War II, Breton was to remarry for the third time, this time to Elisa Claro to whom he dedicated the poetic *Arcane 17* containing four new lithographs inspired by the Major Arcana. These were designed by the Spanish Surrealist Roberto Matta. Matta's *L'Amoreaux* and *L'Etoilles* contain nothing of the peril and fatality, confrontation and crisis of earlier Tarot citations. Rather, they are filled with tenderness and endearment, a *grand jeu* that sustained the couple who remained together at 42 Rue Fontaine for fifty years. Thus it is likely that at the time his works were offered up for auction by Aube and her own daughter, Oona, who were known as *les enfants de nuit et de feu*, Breton's children sought to transcend the circumstances of collective trauma that had engendered the Surrealists' simple offering. In so doing, they succeeded in returning *le grand jeu* to its loftiest metaphysical placement, a hopeful allegory of transformation suspended precariously between the earth and the sky.

Notes

1. Amedeo Amendola, "The Triumphs of Hermes and Wisdom," *Playing Card*, 25 (Feb., 1997)4: 154-160.
2. Arthur Edward Waite, *The Pictorial Key to the Tarot*, (New York: University Books, 1966/1910 rpt.), 317-322. See also Catherine Perry Hargrave, *A History of Playing Cards and a Bibliography of Cards and Gaming*, (New York: Houghton Mifflin, 1930), 31-33.
3. Aubert, Marie, "Jeux de cartes et Tarot de Marseille," in Musées de Marseille, *Le Jeu de Marseille: Autour d'André Breton et des Surréalistes à Marseille en 1940-1941*, (Marseille: Éditions Alors Hors Du Temps, 2003), 71. On hypothetical etymological relationships among the terms *naibe, nabi, na'bi* etc., see Stuart Kaplan, *The Encyclopedia of Tarot*, (New York: U.S. Games Systems, 1978), 20.
4. Court de Gébelin, Antoine, *Le monde primitif*, (Paris: Chez l'auteur, 1773-1782); Alliette, Jean-Baptiste, *Maniere de se récréer avec le jeu de cartes nommées tarots*, (Paris, Chez l'auteur, 1783-1785); Eliphas Lévi,

Dogme et rituel de la haute magie, (Paris: G. Baillière, 1861).

5. See Ronald Decker and Michael Dummett, *A History of the Occult Tarot, 1870-1970*, (London: Duckworth, 2002) and Ronald Decker, Thierry Depaulis and Michael Dummett, *A Wicked Pack of Cards: The Origins of the Occult Tarot*, (London: Duckworth, 1996).

6. Antoine Faivre, *Theosophy, Imagination, Tradition*, (Albany: SUNY Press, 2000), 101.

7. B.P. Grimaud in Paris published its first deck of cards in 1748. See Stuart R. Kaplan, *The Encyclopedia of Tarot*, (New York: U.S. Games, 1978), 178. The oldest existing hand-painted Tarot de Marseille card made from a woodblock engraving was produced by J.P. Payen in Avignon in 1713 and is in the collection of the *Bibliothèque Nationale de France* in Paris. Thierry Depaulis, *Tarot, jeu et magie*, (Paris: Bibliothèque Nationale, 1984), 71.

8. Ibid.

9. André Breton, "Le Jeu de Marseille," *VVV*, Number 1 (June, 1942), 89.

10. Alain Jouffroy, *"Les jeux surrealists entretien avec Jacques Hérold,"* in *XXe siècle, Le surréalisme I, nouvelle série*, XXXVI (June, 1974)42: 152-153.

11. *Le jeu de Marseille*, (Marseille: Musées de Marseille, Éditions Alors Hors Du Temps, 2003), 39. André Breton, *"Le Jeu de Marseille,"* *VVV*, Number 1, June 1942, 89.

12. André Breton, "Prologomena to a Third Manifesto of Surrealism or Else," *VVV*, Number 1, June, 1942, 18-26.

13. Compare these towers with alchemical furnaces appearing in the *Mutus Liber* (the *Trésor Hermétique*) that was owned by Breton: *Trésor hermé'tique, comprenant Le livre d'images sans paroles* (Mutus Liber), (Lyon: Paul Derain, 1914). pl. 14.

14. Martica Sawin, *Surrealism in Exile*, Cambridge, MA: MIT Press, 1995, 130. See also P. Boiteau D'Ambly, *Les cartes a jouer et la cartomancie*, (London: John Camden Hotten, 1859), 47-71.

15. Stuart R. Kaplan, *The Encyclopedia of Tarot*, (New York: U.S. Games Systems, 1978), 7.

16. P. Boiteau D'Ambly, *Les cartes à jouer et la cartomancie*, 133.

17. A trefoil by definition is also a trio of singers and/or instrumentalists.

18. Henry-René D'Allemagne, *Les cartes à jouer du XIVe au Xxe siècle*, (Paris: Librairie Hachette, 1906), I, 235.

19. D'Allemagne, *op cit.*, Vol. I, 269.

20. On distinctions between games of chance and games of skill see Christina Olsen, *Carte da trionfi: The Development of Tarot in Fifteenth-Century Italy*, Dissertation, University of Pennsylvania, 1994, 80 ff.

21. Gerolamo Cardano, *Cardano: The Gambling Scholar*, (Princeton: Princeton University Press, 1953), 111. Amendola also associates Hermetic cosmic associations of the Tarot deck with Hermetic divination with dice. "The Triumphs of Hermes and Wisdom," op. cit., 154.

22. Cardano, *Cardano: The Gambling Scholar*, 126.

23. R. Jütte, *Sharpers and their Tricks in the Late Middle Ages and Early Modern Times*, 1.1 (Gibecière: 2005).

24. Based on the seventeenth-century writings of Guillaume Postel, *Clef des choses caches depuis la constitution du monde*, (1546) transmitted through Eliphas Lévi, *Dogme et rituel de la haute magie*, (Paris: Germer Baillière, 1861), II.341. See also Eliphas Lévi, *The Magical Ritual of the Sanctum Regnum*, 39-40.

25. Antonino Fiorenza, *Comporre Arcano*, (Palermo: Sellerio, 1985), 21, and P. Boiteau D'Ambly, *Les cartes a jouer et la cartomancie*, (London: Hotten, 1859), 22.

26. Legends link some of the earliest Tarot decks in Europe to the city of Ferrara where Andrea Mantegna, working for Isabella d'Este of Ferrara produced a set of cards known as *Trionfi* that Vasari considered among the most beautiful cards created. One of the earliest Ferrarese decks was said to be commissioned by Leonello Guarino Borsa.

27. André Breton, "On Surrealism in its Living Works," (1953) in *Manifestoes of Surrealism*, (Ann Arbor: The University of Michigan Press, 1972), 304.

28. Leah Davidson, M.D. "Foresight and Insight: the Art of the Ancient Tarot," *Journal of the American Academy of Psychoanalysis* 29 (2001)3: 491-501.

29. Ibid., 493.

30. Carl G. Jung, "The Transcendent Function," 1916 in *Collected Works*, Vol. 8, 1957/1960. (Originally written under the title "Die Transzendent Funktion." See Jeffrey C. Miller, *The Transcendent Function*, (Albany: SUNY Press, 2004).

31. Kurt Seligmann, "Prognostication by Paracelsus," *VVV*, Number 1, June 1942, 96.

32. P. Boiteau D'Ambly, *op cit.*, 151 ff.

33. Cennino D'Andrea Cennini, *The Craftsman's Handbook*, Daniel V. Thompson, Jr., trs. (New York: Dover, 1960), 66-67.

The Esoteric Art of Cecil Collins

Arthur Versluis

We take for granted the words "esotericism" and "esotericist," but on reflection, these are actually somewhat awkward terms. Why do we use them, and not "esoterism" and "esoterist"? In English, "esoterism" is actually the earlier term, its first use dating to 1835. In French, the term "esotericism" became prevalent after Martinism, and connoted an experiential dimension; yet by the late twentieth century, because of use by Traditionalists in the wake of Guénon, the terms "esoterism" and "esoterist" had taken on an experiential flavor, whereas "esotericism" and "esotericist" were now prevalent in academe—having been established as the dominant scholarly terms by Antoine Faivre. Yet we will recall that Pierre Riffard's late twentieth-century book on the esoteric is called *L'Ésotérisme*. Here, what I want to suggest does not have to do so much with the specific terminology "esotericism" or "esoterism" as with the nature of the esoteric itself, with how the esoteric is conveyed through images and metaphor, via an "open esoterism" that is visible in the paintings and aphorisms of the British painter Cecil Collins.

As we all know, images played an important role not only in alchemical works and later in Rosicrucianism, but also in Böhmean theosophy, where images accompany the written word and yet represent a separate set of works on their own. Theosophic illustrations in particular, like those accompanying the original German and English editions of Böhme's complete works, represent a visual form separate from and complementing the texts they accompany. Images and words, as I argue in *Restoring Paradise* (2004), function as the primary mode of esoteric transmission in the West. And this is exactly what we see in the works of Cecil Collins (1908-1989), an important and genuinely original British painter.

Cecil Collins is still today comparatively little known, except in some circles—for instance, among those artists and authors associated with the *Temenos* journal founded by Kathleen Raine,

113

Philip Sherrard, and Brian Keeble. In fact, later in Collins's life, his flat in London was in the same building as that of the poet and scholar Kathleen Raine. While at the time of his death and for several decades thereafter, Collins remained comparatively obscure, he nonetheless represents, I would argue, one of the most original and important artists of the twentieth century.

Collins was born in Plymouth, England, in 1908, and he studied at the Royal College of Art in London in the late 1920s. In 1931, he married Elizabeth Ramsden, and for a time in the 1930s he taught painting and drawing at Dartington Hall. He published important essays about the nature of art and about society, including the important work "The Vision of the Fool" in 1947. His work was exhibited in many exhibitions, and he taught part time at the Central School of Art, in later life being featured in films, books, and interviews. He died in 1989, and an excellent collection of his writings, paintings, and drawings was edited and published by Brian Keeble in 1994, and in an enlarged edition in 2002, both under the title *The Vision of the Fool and Other Writings*.

Many of Collins's works were exhibited in a major retrospective in 1989, held in London's Tate Gallery. This was an exhibition that I had the good fortune to see, and I remember well my fascination with those otherworldly images. Almost immediately, I realized that the artist belonged to the same tradition as the writer George Russell, who published under the initials A.E., and that like this contemporary poet, Collins revealed in his work insights into the hidden, higher aspects of nature and humanity. His paintings and drawings reveal more than merely a commodified art work, more even than a way of seeing, for they (by the author's own expressed intent) have an initiatory function: they open up or better, awaken latent possibilities of perception within the receptive viewer. Through them, one glimpses another, archetypal world.

With the publication of Brian Keeble's collection of Collins's art and writing, one could understand much more clearly the nature of Collins's paintings. In his writings, Collins is matter-of-fact in his lapidary aphoristic assertions, such as "art is not about art." In the latter half of the twentieth century, it became commonplace to reject out of hand assertions like Collins's observation that "man is a metaphysical being." What became known as "postmodernism" was a rejection of any metaphysical truth or even "metanarrative." But Collins emphatically did not belong to modernism or postmodernism. As an artist, he asserted, quite clearly, that "art is a metaphysical experience."

Collins's work, like that of his contemporary, George Russell [AE] reflects what we might rightly term a gnostic perspective. In his journals during the Second World War, Collins writes

O holy ones I long for you, I long for my race, I long for my kingdom; we are all exiles. I know of your existence, I remember you, and my life with you. But here I wander, and I know nothing. But you exist, and most holy are you O beautiful servants [14 January, 1945, Totnes, Devonshire][1]

He writes beautifully also of his life in nature, of his solitary walks in the countryside, of how "in the sunlight on the wall in the morning, in the sunlight upon the bark of the tree in the afternoon, there is something speaking ... something to be recovered, a forgotten beauty, a kingdom."[2] Ordinary life in the natural world, for Collins, has spiritual significance; and the task of the artist is to remind us of this, to show us the transcendent beauty of life through art.

Like so many great authors and artists, Collins loved solitude and nature, and was highly critical of insectoid, soulless modern urban life. In Cambridge in 1945 he wrote acidly

What an age to live in! It bites into you with a formless denying of the life in us. A frustration of all that which is growing, of all that which desires to give, to come to fruition. Our time denies, denies all who have inward fruit. Denies the artist, the contemplative, the human being. A winter of the spirit is over all society. The coldness of the vanity of the intellect on one side, and cheap vulgarity of attitude towards life on the other side. It is this official denial of life that confronts us in everything. But deep underneath flows the secret stream.[3]

In 1965, Collins gave a public lecture entitled "The Artist in the New Age," and in it he wrote that

It is part of our democratic self-deception and sentimentality that we vaguely assume we are without an elite, when in fact it is quite clear that we are ruled today by the elite of scientific technocrats and politicians who are quite clearly spiritually and culturally illiterate. They represent a low level of awareness and consciousness; they have no philosophy of life other than the exploitation of nature and of man, and the making of money. This is the same thing actually.[4]

By way of contrast, Collins asserted the critical importance in society of the artist who, with "poised awareness" is awake to the possibilities of resacralising life, of renewing contact with what he terms "the world of archetypes."[5]

Collins is a kind of prophet-artist very much in the tradition of William Blake, and like Blake he calls us out of the insectoid hive-life in industrial society through his art. In his essay "Art and Modern Man," Collins distinguishes between "how" knowledge and "why" knowledge. "How" knowledge refers to the commodification and manipulation of apparently dead objects, whereas "'why' knowledge is concerned with the significance of things, the meaning." "How" knowledge is merely instrumental, whereas

a great deal of 'why' knowledge is known only through nuance of consciousness. Transformation of consciousness cannot be known or be brought about by thinking, by description, by measurement or analysis. It can only be known by inner nuance, rapport, and sensitivity to the vibrations and rays of that livingness which is at the heart of things.

The higher worlds are inaccessible to the insensitive; they cannot be reached by knowledge of them, but only by rapport with those worlds. For like answers to like and creates actualization. ... the instrument of art helps to sensitise the interior nature and to continually re-sensitise it when it grows stale and dull in the world of mere existence—the world of repetition.[6]

Authentic works of art serve as avenues into direct inner spiritual realization, another way of expressing what he calls "why" knowledge. The purpose of art is to awaken an inner rapport with spiritual verities that may be described as the world of archetypes, or as paradisal.

No real artist serves merely to decorate that "empty and mechanical desert we call modern civilization." Rather, the authentic artist offers what Collins calls "rapport" with the transcendent, and thus ultimately nothing less than a awakening of our consciousness to divinity and paradise. In "Art and Modern Man" he describes what art is capable of achieving:

Art is a realization of what is and not of what appears to be[;] art is therefore an instrument of man's inner nature and it enables him to manifest in the phenomena of matter the nuance and living quality of his inner life so that his environment is no longer neutral or alien: a rapport is established.

As our consciousness becomes transformed we become more sensitive to a wider range of nuance and vibration[;] we have a deeper rapport with the earth, trees, rocks, the elements, the answer comes back to us from within them. Art enables us to experience what the French poet René Char calls 'the friendship of created things.' In other words, with the transformation of consciousness our experience of matter undergoes a change, it becomes qualitative, we have communion with it[;] it is consecrated and is now sacramental.[7]

A work of art is thus initiatic: it opens up into "the centre of our being" and reflects at heart a nostalgia, from with our exile in space-time, for paradise.[8] To put it another way, art can serve as a kind of spiritual transmission through the artist to the receptive individual.

In the modern era, which is essentially an era of progressive loss of traditional cultures and religions, art must replace older, canonical religious traditions. Collins writes in "The Artist in the New Age" that although the older cultures of the world are dying, they are replaced by something amazing, by a "lyrical contact with the archetypal world," by the free-flowing, universal, creative spirit of life, the unlocalised god, accessible to all men in all places."

Dawning now is "the age of Holy Spirit."[9] He continues:

> In the past, in the great canonic formality of traditional civilizations there was of necessity a 'closed' consciousness in order to focus upon the sacred. . . .But we have to learn how to concentrate on the sacramental without the use of this 'closed' formality. We must have sacrament everywhere: as Blake says, 'Everything that lives is holy,' if only the doors of perception would be cleansed.[10]

Collins insists that living art is initiation into the realization that all is holy and that our true relationship to nature and to one another is sacramental—the chief problem we face, at heart even the only problem, is how to realize this truth for ourselves.

Collins is an apocalyptic author, albeit in a different, more etymologically grounded way than the word is usually deployed. We live in a "time of the apocalypse, and the word 'apocalypse' means to unveil." We live in

> the time of unveiling, the unveiling of the atom, the opening of man's inner nature, his inner world. But there is something else that has to be opened, and that is the eye of the heart. If the eye of the heart is closed then the whole of the universe is dead, a mere turning of the wheel of existence, of mere desires. Creative art has always been concerned to touch and open the eye of the heart. We are all apt to fall asleep, spiritually, and the eye of the heart is opened by these two artists, the one with the sword, not afraid to wound the heart, make it bleed, and the other with the light. What we are asked to do in the new age is to understand what the function of art is and to give our support and collaboration to the artist, an active support, that we may share each other's creative response to life.[11]

In Collins's insistence on the importance of the "eye of the heart," he draws on a much older tradition, represented especially in the British theosopher and gnostic John Pordage (1608-1681), whose writings emphasized exactly this same image.[12]

Collins's paintings are uncannily unified from beginning to end. All of them can indeed be described as archetypal, showing stylized landscapes and figures. Human forms are elongated and have a

118

geometric quality made more intense in some, like "The Invocation" (1944), by patterns on the limbs and torso. "The Invocation" depicts an invoking angelic human figure, her head bent back and contemplative, her hand outstretched over the land in benediction. It captures, in 1944, the sacramental relationship with nature that Collins discussed in his lectures so many years later. Here, as in many of his visionary paintings, landscape is transformed as well. In "The Invocation," it is as though the black-and-white world of industrial civilization is being transformed before our eyes into the paradisal realm suggested by the awakening colors in its landscape.

Collins's paintings, especially the later ones, are often ecstatic, like "Angels" (1948). In this painting, the landscape seems to be swelling up and rising with energy like an ocean wave, while above it there are golden spirals and a red sun. To the left, we see the sweeping forms of two intertwined angels whose colors partake of the earth's brown and of white, their faces closed in rapt contemplation as they seem but a moment from ascending, around them a halo of golden-yellow light. These paintings are mysterious in their capacity to evoke in us a rapport with something that we cannot quite articulate, but that is uplifting and paradisal, uniting an archetypal humanity and nature in golden illumination.

We might also observe that in many of Collins's later paintings, the figures' eyes are opened as if to reflect Collins's own opening sense of inner vision, but also to awaken this sense, or a rapport with this inner vision, in the contemplative viewer. The strange, dreamlike, hieratic nature of these images is revealed very clearly in his masterwork, "The Music of Dawn" (1988). Here the entire image is awash in golden light, to the left the orb of the sun, to the right a human figure with a sweeping robe that looks as though it rises out of the earth like the hill behind it. The figure gazes into the distance, its features smooth and surrounded by a mane of hair, in its hand a staff topped by an orb. To gaze at this painting is to experience for oneself Collins's expectation of a new era, in which we experience a new humanity gazing on mysteries with serene contemplation.

These paintings indicate Collins's extraordinary ability to reveal, through the image, something that transcends image. In

another book, *Meditations, Poems, Pages from a Sketchbook* (1997),
Collins wrote that Divine Reality

is so powerful that we cannot look on it and live—therefore we need a
buffer, a world between us and it, like an electrical transformer, to take the
impact and transform it to our dimension. This buffer world is called the
archetypal world, by which we make contact with reality through images.
… If this participation in reality through images is brought down into our
environment, so that God becomes a table, chair, or altar, we then have
'sacred space,' *sacred* images, instruments for transmitting a reality higher
than ourselves.[13]

A living work of art serves as a transmitter to us of the higher,
archetypal world; it offers nothing less than "transmissions of the
nature of reality."[14]

And so Collins's paintings, drawings, and writings represent a
fundamental challenge to us, not only as scholars, but also as human
beings living in an industrial or perhaps, post-industrial era. As
scholars, he challenges us directly to consider anew the nature of
art and, beyond that, of what reality we take for granted. In the
face of relativism and nihilism, he asserts confidently that there are
metaphysical truths, and that it is possible to experience intimations
of these truths—which are archetypal in a Platonic sense—directly
for ourselves in art. Furthermore, only through such recognition
and experiential awakening can we find our way beyond the cultural
decadence and deadness in which moderns are otherwise surrounded.
These are direct challenges for the scholar, but more fundamentally
yet, for all of us as human beings. How are we to respond to them?

Collins's challenge does have implications for scholarship on
esoteric works. It became commonplace in the late twentieth and
early twenty-first centuries to use the term "esotericism" to refer to
the esoteric currents or traditions of the West, primarily to establish
this long-neglected area as a respectable domain within academia.
Prior to the academic field of "esotericism," which really dates from
the 1990s onward, we do see some use, chiefly among perennialists,
of the term "esoterism." This other word, "esoterism," has religious
connotations—it refers to the esoteric spiritual path within various

religious traditions, like Sufism in Islam, or Kabbalah in Judaism. As an academic domain, an area of empirical study, the word "esotericism" is no doubt useful, but when we turn to the work of Cecil Collins, I find the word wanting. Does Collins belong to "Western esotericism"? Perhaps, if William Blake does. But that tells us virtually nothing about Collins's paintings, does it?

What matters is the direct visual transmission in the paintings themselves, the experience of the painting. When we perceive "The Music of Dawn," what we perceive is esoteric, intuitive, and belongs, I think, to the realm of esoterism. We may not want to acknowledge this, but the fact is that "esoterism," better than "esotericism," describes the intuitive understanding of a Collins painting which, as we know directly from Collins himself through his aphoristic writing, was meant to "transmit" a "higher reality than ourselves," and ultimately to open within us the "eye of the heart." I am quite sure that this kind of language and these kinds of ideas will make many scholars uncomfortable, especially if they are concerned about establishing esotericism as a field in the realm of academia.

But does anyone think Collins himself gave a hoot about establishing esotericism as an academic field of study? It is abundantly clear that what mattered to him was to convey, through his painting and writing, what might be called an "open esoterism," an openness to what he termed the "secret stream" of creative symbolic or metaphysical life. Collins's esoterism is open to all, just as his paintings are there for anyone to see. They are meant, he tells us, as a kind of inner attunement, as a reminder of a particular kind of inner resonance. They represent an opening into a renewed understanding not of how to live, but of why, that is, an entryway into the hidden kingdom of the imagination. Collins's work represents an open challenge to the mentalities that see in education, as Michael Oakeshott put it, merely a "certificate to let them in on the exploitation of the world."[15] It is, in other words, exemplary not of esotericism, but of esoterism. That is its particular challenge for us.

Notes

1. See Cecil Collins, *The Vision of the Fool and Other Writings*, Brian Keeble, ed., (Ipswich: Golgonooza, 2002), 63. On esoteric transmission by way of images, see Arthur Versluis, *Restoring Paradise: Western Esotericism, Literature, Art, and Consciousness*, (Albany: SUNY Press, 2004). Collins's beautiful paintings can be found easily online in a variety of collections across Britain, and I encourage readers to look them up at, for instance, the Tate collection website.

2. Collins, 51.

3. Collins, 63.

4. Collins, 117.

5. Ibid., 120-121.

6. Collins, 108-109.

7. Collins, 109-110.

8. Collins, 112.

9. Collins, 122.

10. Collins, 123.

11. Collins, 123-124.

12. See Arthur Versluis, ed., *The Wisdom of John Pordage*, (St. Paul: New Grail, 2004). The eye in the heart is featured on the book's cover, and in the text.

13. See Cecil Collins, *Meditations, Poems, Pages from a Sketchbook*, (Ipswich: Golgonooza, 1997), 83-84.

14. Collins, *Meditations*, 82.

15. Michael Oakeshott, *The Voice of Liberal Learning*, (New Haven: Yale UP, 1989), p. 104.

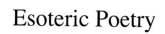

Esoteric Poetry

William Blake, George Cumberland, and the Visionary Art of Exotic Erotica

Marsha Keith Schuchard

It has long been recognized that the rise of British Oriental studies in the late eighteenth century had a significant influence on the Romantic movement, but recent research into earlier Moravian and Swedenborgian interests in "exotic erotica" reveals their previously unknown influence on the esoteric art and radical philosophy of William Blake and his good friend George Cumberland.[1] Through his family's association with the Moravian Church in the 1740s and 50s, Blake had early access to reports about "Oriental" art and mysticism (i.e., from North Africa to India), brought to the Fetter Lane congregation in London by missionaries, scholars, merchants, and soldiers. Like Emanuel Swedenborg, who also attended Moravian services, Count Nicolaus Ludwig von Zinzendorf (the Moravian leader) assimilated these exotic and erotic notions into a heterodox system of Christianity, in which meditative techniques opened the Blakean "doors of perception" through "an improvement of sensual enjoyment."[2] Inspired by Blake's passionate statements and artistic expressions of sexualized spirituality, Cumberland further explored the role of the sexual body as stimulus to the visionary imagination, and his unpublished drawings and interpretations shed new light on several of Blake's most explicit but puzzling sketches.

It was the daring and charismatic Zinzendorf who first opened the Moravians' "doors of perception." As a child in early eighteenth -century Germany, he had listened with wonder to the tales of Lutheran missionaries, who returned from India and visited his grandmother, an erudite Pietist, who was raising him. Later at the University of Halle, he heard and read the uncensored reports of Bartholomaeus Ziegenbalg, who served as a Pietist missionary in Malabar in south India. Ziegenbalg was fired with conversionist zeal, but he also described fully the religious beliefs and practices of the local Hindus, which—ironically—made them seem more attractive

125

than those of the Christian missionaries.[3] For young Zinzendorf, the revelations about Hindu reverence for the human sexual organs, the male *Lingam* and female *Yoni,* and their artistic depiction in religious art and architecture, would make a lasting impression. Moreover, the Hindus' tolerance toward other religions reinforced his growing ecumenical notions. When the count's Halle mentor, Auguste Hermann Franke, realized that Ziegenbalg's reports might become counter-productive to Pietist ideals of Protestant conversion and sexual asceticism, he ordered that the reports be censored before publication: "The missionaries were sent out to exterminate heathendom in India, and not to spread heathen nonsense throughout Europe."[4] But, it was too late for Zinzendorf, whose imagination had been fired by the esoteric and erotic beliefs of these exotic devotees.

After leaving Halle, Zinzendorf made a European study tour in which he examined religious paintings and conversed with liberal Catholics and mystical Jews. After his marriage, he became the leader of the Moravian Brethren, who settled on his estate and established the community of Herrnhut. Emboldened by what he was learning about Kabbalistic and Yogic traditions, which expanded the sexual and imaginative horizons of religion, Zinzendorf sent his "diaspora" missionaries to Jewish, Asian, and African communities, whose meditation rituals and symbolic systems began to influence his own beliefs about the role of religious art in stimulating spiritual vision.[5] By the 1740s, when William Blake's mother Catherine and her first husband, Thomas Armitage, joined the elite inner congregation of the Moravian church in London, Zinzendorf had commissioned his artists to embellish the meeting rooms with intense, even lurid, paintings of the wounded body of Christ and the passionate devotion of his worshippers. He espoused a Christocentric theology that was heavily infused with Kabbalistic and Yogic reverence for human sexuality, which was embodied in the fully humanized Jesus, the God-Man, who possessed many of the qualities of the Jews' *Adam Kadmon* and the Hindus' *Siva.*[6] Central to Moravian teaching was the sacramental importance of the male and female sexual organs, for in reverent marital intercourse the human couple replicated on earth the heavenly marriage of God and the female Holy Spirit,

126

who was Zinzendorf's version of the Kabbalists' *Shekhinah* and the Hindus' *Sakti*.[7]

Inspired by his association with the Moravians, the Swedish scientist-theosopher Emanuel Swedenborg went even further than Zinzendorf into Kabbalistic and Yogic mysticism and meditation practices. Swedenborg's studies in anatomy and physiology helped him master the difficult breathing techniques and genital muscle controls that enable the adept to transmute sexual arousal into ecstatic vision. Like the Tantric Yogis, he learned to control the cremaster muscle which raises the testicles and allows or prevents ejaculation.[8] Zinzendorf observed that the Moravians' "Notion of Divinity is apt to appear almost like Alchemy," for the body of a human and of Jesus serves as "the outward Taberncle," which will be refined by "a more than Chymical Process," until it becomes a "concentrated heavenly Body, which is to last forever."[9] Swedenborg went further and echoed Tantric beliefs in sexual alchemy. Praising the divine perfection of the chemistry and structure of the male genitals, he referred to "the alchemical preparation of the seed in the testicles."[10] Through intense visualization and meditation on the male and female polarities within the Divine Body, coupled with controlled breathing and genital arousal, Swedenborg received the visionary revelation that "the uttermost love for the holy" consists in sacramental "projection of the semen"—that is, the alchemical movement of the seed (the Tantric *bindu*) from the genitals up the spine into the brain, where it is transmuted into mystical, mental orgasm.[11] He also echoed Tantric beliefs that this altered state of consciousness makes possible communication with spirits, celestial travel, prophetic vision, physical rejuvenation, and even immortality.[12] Noting that he has now been initiated into the "Society of Immortals," he hinted at the infusion of Kabbalistic and Tantric esoteric eroticism into current Rosicrucian and Masonic rituals.[13] Swedenborg later urged illuminated initiates to meditate on Asiatic emblems of divine copulation pictured on walls and cast in silver.[14]

After Zinzendorf's death in 1760, the more conservative Moravian Elders tried to suppress the psycherotic themes of the "Sifting Time," but many members continued to cherish them and to teach them within their familes.[15] In the meantime, the widowed

Catherine Armitage left the inner congregation and married James Blake, who became the father of William. According to Thomas Muir, the 19th-century Blake facsimilist, the Blakes continued to attend the public services at the Fetter Lane chapel, until they moved on to Swedenborgianism.[16] For young William, exposure to the Moravian-Swedenborgian notions of sexualized spirituality influenced his own curiosity and openness to exotic erotica. By the 1780s and 90s, his interest was further fuelled by the oral reports and publications of radical antiquarians and scholarly Orientalists, who argued that sexual desire and pleasure were the basis of all religions and that an intellectually arid and psychologically crippling Christianity could be regenerated by unleashing the emotional and imaginative energy of erotic art and ritual.

This provocative challenge led Blake and his friend Cumberland to explore the esoteric and erotic visions of India and Ethiopia, which the more radical Swedenborgians now claimed as reinforcement for their master's sexual and spiritual revelations. When the increasingly puritanical conservatives of the New Jerusalem Church began to persecute the radicals (called the *Illuminés*), Blake issued *The Marriage of Heaven and Hell* (1790-93), a blistering satire on the prudes. Praising unrestrained sexuality as the vehicle of spiritual vision, he sought beyond Swedenborg for further psychoerotic liberation. Thus, he and the *Illuminés* were thrilled by the arrival in London of a manuscript of the *Ethiopian Book of Enoch*, brought from Africa by the Scottish explorer and Freemason, James Bruce, who worked on an English translation throughout the 1780s. Through the Moravian and artistic friends of Bruce, Blake evidently gained access to the manuscript's erotic mysticism by 1796, when he sketched highly explicit illustrations of the Enochian text, in which the angelic Watchers copulate with the Daughters of Men.[17]

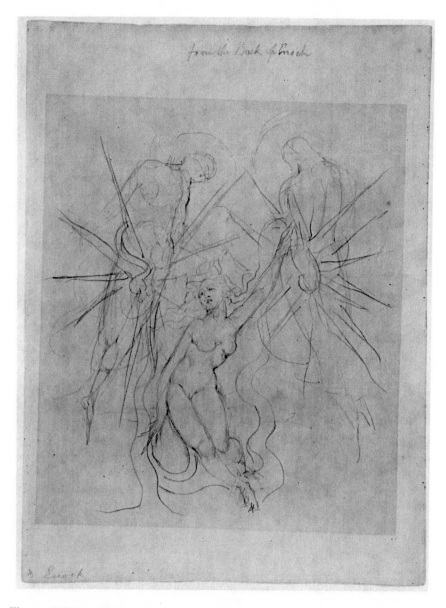

Fig. 1. William Blake, "The Descent of the Angels to One of the Daughters of Men," Lessing Rosenwald Collection, National Gallery of Art, Washington, D.C.

Fig. 2. William Blake, "An Angel Teaching a Daughter of Men the Secrets of Sin," Lessing J. Rosenwald Collection, National Gallery of Art, Washington, D.C.

What most intrigued Blake was the notion that the angels' divinity resides in their organs of generation. He portrayed them with enormously enlarged, star-like phalluses, which can transmit mystical knowledge to the females.[18] In one drawing, he showed a seductive angel stretching his arm downwards to touch the vulva of a woman, who thus received the forbidden knowledge of "sorcery, incantations, bracelets and ornaments, the use of paint, the beautifying of the eyebrows, the use of stone, so that the world became altered." Unlike the original Hebrew author, Blake did not condemn this angelic-human transmission of erotic *gnosis*.

Blake probably showed his Enochian drawings to George Cumberland, who happily maintained an unconventional sexual life (he lived with another man's wife and sired several illegitimate children).[19] Cumberland had long been interested in Bruce's experiences and would have been interested in his manuscript translation of *Enoch*.[20] In 1796, the watermarked date on the drawings, Cumberland commissioned Blake to engrave his genitally-explicit illustrations of ancient Greek art that Cumberland included in his book, *Thoughts on Outline*. Praising the unashamed nakedness of the Greeks, who freely displayed "the masculine parts" in their statues, Cumberland chastised the increasing prudery of conservative art critics: "today the index of a narrow mind … has a cruel tendency to depress the hand of Art, which is never more elevated than when describing the *human form divine* as it came from the hands of the mysterious first Cause."[21] Cumberland then began writing a utopian novella, *The Captive of the Castle of Sennaar,* in which he portrayed a libertarian commune, situated near Ethiopia, where the deistic citizens (called the Sophis) enourage a simple, natural life of sexual freedom and religious toleration. The Sophis revere the sexual drive, which they deem "the good Energy, whose office is to create"; thus, they chant, "O Holy Energy … thou art Love!"[22]

In Cumberland's volume of *A Code of Gentoo Laws* (1776), by the Orientalist Freemason Nathaniel Brassey Halhed, he read about the visionary practices of Hindu Yogis (who become "absorbed in a State of Unconsciousness, — a Kind of Trance") and their associated sexual beliefs ("A Woman is never satisfied with the Copulation of Man, no more than Fire is satisfied with burning fuel, or the main

131

ocean with receiving the Rivers").[23] Blake was possibly familiar with Halhed's graphic sexual descriptions, for the plates were engraved by Basire's studio while Blake served as his apprentice. These Hindu beliefs now became relevant to the *Ethiopian Book of Enoch*.

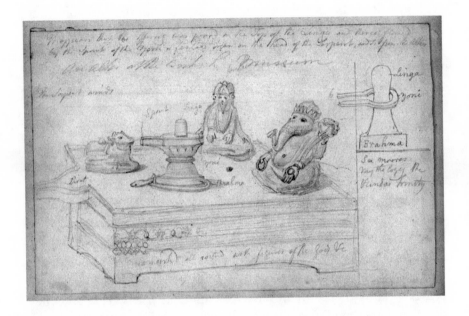

Figure 3. Hand Drawn Image by Cumberland, From George Cumberland, *Sketchbook*, f. 29; Bentley Collection, Victoria College Library, University of Toronto. Reproduced by the kind permission of Professor Bentley and Dr. Robert Brandeis.

Cumberland also owned Quentin Craufurd's *Sketches...of Hindustan* (1790), which revealed that the naked Gymnosophists or holy visionaries of Ethiopia originally came from India and that they brought with them the worship of the phallic god Siva, the Lord of Desire.[24] Cumberland similarly traced the Sophis' origins from India, and he hinted at his studies of African and Asian art, praising those ancient, exotic statues that "still remain" and which "glory in the form the Creator had asssigned them."[25] The Sophis "would have spurned at the unnatural depravity that affixed ideas of shame to the most necessary, wonderful, and noble organs of the human superstructure." When he sent copies of his text to several friends, they were so shocked that they persuaded him to withdraw it from publication. Blake, however, was delighted and wrote Cumberland, "Your vision of the Happy Sophis I have devourd. O most delicious book."[26]

Both Cumberland and Blake were familiar with Richard Payne Knight's controversial book, *An Account of the Worship of Priapus ...and its Connexion with the Mystic Theology of the Ancients* (1786), which argued that the phallic drive was the basis of all religions, including Christianity, and that remains of it could still be deciphered in medieval church carvings and Maypole ceremonies. Knight lamented that hypocritical priests destroyed the joyful and natural religion of its originators and fulminated that "one of the greatest curses that ever afflicted the human race is dogmatical theology."[27] Inspired by Knight's bold argument, Major Edward Moor, a returned soldier-scholar from India, decided to publish the early fruits of his own study of Indian erotic art and Yogic meditation. He used Blake's publisher Joseph Johnson to issue *A Narrative of the Operations...of the Maharatta Army* (1794), and he evidently met Blake while he sought engravers for his many drawings and sculptures of Indian art.[28]

To avoid the opprobrium heaped upon "Priapus Knight," Moor pretended to be shocked by the "indecent" erotica that he described, but he obviously found it fascinating and healthy. Linking the worship of Siva's *Lingam* with the "divine *absorption* of the pious Yogees," he hinted at his own study of Tantric rituals, in which the meditating Yogi maintains an erect penis in order to energize his visionary imagination.[29] With tongue-in-cheek, Moor conceded that "the continual contemplation" of the attributes of the *Lingam* may cause concern for "virgin innocence;" nevertheless, its defenders "acquit the votaries of this worship, not only of criminality, but of any immoral tendency, in their sensual and voluptuous excesses."

In *The Marriage of Heaven and Hell*, Blake expressed his yearning for a similar visionary breakthrough, in which "the whole creation will be consumed and appear infinite and holy." (E, 39). He affirmed that "This will come to pass by an improvement of sensual enjoyment." In the late 1790s, while he drafted the hallucinative, psychoerotic epic of *The Four Zoas*, he sketched a huge erect penis with three female figures bowing down before it.[30] He gained access to the erotic art brought from India to London not only by Moor but by his artistic friends Thomas Daniell and Ozias Humphrey. While Cumberland worked on a new version of his Sophian novella, he referred to the grand erotic sculptures carved in the "caves at Elephanta," and he inspected the drawings made by Moor and Daniell of the joyful copulatory images which abounded in Elephanta, Ellora, and other Hindu temples.[31]

Blake and Cumberland also learned more about the female component of *Lingam* worship, which was rarely mentioned in previous Orientalist publications. Adoration of the *Yoni* or vagina was complementary to *Lingam* worship, and Edward Moor possessed sketches of *Yoni* emblems and sculptures, in which he took an increasing interest over the next decades.[32] For Blake, these must have evoked memories of similar images drawn by the Moravians, in which their artists made brilliantly colored cards featuring a vulvic shape which enclosed domestic and marital activities (such as the bed and chair designated for sacramental conjugal intercourse in the special "Sleep Chamber").[33] Moravian married couples had used these "devotional images" in preparation for their Love Feasts, which—in retrospect—took on a new significance from the Indian studies of Moor. He argued that early Christian Love Feasts or *Agapes* grew out of Hindu traditions and that the "nocturnal vigils" often resulted in "spiritual raptures and divine extacies" which unleashed "the passions and appetites of men" during what "were at first, pure exercises of devotion."[34] Their suppression by church officials "may be considered the final subversion of that part of the ancient religion here examined." Moor went on to trace the *Yonic* image in British church regalia and mystical Masonic symbolism.[35] But a sexually frustrated Blake, angry at his wife's rejection of his passionate overtures, drew an empty *Yoni*, with no image of conjugial love or domestic bliss portrayed inside it.[36]

In the early 1800s, while Blake struggled to assimilate the eclectic theosophies of Ethiopia and India into his own Christian-Kabbalistic belief system, he portrayed the *Lingam* and *Yoni* in many guises. His drawings began to suggest a happier marital situation, in

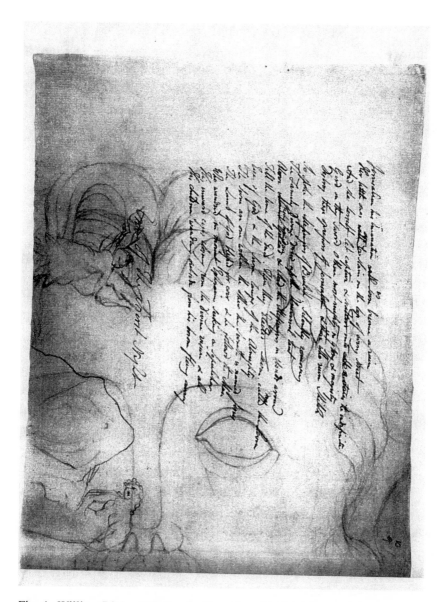

Fig. 4. William Blake, *Vala, or the Four Zoas*, British Library, Add. MS. 39,764, f. 13v. Infrared photograph. Courtesy of British Library Board.

which his devoted wife accepted his erotic theosophy and practice. In a mythic portrayal of himself and Catherine, nude and reclining on a bed of rocks, he seemed to draw on the Hindu-Tantric technique of delayed ejaculation or *coitus interruptus*, which enables him to achieve a vision of the eagle of inspiration.[37] In another drawing, the loving couple are positioned in a Tantric-style sexual embrace, while they sit on an Indian lotus blossom, traditional emblem of the *Yoni*.[38] Echoing both Zinzendorf and the Tantrists, he drew a nude woman with a Gothic chapel in her *Yoni*.[39]

In the meantime, a more cautious Cumberland revised *The Captive of the Castle of Sennaar* to reflect conventional Protestant beliefs, but he continued to study the erotic art of India and Egypt. Among the drawings in his sketchbook is a copy of a carved *Lingam* with encircling *Yoni*, next to an altar with a similar sculpture, surrounded by worshippers.[40] Cumberland wrote on the top of the drawing that "It appears that the offering was poured on top of the Linga and then flowed by the spout of the Yoni or female organ on the head of the serpent and so from the altar." On the bottom, he noted that it is "ornamented all round with figures of the God Vi." He added, see Moor's book. His unusual appreciation and comprehension of Blake's difficult poetry and visionary art was enhanced by his recognition that the esoteric was integral to the erotic and that one must decipher the hieroglyphics and symbols encoded in exotic religious art.

On a previously unknown manuscript scroll, now in the British Library, Cumberland provided provocative clues to some of the most puzzling symbols in Blake's works, when he copied and interpreted the images carved inside an Egyptian granite sarcophagus.[41] Drawing on Moor's *Hindu Pantheon*, he interpreted the emblems in terms of Hindu theosophy:

The *interior part* ... seems to include the most recondite Mysteries, as it contains the image placed over the doors of all the Temples, as the *key stone of Creation*—the Winged Serpent or Wisdom the *first Cause* brooding over the Waters—also a guardian or presiding Cherubim, kneeling with emblem of vigilance behind ... The ornament on the breast of the serpent seems to be a tablet for the *unknown name*.

136

Quoting Moor on "the most venerable text in the Indian scripture," which describes AUM and the radiating sun as the universal intellect, Cumberland added comments on KNEPH as the Demiurgos, which he wrote in Hebrew letters.

More striking and relevant to Blake's preoccupations were Cumberland's intricate and elaborate drawings of the rows of erotic emblems on the sarcophagus, which illustrated "The Mysteries of Isis and Osiris." On the top row of the scroll were phallic pillars, which he described as "the Garden of Priapus." On the next row were vials, flasks, and furnaces, which he attributed to "Chemistry" (alchemy). At the right and left ends, a nude Isis and an aproned Osiris each worship a phallus. In the middle row, the largest design portrays "Syrius or the dog Star presiding over the flowing of the Nile," which features a headless man lying naked on his back with an erection, while his ejaculated semen goes up in an arc to a crab, which Cumberland annotated as "the Pudendum muliebra." However, the crab emblem was difficult to decipher, because someone tried to erase it with a chisel. In his own manuscript copy, some prude has cut out a square right next to the erect penis. Cumberland wrote about this ejaculatory image, "This is I think the Nile originating from an unknown head, Orus or the Spring, receiving his *efflux under the form of the Crab.*"

Cumberland possibly discussed his drawing and interpretation with Blake, for in *The Four Zoas* Blake sketched " a crab standing on a sort of toy penis," just below a nude woman's vulva.[42] Again, some censorious reader tried to erase Blake's image. On Cumberland's sarcophagus, the sacramental and illuminative role of the semen was further emphasized in a design to the right of the crab, in which the head of Isis becomes an upward flowing river, while a male perched on her finger tips pours water onto a cosmic globe which sits on the head of a judge, who represents wisdom and enlightenment. Drawing on similar symbolism, Blake drew a woman holding an erect penis that spurts "balmy drops" of semen onto her forehead, producing a vision of fallen but redeemable sexuality.[43]

The complexity of the Egyptian emblems perplexed Cumberland, who viewed them through the eclectic mythological lens of the Priapic antiquarians and Yogic orientalists. As he tried to

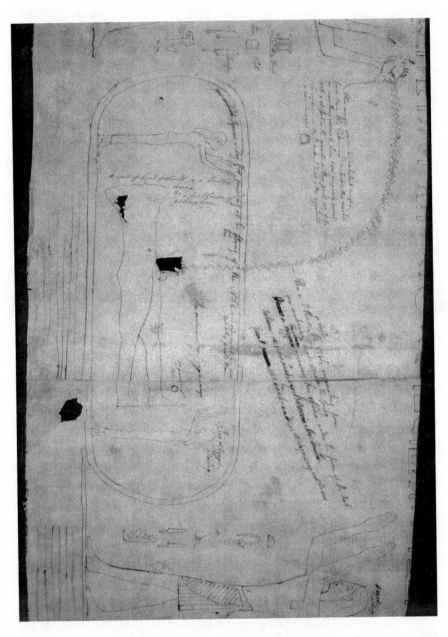

Fig. 5. George Cumberland, "Sketch of Egyptian Sarcophagus," Courtesy of the British Library. British Library. Add. MS. 36, 522

explicate a blank tablet placed on a cobra, he wrote:

> This *Tablet* seems to be the Emblem of Creation in the Ens, or mind of the Creator, a *Two from One, Male and Female...* The Hindus have a Mythological Serpent called *Naga*...also called *Sesha*, emblem of Eternity, Regent of the lower regions—born on the head of *Siva,* who has been incarnated, *Siva* is the destructive energy.

Cumberland vaguely sensed the similarities with Jewish mysticism, noting that a winged Isis seemed to be a Cherubim, guarding a planet or globe, but he did not elaborate on the Kabbalistic tradition of the sculptured Cherubim in the Holy of Holies of the Jerusalem Temple. Blake, however, was aware that the male and female Cherubim were locked in copulatory embrace, representing the blissful marriage of God with his *Shekhinah.*[44]

Like Cumberland, Blake was perplexed by the increasing complexity of these esoteric-erotic theosophies, as they flowed into London from faraway Ethiopia, India, and Egypt. Thus, he affirmed, "I must Create a system, or be enslav'd by another Mans/ I will not Reason & Compare: my business is to Create." (E, 153). In his later years, he assimilated the Asiatic exotica into a Christian-Kabbalistic system, in which the great works of esoteric-erotic art expressed the supreme values of the human imagination. At his first and only art exhibition in 1809, Blake proudly affirmed:

> The Artist having been taken in vision into the ancient republics, monarchies and patriarchates of Asia, has seen those wonderful originals called in the Sacred Scriptures the Cherubim, which were sculptured and painted on the walls of Temples... Those wonderful originals seen in my visions, were some of them one hundred feet in height; some were painted as pictures, and some carved as basso relievos, and some as groups of statues, all containing mythological and recondite meaning. (E, 531).

He further praised the "sublime conceptions" of India and Israel—the source of all works of "Inspiration or Imagination." Thus, the Hindus' *Lingam* and *Yoni* became one with the Jews' male and female Cherubim, and all were subsumed in the androgynous body of Blake's Jesus, whom he portrayed with female breast and erect penis.[45]

Blake did indeed create "a System," which enabled him to express his psychoerotic visions and intense spirituality in luminous works of art—and to transform his wife into a partner in his explorations of exotic erotica. For the non-visionary Cumberland, this System produced "devilish Works," which inspired both admiration and amusement.[46] Thus, when his son reported on the violent radicalism of the elderly Blakes, Cumberland responded wryly that Blake, "still poor still Dirty," was "a little Cracked, but very honest—as to his Wife, she is the maddest of the two."

Notes

1. For the late eighteenth-century context, see David Weir, *Brahma in the West: Blake and the Oriental Renaissance* (Albany: State University of New York Press, 2003). For the Moravian-Swedenborgian background, see Marsha Keith Schuchard, *Why Mrs. Blake Cried: William Blake and the Sexual Basis of Spiritual Vision* (London: Random House/Century, 2006).

2. David Erdman and Harold Bloom, eds., *The Complete Poetry and Prose of William Blake,* rev. ed. (New York: Doubleday/Anchor Press, 1988), 39. Hereafter ctied as E in text.

3. H. Grafe, "Hindu Apologetics at the Beginning of the Protestant Mission Era in India," *Indian Church History Review,* 6 (1972), 43-69.

4. Wilhelm Halbfass, *India and Europe: An Essay in Understanding* (1981; Albany: State University of New York Press, 1988), 47.

5. Zinzendorf's teachings on the use of religious art for meditation and sensual arousal are discussed in Marsha Keith Schuchard, "Young William Blake and the Moravian Tradition of Visionary Art," *Blake: An Illustrated Quarterly,* vol. 40 (2007), 84-100.

6. For Kabbalistic influences on Zinzendorf, see Christiane Dithmar, *Zinzendorfs Nonkonformistische Haltung zum Judentum* (Heidelberg: C. Winter, 2000).

7. Jacob Sessler, *Communal Piety Among Early American Moravians* (New York: Henry Holt, 1933), 176; Craig Atwood, "Sleeping in the

Arms of Jesus: Sanctifying Sexuality in the Eighteenth-Century Moravian Church," *Journal of the History of Sexuality*, 8 (1997), 25-51.

8. Emanuel Swedenborg, *The Generative Organs*, trans. J.J.G. Wilkinson (London: W. Newberry, 1852), 20-28, and *The Delights of Wisdom Concerning Conjugial Love*, trans. Alfred Acton (1768; London: Swedenborg Society, 1970), 107n.1; Schuchard, *Why Mrs. Blake Cried*, 78-83, 95-97, 114-21

9. Nicolaus Ludwig von Zinzendorf, *Maxims, Theological Ideas and Sentences, Out of the Present Ordinary of the Brethren's Churches ... 1737 till 1747* , ed. J. Gambold (London: J. Beecroft, 1751), 173, 175.

10. Emanuel Swedenborg, *The Animal Kingdom*, trans. J.J.G. Wilkinson (1744; London: W. Newberry, 1843), I, 235.

11. Emanuel Swedenborg, *Emanuel Swedenborg's Journal of Dreams*, trans. J.J.G. Wilkinson, ed. W.R. Woofenden (New York: Swedenborg Foundation, 1986), passage # 172. The MS. reveals that the elided word was "ejaculation."

12. Douglas Renfrew Brooks, *The Secret of the Three Cities: An Introduction to Hindu Sakta Tantrism* (Chicago: Chicago University Press, 1990), 56-58; Hugh Urban, *The Economics of Ecstasy: Tantra, Secrecy, and Power in Colonial Bengal* (Oxford: Oxford University Press, 2001), 47, 88, 113, 148.

13. Swedenborg, *Journal*, #243, 260, 268; Schuchard, *Why Mrs. Blake Cried*, 154, 264-65.

14. Swedenborg, *Conjugial Love*, # 76.

15. Craig Atwood, "Interpreting and Misinterpreting the *Sichtungzeit*," in Martin Brecht and Paul Peucker, eds., *Neue Aspekte der Zinzendorf-Forschung* (Göttingen: Vandenhoeck & Ruprecht, 2006), 174-87.

16. Thomas Wright, *The Life of William Blake* (1929; rpt. New York: Burt Franklin, 1969), I, 2.

17. The Moravian artist/architect Benjamin Henry La Trobe worked closely with Bruce in the 1780s, while the explorer translated most of Enoch. For Blake's access to the Ethiopian work by 1796, see Schuchard, *Why Mrs. Blake Cried*, 270-75.

18. Gerald Bentley, "A Jewel in an Ethiop's Ear: The Book of Enoch as Inspiration for William Blake, John Flaxman, Thomas Moore, and Richard Westall," in Robert Essick and Donald Moore, eds., *Blake in His Time* (Bloomington: Indiana University Press, 1978), 213-40.

19. Gerald Bentley, *A Bibliography of George Cumberland (1754-1848)* (New York: Garland, 1975), xviii.

20. George Cumberland, *The Captive of the Castle of Sennaar*, ed. Gerald Bentley (Montreal: McGill-Queen's University Press, 2001), xiv-xv, 300-15.

21. George Cumberland, *Thoughts on Outline* (London: W. Wilson, 1796), 17, 29, 44-45.

22. George Cumberland, *The Captive of the Castle of Sennaar* (London: printed for the author; and sold by Egerton, 1798), 52, 61.

23. George Cumberland, list of books in his library, Eng. MS. 420, John Rylands Library, University of Manchester, England. Nathaniel Brassey Halhed, *A Code of Gentoo Laws* (London, 1776), xxxv, 283. See also British Library Add. MS.36,497.f. 95, in which Cumberland discusses "Hindu literature and laws; he orders more "Asiatic publications," which open "a new field of Discovery," especially in "Philosophy."

24. Cumberland, list of books; Quentin Craufurd, *Sketches Chiefly Relating to the History, Religion, Learning, and Manners of Hindostan* (London: T. Cadell, 1790), 168-77, 191n.

25. Cumberland, *Captive*, 83.

26. Robert Essick and Morton Paley, "'Dear Generous Cumberland': A Newly Discovered Letter and Poem by William Blake," *Blake: An Illustrated Quarterly*, 32 (1998), 4-5.

27. Nikolaus Pevsner, "Richard Payne Knight," *Art Bulletin*, 32 (1949), 297-98.

28. For Blake's probable friendship with Moor, see Weir, *Brahma*, 74-79; Schuchard, *Why Mrs. Blake Cried*, 283, 395.

29. Edward Moor, *A Narrative of the Operations of Captain Little's Detachment, and of the Maharatta Army* (London: Joseph Johnson, 1794), 54, 393.

30. See Figure 4, William Blake, *Vala, or The Four Zoas* (ca. 1797-1807), British Library, Add. MS. 39,674, f.48v. Infrared photograph. Courtesy of the British Library.

31. Cumberland, *Captive* (ed. Bentley), 112, 300.

32. Edward Moor, *Oriental Fragments* (London: Smith, Elder, 1834), 79, 98, 133, 283.

33. Aaron Fogleman, "Jesus is Female: The Moravian Challenge to the German Communities of British North America," *The William and Mary Quarterly*, 60 (2003), 309.

34. Moor, *Narrative*, 398.

35. Moor, *Oriental*, 79, 285, 293, plate 4.

36. See Figure 4, William Blake, *Vala, or the Four Zoas*, British Library, Add. MS. 39,764, f. 13v. Infrared photograph. Courtesy of British Library Board.

37. David Erdman, *The Illuminated Blake* (London: Oxford University Press, 1975), 258; Schuchard, *Why Mrs. Blake Cried*, 310-12.

38. Erdman, *Illuminated*, 399; Schuchard, *Why Mrs. Blake Cried*, 331.

39. Erdman and Magno, *Four Zoas,* 158.

40. See Figure 3. George Cumberland, Sketchbook, f. 29; Bentley Collection, Victoria College Library, University of Toronto. I am grateful to Professor Bentley and Dr. Robert Brandeis for permission to reproduce Cumberland's drawing of the Indian altar.

41. British Library, Add. MS.36,522. Cumberland's drawing of the hieroglyphs and images on an Egyptian sarcophagus in "the museum at Oxford." See Figure 5, courtesy of the British Library.

42. Erdman and Magno, *Four Zoas,* 62, 178.

43. Ibid., 47, 155. I refer to Erdman's enhanced drawing because the MS. image has been so heavily erased.

44. See Blake's references to the sexual "secret Cherubim" in the Tabernacle, in *Jerusalem* (E, 166, 193).

45. Erdman and Magno, *Four Zoas,* 222; Peter Otto, *Blake's Critique of Transcendence: Love, Jealousy and the Sublime in The Four Zoas* (Oxford: Oxford University Press, 2000), 270.

46. Gerald Bentley, *Blake Records* (Oxford: Clarendon Press, 1969), 232, 236.

Vladimir Solovyov's Poems of Wisdom, Mystery, and Love: "Three Meetings"

George M. Young

The twentieth-century Russian philosopher Nikolai Berdyaev detected in his paradoxical but most celebrated nineteenth-century predecessor two distinct identities: a Vladimir Solovyov of the day, and a Vladimir Solovyov of the night.[1] The "day-Solovyov" was—by nearly unanimous consent—nineteenth century Russia's greatest philosopher, a rationalist, in the broad sense, a Christian idealist, who, in the books and essays translated into many languages presents his religious and ontological conceptions in the metaphysical terminology current in philosophical discourse of the time; the "night-Solovyov" was a mystic who presented his personal revelations, the immediate feelings that underlay his philosophical concepts, primarily through the images and cadences of poetry. Most commentary on Solovyov, both in English and in Russian, has focused on the ideas and ecumenical activities of the "day-Solovyov," on such works as *Lectures on Godmanhood*, *The Meaning of Love*, *The Justification of the Good*, and *Russia and the Universal Church*, as well as on key facets of his biography, such as his stand as an early opponent of capital punishment, his relationships with Dostoevsky and Tolstoy, and his attempts, with Bishop Strossmayer, to reunite the Orthodox and Catholic churches. These are all well covered topics. But it is the "night-Solovyov," the mystical poet, the Gnostic seer, the earthly friend of Divine Sophia, whose work, and particularly one work, "Three Meetings," I will discuss here.[2]

Solovyov, who was born in 1853, began to write non-juvenile poetry as a very young boy, but his most significant poems date from the mid seventies, when he was in his early twenties, and continue into 1900, the last year of his life. Throughout his poetry, the self-image he projects is not so much that of a lover seeking his beloved, but rather that of a male friend waiting for his female friend and benefactress to reappear. He is on this shore; she is from elsewhere, beyond, Russian *nezdeshnaya*, not here, known by flower petals and other tokens, by memories of her from other places, other times, other lives. He is a mortal poet, an ascetic devotee, gifted with clairvoyance and a view that penetrates the world of matter. She is a Queen, a Goddess, an Empress, Tsaritsa, the Eternal Feminine, Sophia, in both her aspects as Wisdom of God and as Soul of the World, Third Member of the Trinity, in a few poems Isis, Eurydice, the resplendent seven-crowned figure in an icon—but for Solovyov, seldom is she Venus, never the Dark Lady, never Mary Magdalene. Solovyov calls to her, and speaks to us, in a voice unique for its combination of earnest, lofty sincerity and modest self-deprecation. As Berdyaev and others have noted, he often uses a slightly humorous, self-satirizing tone when discussing the very subjects he cherishes most—partly from natural shyness, partly from a desire not to sound teachy or preachy, partly as a gesture of self-defense, out of a fear that the ideas dearest to him might seem ridiculous to others, but also sometimes seems to be using humor in its Gnostic function, as "luminous substance," one of the passions that created the material world, the laughter of the Christos at the moment of the crucifixion.

His 1898 poem, "Three Meetings," is a prime example of his double attitude, humorous and serious, earnest and ironic, toward a mysterious, life-altering experience. In a note at the end of the poem, he wrote: "An autumn evening and the dense forest inspired me to reproduce in humorous stanzas the most significant moments of my life up until today. Memory and consonance rose up irrepressibly in my consciousness for two days, and the third day delivered this small autobiography that has appealed to some poets and ladies." This "small autobiography" of interest to "some poets and ladies" is probably his most important, certainly his best known poem, the one most often cited in the literature about him. It describes his three personal encounters with Divine Sophia, though here, as elsewhere in his poetical works, she is not named. Why three meetings? Perhaps biographically he actually did see her three times, but probably also because, since Dante, three has always appeared to be the right number for such encounters, and Solovyov may have felt that at least in quantitative terms his Sophia should not take a back seat to Beatrice. The full title is: "THREE MEETINGS: (Moscow-London- Egypt. 1862-75-76)," and it begins:

Over all death, long in advance victorious,
And freed by love from temporality's chains,
Eternal companion, I need not invoke you
For you to sense my hesitant refrain....

Not trusting in the gross world of deception,
Beneath materiality's coarse rind
I have touched the deep, imperishable porphyry
And recognized the glow of the divine...

And have you not, three times, granted one living
A glimpse of you — not as illusion, — no!
Whether presage, aid, or reward, you came, giving
An answer to the pleading of my soul.

Victory over death, in Solovyov, means more than, for instance, the literary immortality that is a theme in Shakespeare's sonnets. From the early 1880's on, Solovyov and an eccentric thinker, the Moscow librarian Nikolai Fedorov (1829-1904), shared a unique interpretation of the traditional Christian idea of resurrection — they believed that all people should not merely commemorate Christ's resurrection but should themselves become active resurrectors of the dead. Victory over death would not be merely symbolic, but literal — people would collaborate in a universal project, a "common task" that would unite all art, religion, and science in an effort to achieve, eventually, individual immortality for everyone then living and to restore life to everyone who had lived before, generation after generation. Children would resurrect their parents, who in turn would resurrect theirs, and so all the way back to Adam and Eve. Solovyov addressed Fedorov as his master and spiritual father, and declared that he accepted the project without hesitation or discussion, and that since the beginnings of Christianity, Fedorov's project was the first forward movement of the human spirit along the path of Christ. The major difference that became more apparent the longer they tried to collaborate was that Fedorov insisted on a physical resurrection using projected advances in future scientific technology (as early as the mid-1860s he foresaw such possibilities as space travel, cloning, and genetic engineering), whereas Solovyov insisted that the project of resurrection should be primarily a spiritual process, involving future highly advanced versions of spiritual techniques long known to certain saints, ascetics, and mystics of every religion. Fedorov proposed that we would eventually leave our planet in search of the dispersed particles of departed ancestors, and would colonize other planets as those resurrected began to overcrowd the earth. Solovyov's idea was closer to that of Gnostics and theosophists, that the divine spark within each of us is already immortal, and what Fedorov called the common task of resurrecting is actually a task of realizing and universalizing the divine immorality already within us—we may not need reconstituted material bodies after the ones we are now in are used and discarded, or if we do need new bodies of some kind our immortal spirits can fashion the appropriate vessels, which may be entirely different from the ones we know now.

So in the first line of his poem, we learn that it is through the one the poet addresses, Sophia, though she will remain nameless, that death is—in advance— overcome. For Solovyov, her guarantee of immortality is more realistic than Fedorov's vision of ever-renewable body parts. In the ten iambic syllables of the second line, Solovyov states the core thesis of "The Meaning of Love." It is love—nothing else —not a futuristic mechanical time machine,— that liberates us from the chains of temporality. How does this work? Following Fedorov, Solovyov emphasizes not just the horizontal love between persons of the same generation, but the vertical love of child for parent, parent for child, human for divine, divine for human. As the exercising of the divine spark inside each of us and the acknowledgement of and attraction to the divine spark in others, love expands the eternal in us and diminishes the temporal. Love, in Solovyov, is the overcoming of the isolation of the human particle, the force that brings individual atoms into coherent all-unity, in Russian *vseedinstvo*. In socio-political terms, love is what makes possible *sobornost'*, the Russian term for the spiritual consensus that is the perfect synthesis of democracy and autocracy. Love, joining us to others on both the vertical and horizontal planes, frees us from our material, temporal, individual selves and unites us with the universal and eternal.

In the third line, the word I translate as "eternal companion" is *podruga*, the female friend, not in the sense of our English "girlfriend", but a female person who is a close, longtime friend of another person, whether male or female. And this term of "friend" or "companion" is the one Solovyov most often uses in reference to Sophia in his poems. Sometimes she is also a queen or an empress, other times a goddess, a wandering traveler, sometimes even a body of water—but always she is a friend. His love for her does not imprison him in carnality, but frees him from bodily attachment. The word that I translate as "invoke" is ambiguous in Russian—it means "to name" as well as "to invoke or summon". One thing he is telling us here, then, is that unlike Homer and Virgil, he does not need to invoke his goddess as he begins his longest poem. But also he is saying that either he cannot or dare not name the one he is addressing—for she is of the ineffable. In the Gnostic system of Valentinus, which Solovyov echoes and borrows from but does not strictly adhere to, Sophia is both "Agia Sophia, the Holy Wisdom of God that remains in the glory and perfection of the Pleroma, and her antitype, the Sophia Proneikos, Wisdom the Whore," whose fall initiates our human history. But her origins, in both aspects, are in the All-Unity, the Pure Light, the Unknowable, the Unutterable. In Solovyov, the color associated with Vseedinstvo, the Pure Light, the Unknowable, is azure, the color of the cosmic vault. So when Sophia appears in Solovyov's poems, she is unnamed, and usually surrounded by an azure glow.

The fourth line tells us that even without being named or summoned, she will "sense"—an accurate translation of the Russian word—what the poet is saying, no matter how weak or hesitant his refrain. As the poem will show, Sophia has always before responded to the poet's summons, whether verbal or telepathic, and their relationship is such that the poet knows she will "sense" the purpose and meaning, even if his verbalizing is wobbly and inept.

The second stanza presents the classic Gnostic formula of divine truth hidden under the "coarse rind" of the material. The "imperishable porphyry" that his diggings through surfaces have uncovered may refer not only to the hard, royal purple metal, but could also be a punning reference to the Neo-Platonist philosopher of that name. Solovyov's usual word for "purple-crimson" is *purpur*, so his use of *porfir* modified by imperishable and divine could be his clever way of mentioning and at the same time not mentioning a name that could raise the hackles of the Orthodox Church censors.

After reminding Sophia, in the third stanza, that she has granted him, a living earthling, three glimpses of what he will later refer to as "all of her," he moves on to the details of the first of the three meetings.

The first time—ah, how long ago, how distant,
So many years now, thirty-six, it seems
Have passed since a child's soul felt unexpected
Love's heartache paired with disturbing dreams.

I was just nine, and she—she was nine also.
"A day in May in Moscow," to quote Fet.
I confessed my feelings. Why was she so silent!
Perhaps a rival!—requiring a fight to the death!

A duel. On Ascension Day a duel!
My soul was seething. Feelings gnawed inside.
All worldly care ... from us... shall be banished...
The sounds grew longer, quieter, then died.

An empty altar... and the priest, the deacon?
The praying congregation —gone, where to?
The flood of feelings, passions—all now vanished.
Inside my soul and outside, azure blue.

A tint of gold then permeated the azure,
And holding, from some land other than this,
A flower, you stood smiling at me, radiant,

Then nodded once and vanished in the mist.

And love as children know it became alien
To me, and to this world my soul turned blind...
I still can hear my German governess saying
"Ach, little Volodenka—poor feeble mind!"

Here we see Solovyov's gentle, self-deprecating irony at work. The purported childhood experience of the first meeting with Sophia is told through layers of literary allusion and convention: nine, the age of both Solovyov and his first little love, was also the age of Dante and Beatrice at their first meeting; the day of their meeting is couched as a line borrowed from Solovyov's friend the poet Fet; the duel that immediately springs to the nine year old lover 's mind as a way to settle scores with his hypothetical rival springs directly out of Pushkin, Lermontov, Dostoevsky, Tolstoy and nearly every other major figure in nineteenth century Russian literature; the refrain that counters and seems to calm his seething nine year old passions is from the Orthodox liturgy for Ascension Day. Then, in silence, in an empty place, accompanied by azure, "she" appears— and in a footnote, Solovyov clarifies that the "she" who appears to him inside the church is not the same "she" as the nine-year-old girl in the preceding stanzas. The boy's earthly love for an earthly girl has resulted—he feels—in rejection, frustration, anger, confusion, now replaced mysteriously by something higher that he enjoys but does not yet understand. The unfathomable azure that accompanies her and is her attribute has now entered him as well—as above, so below, as outside, so inside—and the flower from beyond, *nezdeshny* enters his memory as her token and symbol. Her radiance—gold in the azure—is like the sun against a cloudless blue sky, and also like the crown of gold stars on the azure field in both Russian icons and Italian paintings of the queen of heaven. Already now, at age nine, alien to earthly love and blind to this world's attractions, he has become sort of a juvenile version of the Russian holy fool, in the German governess's words "slishkom on glupa," which I've translated as "poor feeble mind." This is a fine irony. Solovyov's father was a leading academic, the author of a still classic twenty-

151

nine volume *History of Russia*, and his mother was a highly intelligent poetically and spiritually sensitive descendent of Grigory Skovorada, the wandering mystic generally regarded as Russia's most original eighteenth-century thinker. Vladimir Solovyov was their highly precocious favorite child, by age nine already reading literary and religious classics in several languages, but instead of presenting an assessment of his own youthful intellect from the point of view of either of his parents, or from one of his academic tutors, he lets us see how stupid he seemed to an ordinary representative of the outside world. He will do this again, after his third meeting with Sophia, when he tells us the advice he received from a retired Russian general.

In 1875, after a brilliant defense of his university thesis and a term of advanced study at a monastery noted for hesychastic devotions, Solovyov was awarded a fellowship to London for the study of "the Gnostic, Indian, and medieval philosophies" and to investigate what he had heard of the beginnings of psychical research. He read English well, but, like Pushkin before him, spoke it with a Latin-inspired eloquence, so that neither what he said nor what was said to him ever seemed to register. He lived alone in an upstairs flat at 39 Great Russell Street, attended a few unconvincing séances, but spent most of his time in the reading room of the British Library poring over the two-volume *Kabbala Denudata* or staring at a single page of the Rosicrucian *Splendor Solis*. As he writes:

> In the reading room, I was alone most often
> And whether you believe or not—God sees —
> Powers hidden from me were making choices
> Sending everything about Her I could read.
>
> When sometimes I succumbed to a temptation
> To read "from another opera," as they say,
> The stories would produce only confusion
> And I would trudge home, feeling guilty all the way.
>
> But then it happened once—it was in autumn —

I said to her: "I sense you, know you're here—
Oh why, divinity's full flower, since childhood
Have you been so reluctant to appear?"

This thought, inside my head, had just been uttered
When suddenly the golden azure shone
Filling all space around, and She was present,
Her face glowing—only Her face, alone.

And that moment of bliss was long extended,
And once more to this world my soul turned blind,
And if my speech had been heard by someone "serious"
It would have seemed babble from a feeble mind.

Again, as in the first meeting, she is surrounded by the golden
azure that fills all space. This time she is not holding a flower but
is herself addressed as "divinity's full flower." And, like the sun
against the blue background, only her face appears. Again his soul
becomes blind to things of this world, and to any outside "serious"
listener, his speech would seem only an idiot's babble.

I said to Her: "Your face appears before me,
But I would now like to see all of you.
Why to a child would you reveal entirely
What to a young man you withhold from view?"

"Then be in Egypt!" rang a voice inside me.
First Paris! then off by steam toward the south.
My feelings didn't have to quarrel with reason,
For, like an idiot, reason sat close-mouthed.

Her voice, then, instructs him not from somewhere overhead,
in the vault of the reading room, but from inside himself—her truth
internalized into the voice within. And the old eighteenth century
quarrel between reason and passion does not even have a chance
to begin here, since in the presence of Sophia mere human reason,
like an idiot, is not even able to open its mouth. In real life, the trip

to Egypt was not quite as sudden as in the poem, and, since he had almost run out of money and needed to find somewhere cheaper than London to continue his researches, the trip may have been motivated by urgencies less esoteric than in the poem.

> To Lyon, Turin, Piacenza, and Ancona
> To Fermo, Bari, Brindisi, and then
> Over the trembling surface of blue water
> My British ship, trailing steam in the wind.
>
> Supplied with credit and a roof in Cairo
> At the Hotel Abbat—alas, gone now!
> So cozy, modest—best I've yet encountered...
> And there were Russians, even from Moscow.
>
> A general in Room Ten entertained us
> With stories of the Caucasus of old...
> To name him is no sin—he's long departed
> And of him nothing shameful will be told.
>
> This was the famous Rostislav Fadeev
> Retired from battle, he now wielded pen.
> For names of local courtesans or cathedrals
> He had secret sources without end.
>
> We sat together for *table d'hote* twice daily.
> His words abundant, mood and spirits good.
> He related dubious anecdotes with relish,
> And philosophized as best he could.

Interestingly, the retired general with the "secret sources" was an uncle of Helena Petrovna Blavatskaya, Madame Blavatsky, HPB, who was probably starting to write her first major book, *Isis Unveiled,* at about the same time Solovyov was in Egypt awaiting his third meeting with Sophia.[3] From memoirs of some of the other Russians in Egypt at the time, we learn that Solovyov visited Coptic monasteries in the vicinity of Cairo and had at least brief discussions with certain ascetic hermits in the desert. Whether he had contact with any of the individual European occultists or esoteric brotherhoods then active in Egypt is not known. According to Paul Johnson, in *The Masters Revealed*, one of HPB's future Mahatmas was based in Cairo at precisely this time. In his public writings, the "day-Solovyov" mentions HPB and "her miracles and tricks" only in disparaging terms, but as the circumstantial evidence of this poem suggests, the "night-Solovyov" may have shared more common ground with the figure his older brother Vsevolod Solovyov wrote about as "A Modern Priestess of Isis" than previously has been suspected.

The third meeting, which he later always considered the most important moment of his life, and which informed all his subsequent writings as the "night-Solovyov" and much of his work as man of the day, is described with playful literary echoes, and treated almost as a light-hearted adventure, a comical event.

I waited, meanwhile, for the promised meeting,
Then one night, at the quiet hour, suddenly
Like the whisper of a cool breeze, came her breathing:
"I am in the desert—come to me."

I had to walk (from London to the Sahara
They don't give rides to young people for free—
Dust balls were all that rolled inside my pockets,
For life had long been "on the cuff" for me.)

To God knows where, with neither food nor money,
I set off one fine day, walked a long time,
As in Nekrasov, Uncle Vlas's journey....
(Oh well, at least I almost made it rhyme.)

You must have laughed at me, there in the desert
Dressed in my overcoat and high top hat —
A frightened Bedouin took me for a devil
And very nearly murdered me for that,

With noise and gesture, in the Arab manner,
The sheiks of two assembled tribes conferred-
What would they do to me? —hands tied together
I was hauled off, slave like, without a word

For some distance. Then , nobly, in high humor,
They unfastened my hands and walked away.
I can laugh with you now: for gods and humans
Misfortunes that are long past cease to weigh.

Meanwhile, over the land the dark descended
At once, no time wasted , just day, then— night
And all I sensed was silence around me
And thick blackness surrounding points of light.

And lying on the earth, I watched and listened....
A jackal raised a stomach-turning howl;
He no doubt dreamed of having me for dinner!
I threw no stick—didn't have one, anyhow.

But what's a jackal! The cold was what was terrible...
Zero for sure—after such heat all day...
The stars were glaring down with ruthless clarity,
That cold brightness kept friendly sleep away.

For a long time I lay there, weirdly drowsy
And then on a breeze: "Sleep, my poor dear friend!"
I fell asleep; and when I was awakened
The scent of roses rode the gentle wind.

And in the purple splendor of the heavens
With eyes of azure radiance, Your gaze
Was like the matchless, shining luminescence
That filled the universe on the first day.

What is, what has been, and will be forever
That steady gaze has seen and understood...

Beneath me now stretch the blue seas and rivers
The snowy mountain peaks, the distant woods.

I saw it all, and all was one thing only —
An image of a woman's loveliness...
And it was you, you who appeared before me
Showing in finite form the limitless.

O radiant one! You cannot have deceived me:
In the desert I know I did see all of you...
These roses in my soul will never wither
No matter where this life's waves toss me to.

A single instant! The vision now was over
And in the sky the sun resumed its round.
In the desert—silence. My soul said prayers
While inner church bells tolled in joyous sound.

By mentioning Uncle Vlas, Solovyov not only recalls Nekrasov's narrative poem about a sinful peasant who falls ill, and after a dream in which he sees black Ethiopian devils tormenting sinners in hell, wakes up, and becomes a wandering saint, but also a famous passage from *Eugene Onegin* in which Pushkin explicitly points out that he has chosen a particular word only because it provides a needed rhyme. Another allusion, which Solovyov points out in a footnote, is that her "eyes of azure radiance" shine not only from the night sky, and from the pages of Gnostic parchment, but also are from a line in a Russian poem by Lermontov. This is the all-inclusive vision of the awakened adept: the royal purple splendor, the boundless azure, the aroma of roses, the view of mountains and woods as if from a position of levitation, the infinite within the finite, all time beheld in an instant—all encompassed within the beauty of the eternal feminine. The poet has, indeed, seen "all of her." But the entire vision is conditioned by the irony of expression. The inner rose is eternal and will not wither, but the radiant face fades, the hot desert sun now resumes its round and the outer man must trudge back through time and sand to the Hotel Abbat, tired, hungry, and in perforated shoes.

> Strong in spirit, but two days I had fasted
> And my lofty views began to fade away.
> Alas, your soul can be ever so sensitive,
> But hunger is not your dear aunt, as they say.
>
> To reach the Nile I followed the sun's path westward
> And was back in Cairo by evening. My soul
> Retained some of its rosy smile of pleasure
> But my poor boots showed more than one new hole.
>
> From the outside the whole thing appeared quite stupid
> (I told the facts, but not what I had seen)
> In the silence after laying down his soupspoon
> The general, eyeing me, in solemn mien:
>
> "The mind, of course, has its right to be stupid,
> But best not over-exercise that right.
> For it is not easy, given human obtuseness,
> To discern madness, judge dark minds from light.
>
> If you do not wish to be thought a madman,
> Therefore, or be considered an outright fool,
> Then never to speak again about this matter
> Might be, for you, a very prudent rule."
>
> He made more witticisms, but already
> A light blue mist irradiated me,
> And overcome, by a mysterious beauty,
> Into far distance receded this life's sea.

The suggestion, from Madame Blavatsky's worldly and practical uncle, that Solovyov not say another word about his vision in the desert, is advice that the "day-Solovyov" scrupulously followed. Though he believed he had seen all of her, he did not go on to write "Sophia Unveiled," at least in prose. In Solovyov's life, as in this poem, General Rostislav Fadeev has only the penultimate word. After the witticisms, a blue mist and a mysterious beauty spread over this life's receding sea. And having told his story, the poet ends with verses repeating, with slight changes, the opening lines of the invocation. The "night-Solovyov" who near the end of his life returns to the source of his lifelong inspiration, has in "Three Meetings" revealed not a secret doctrine itself but a previously untold account of the obscure origins of his daytime teachings.

The higher, Neoplatonist love story of Solovyov and Sophia does not end here. After the first three, there were many more — perhaps forty or fifty meetings, at least requested, if not always held. But what happened in those meetings is another story for another day.

Notes

1. Nicolas Berdyaev, *The Russian Idea,* (Boston: 1962), 167
2. Works in English that discuss Solovyov's poetry and mystical side include: Paul Marshall Allen, *Vladimir Soloviev, Russian Mystic,* (Blauvelt: Steinerbooks, 1978); Maria Carlson, "Gnostic Elements in the Cosmogony of Vladimir Soloviev," *Russian Religious Thought,* edited by Judith Deutsch Kornblatt and Richard F. Gustafson, (Madison:University of Wisconsin Press,1996); Judith Kornblatt, "Soloviev on Salvation: The Story of the "Short Story of the Antichrist," *idem;* Samuel D. Cioran, *Vladimir Solov'ev and the Knighthood of the Divine Sophia,* (Waterloo, Canada: Wilfrid Laurier University Press, 1977).
3. John Algeo of the Theosophical Society pointed this out to me in a private email.

Mirror, Mask and Anti-self:
Forces of Literary Creation
in Dion Fortune and W. B. Yeats

Claire Fanger

In what follows, we will explore some of the links between self-creation and artistic creation in the works of two early twentieth-century occultists who were also responsible for works of fiction and poetry: the novelist Dion Fortune, and the great modern poet W. B. Yeats. A part of my concern will be to show how the functions and processes of creative activity documented by these authors may be mapped onto a set of essentially Freudian ideas, particularly those surrounding narcissism.

Freud, Narcissism, and the Occult

While it is obviously beyond our scope to summarize all that has fallen out from Freud's brief but seminal article "On Narcissism: An Introduction," it is necessary to lay out a few key aspects of his version of narcissism here. In the most basic terms set out by Freud, narcissism is a libidinal cathexis of the self (or ego); however implicitly in the form described by Freud, and ever more explicitly in the works of those following him, what this really means is a libidinal cathexis of a self-representation (since only in the state of primary narcissism, i.e., babyhood, does the subject lack distinction between "self" and "object" to the point where a simple and undivided self-love is possible). A narcissistic cathexis thus involves in essence an image (or reflection, mirroring) of the self to which love (libidinal energy) is directed (as in the myth of Narcissus).

Both in Freud's work and later elaborations of his ideas by other authors, ideas of the self as healthy and mature tend to emphasise a balance of cathexis of self and object representations. To simplify somewhat Freud's schema of individual development, maturation of the self involves moving from a state of primary narcissism where ego is all, to a perception that there is a difference between ego and all, and ultimately to a respectful understanding of the difference between self and other, which enables the morally conscious social human being.

Within the Freudian framework, development of a mature ego and of successful object relations are intimately connected. Narcissistic love can be seen within this context as part of a continuum of activity that becomes pathological (both in the views of Freud and later writers, though differently so) only when individuals are so dominated by narcissistic love that realistic object relations are to a greater or lesser degree excluded from their experience. While neither Freud nor others following him suggest that narcissistic cathexis *per se* is bad for the health, there is a tendency within the general conversation on narcissism to see the ability to maintain successful object relations as a sign of health. Narcissistic cathexes have tended from the time of Freud to be more associated with pathologies of the self at the outset; the notion that narcissistic love has positive aspects is upheld throughout the theoretical discourse, but nevertheless upheld with some difficulty.

In post-Freudian elaborations of narcissism, narcissistic pathologies are those characterized by the subject's inability to maintain successful object relations, and concomitantly by weak self-boundaries and an ongoing difficulty maintaining a sense of self without help from other people. In essence, from the individual point of view, narcissism becomes pathological when self-representations canot ever be left alone, but require ongoing energy and attention to keep them from falling apart. However, recurrent anxieties about self representations in some degree are normal. A useful definition of narcissism is offered by Robert Stolorow: "Mental activity is narcissistic to the degree that its function is to maintain the structural cohesiveness, temporal stability and positive affective colouring of the self representation."[1]

My primary interest in this essay is the way in which the creation of literary works—poetry in the case of Yeats, novels in the case of Dion Fortune—is theorized by these two writers as having a narcissistic function in the sense defined by Stolorow: the literary work involves an act of creating a psychically active (i.e., narcissistically cathected) representation of the self, which is, as Stolorow says, structurally coherent, temporally stable, and positively affectively coloured. What I want to do is not simply to show that the literary works of Fortune and Yeats are narcissistically cathected (something which Freud and those following him would see as normal for artists), but that their ways of thinking about — theorizing — what is going on when art is created is structurally similar to Freudian ways of thinking about — theorizing — narcissistic activity.

How much these authors may actually have known of Freud is open to question. Fortune drops Freud's name often, though to my knowledge her only citation of one of his actual works is to *The Interpretation of Dreams*. It is clear from the bibliography in her *Machinery of the Mind* that she was familiar with many popularizing digests of psychoanalytical and biological theory, and it seems probable that her absorption of Freudian thought was at least partly indirect, informed by these secondary sources. The same may be true of Yeats, who never mentions Freud by name, but clearly has independent acquaintance with many of ideas referred to by Fortune as Freudian.

Both Fortune and Yeats refer frequently to the "subconscious" mind, which is not only the realm of things that cannot be consciously thought (for Fortune, at least, contiguous with Freud's unconscious), but also the realm where the soul goes after death, inhabited by the dead as well as our own inactive memories. Through the subconscious mind we can also reach other entities — the dead and discarnate spirits — who belong to us or have something to do with us. (This idea of "subconscious" material belongs to the realm of psychology as well as occultism, but in a way that is pre-Freudian.) Fortune and Yeats also assume the reality of reincarnation; they share similar ideas of life to life expiation — that is, some of our karma in each life belongs to things not fully expiated or completed from past lives.

Neither Yeats nor Fortune speak of narcissism, nor do they have much use for the Freudian terminologies of self structure (id, ego, super ego, ego ideal); they also do not use the parallel Jungian terminologies (ego, persona, shadow, anima, self). Rather, both have highly idiosyncratic terminologies describing structures of the self, which are clearly informed by their training in theosophy and ritual magic.

My aim here is to triangulate the Freudian understandings of the self and its narcissistic representations with occultist ideas of the way self representations worked in magical and artistic creation, especially as these are elaborated in Yeats and Fortune. All three writers are more or less contemporary, Freud and Yeats dying in the same year (1939) and Fortune, the youngest of the three, just seven years later (1946). Fortune took an active interest in psychology at a time when Freud's name had begun to be firmly identified with an idea of "science" and she uses Freud's name often as a kind of metonymy for the (scientific) psychological and neurological disciplines as a whole. However Freud himself emerged from a milieu where psychology and psychical research were interlinked disciplines; the objective and secular understanding of the psyche evident in Freud's psychoanalysis was partly the result of a deliberate distancing from magic and spiritualistic phenomena—areas where other psychologists were still engaged in active research. Alex Owen gives a lucid overview of the relations between concepts of consciousness and dream interpretation in Freud, F. W. H. Myers, and several occultist thinkers, including Yeats; however it is worth looking a little more closely at a particular moment in the history of these relations.[2]

As noted in a useful article by James Keeley, Freud agreed to publish a seminal article, titled "A Note on the Unconscious in Psycho-Analysis," in the 1912 *Proceedings of the Society for Psychical Research* at the invitation of F. W. H. Myers, a psychologist of voluminous output, better known at that time than Freud.[3] Writing of emergent theories of human personality, Myers notes certain commonalities of thought:

> Conceptions of what I have called stratified consciousness are now coming to the front in so many places that it may be of interest to remark that (so far as I know) such a conception first presented itself independently to three observers as the result of three different lines of experiment. Mr. Gurney was led that way by experiments on hypnotic memory; M. Pierre Janet by experiments on hysteria; and to myself the observation of various automatisms neither hysterical nor hypnotic– as

automatic script and the like—brought a still more developed (I do not say a better established) conception of the stratified nature of our psychical being, of the higher faculties discernable in the deeper strata, and of the unity which comprehends them all.[4]

Clearly Myers's notion of stratified consciousness as he describes it here (without reference to Freud) bears more resemblance to the occultist notions than to Freud's; however Freud's own version of the unconscious was given an important push by Myers invitation, and almost certainly as well by a certain resistance to Myers's own thought. Freud's "Note on the Unconscious," written at Myers's instigation, propounds a theory radically different from the broader and more fluid ideas shared by Myers and the occultist thinkers.[5] Perhaps the most salient difference between this picture of stratified consciousness and Freud's is that, as Keeley intelligently describes it, for Myers, et al., ideas can emerge from preconsciousness to consciousness *if they are strong enough*—there is a constant commerce between conscious and subconscious material—whereas for Freud, unconscious ideas and impulses remain unconscious *no matter how strong they are*; they can only be recuperated from the realm of the unconsciousness by analysis of the patterns they leave on the subjects dreams and behavior. Myers's notion of personality is thus a more fundamentally integrated entity; in essence Freud argues for a "human personality composed of irreconcilable parts."[6]

Subconscious action and material as evident in the idea of Yeats and Fortune tend to resemble those of Myers, et al., rather more than they do Freudian ones. However, there are points in the writings of both occultists where we see a concept of the structure of human personality with more marked resemblances to Freud in their implicit understanding of the "irreconcilable parts" of the human self. These occur notably around the concepts of what happens in the process of artistic creation, and in the uses of art and poetry as a repair for states of functional damage to the self occasioned by normal life. In this area occultists seem to think with concepts innately closer to Freud's.

Union with Anti-self in the Work of W. B. Yeats

In an early essay on magic, Yeats speaks of magic as a manifestation (and manipulation) of several minds working collectively, or of the operation of the "great mind":

> I believe in the practice and philosophy of what we have agreed to call magic, in what I must call the evocation of spirits, though I do not know what they are, in the power of creating magical illusions, in the visions of truth in the depths of the mind when the eyes are closed; and I believe in three doctrines. . .
>
> (1) That the borders of our mind are ever shifting, and that many minds can flow into one another, as it were, and create or reveal a single mind, a single energy.
>
> (2) That the borders of our memories are as shifting, and that our memories are a part of one great memory, the memory of Nature herself.
>
> (3) That this great mind and great memory can be evoked by symbols.[7]

While Yeats embraces several different versions of his own metaphysics over the long course of his life, he seems to adhere to the basic principles here stated in both his early and his late writings. The notion that "the borders of our mind are ever shifting" belongs what I have come to think of as his theorization of "weak boundaries" of the self—that is, he understood that all minds were in a state of some interpenetration at all times, the degree of interpenetration being governed by strength of imagination. It is evident here and elsewhere that Yeats does not distinguish between psychic and imaginative phenomena, for in the magical workings he describes here, he says that the magically induced visions that occurred when his imagination "began to move of itself." Though the images he saw were "never too vivid to be imagination, as I had always understood it, [they] had yet a motion of their own, a life I could not change or shape."[8] And later in the essay he adds,

> If all who have described events like this have not dreamed, we should rewrite our histories, for all men, certainly all imaginative men, must be for ever casting forth enchantments, glamours, illusions; and all men, especially tranquil men who have no powerful egotistic life, must be continually passing under their power.[9]

By the "powerful egotistic life," it seems that Yeats means to indicate in a general way whatever is independent in the processes of the self. The power to cast "glamours," "illusions" derives from the fact that the processes of the self in those who are "imaginative" cannot contain themselves; they keep on working, even when not willed to work, and they overflow onto other people, sometimes causing intended or unintended intersubjective effects. Only from magic, understood as an imaginative act performed in co-operation with other linked minds, does Yeats derive evidence that the power of the imaginative self can be guided, making a continuous experience which is validated by the fact that it is shared.

If Yeats's imagination has "a will of its own" that enables him to participate psychically in the experiences of others, the state of his conscious mind alone and at rest he describes as distressingly fragmented, lacking in continuity. In extracts from a diary kept in 1909 (eight years after the essay on magic) which are published in his autobiography, he writes:

The pain others give passes away in their later kindness, but that of our own blunders, especially when they hurt our vanity, never passes away. Our own acts are isolated and one act does not buy absolution for another. They are always present before a strangely abstract judgment. We are never a unity, a personality to ourselves. ... Vanity is so intimately associated with our spiritual identity that whatever hurts it, above all if it came from it, is more painful in the memory than serious sin, and yet I do not think it follows that we are very vain.[10]

This inability to put his own personality together on an experiential level (the sense that he is "never a unity", that his acts are "isolated" from each other, and that the bad acts or "blunders" must always remain an unabsolved part of his consciousness) he links to the need for creative activity:

I think that all happiness depends on the energy to assume the mask of some other self; that all joyous or creative life is a re-birth as something not oneself, something which has no memory and is created in a moment and perpetually renewed. We put on a grotesque or solemn painted face to hide us from the terrors of judgment. . . a game like that of a child, where one loses the infinite pain of self-realisation.[11]

There is an ongoing tension between the mask and the self (or the *Mask* and the *Will*[12]), for if the Will is "self," the mask is simultaneously "not oneself" and an "other self," and the entry into it is described at once as an escape into child's play and as a rebirth. Both self and not self, the Mask is something which can be experienced as free from the "terrors of judgement" and which "has no memory" (therefore knows no past to judge). It is a kind of projection which enables freedom from the condition of incoherence normal to Yeats (and surely in some degree part of the human condition).

Elsewhere Yeats indicates that this experience is not always as easy as the metaphor of child's play would suggest; in "Hodos Chameliontos" (1922), the union with Mask or Image is described as something brought about by a kind of crisis generated by the interaction with "personifying spirits":

There are indeed personifying spirits that we had best call but Gates and Gatekeepers, because through their dramatic power they bring our souls to crisis, to Mask and Image. . . They have but one purpose, to bring their chosen man to the greatest obstacle he may confront without despair.[13]

And speaking of the greatest of all poets — Villon and Dante — he writes:

The two halves of their nature are so completely conjoined that they seem to labour for their objects, and yet to desire whatever happens, being at the same instant predestinate and free, creation's very self. We gaze at such men in awe because we gaze not at a work of art, but at the re-creation of the man through that art, the birth of a new species of man, and it may even seem that the hairs of our heads stand up, because that birth, that re-creation, is from terror.[14]

There is an interesting ambiguity in this passage inasmuch as Yeats seems to keep deliberately vague any sense of distinction between the self of the poet and the poem of the self: what is created in the greatest poetry is not a "work of art" but "a new man" or perhaps "a new species of man"; yet of course it must be a work of art too. What gives such poetry its enormous power is the completeness of the melding of the "two halves"—the self and the Anti-self—resulting from the crisis brought about by the "personifying spirits" (a curious term by which he appears to mean spirits whose work is to concretize and realize human personality). But does this melding occur in the poet or in the poem? Characteristically, Yeats prefers to leave us with the question; and it is with all humility that I would suggest that perhaps the poem itself is the mask with which the poet joins; the poem becomes as he writes a part of the architecture of his identity—a part which *was not there before*, and yet is, indisputably, *himself* from the moment of its creation.

Yeats elsewhere admits that such a union cannot remain a part of one's experience of the self in this life:

A poet writes always of his personal life, in his finest work out of its tragedy, whatever it be, remorse, lost love, or mere loneliness; he never speaks directly as to someone at the breakfast table, there is always a phantasmagoria. … . he is never the bundle of accident and incoherence that sits down to breakfast; he has been reborn as an idea, something intended, complete. … He is part of his own phantasmagoria, and we adore him because nature has grown intelligible, and by so doing a part of our creative power.[15]

By his personal tragedies, the poet is brought to crisis, generating the poem in which the poet experiences his "rebirth as an idea." Here, as in the passage above, we note how the act of writing a poem is (simply assumed to be) an act of self-construction or self creation; there is not anywhere a clear distinction made between the written object and the self of the author, except that the self constructed in the poem is not the ordinary man "who sits down to breakfast"; but it is not the poem that is called intended and complete (as though it were something separate from the author): it is the poet himself.

In this respect, what Yeats describes as the function of poetry maps closely onto the function of what Freud describes as the ideal ego in his essay "On Narcissism." Freud notes first that there is a force which watches over our actions and judges them; it is internal to the self, but sometimes feels external; paranoia is a regressive manifestation of this power (for which Freud has not yet developed a terminology, but will later be called 'superego'). This power at bottom is an internalized embodiment of parental criticism, which continues its development through the absorption and internalization of cultural and institutional ethical systems and renders impossible the original self love of primary narcissism. The power is directly responsible for the formation of the ideal ego—a representation of the self, like the ego but more perfect, and still capable of cathexis. Freud writes:

libidinal instinctual impulses undergo the vicissitudes of pathogenic repression if they come into conflict with the subject's cultural and ethical ideas. ... Repression, we have said, proceeds from the ego; we might say with greater precision that it proceeds from the self-respect of the ego. . . For the ego, the formation of an ideal would be the conditioning factor of repression.

This ideal ego is now the target of the self-love which was enjoyed in childhood by the actual ego. The subject's narcissism makes its appearance displaced onto this new ideal ego, which, like the infantile ego, finds itself possessed of every perfection that is of value. ... [Man] is not willing to forgo the narcissistic perfection of his childhood; and when, as he grows up, he is disturbed by the admonitions of others and by the awakening of his own critical judgment, so that he can no longer retain that perfection, he seeks to recover it in the new form of an ego ideal. What he projects before him as his ideal is the substitute for the lost narcissism of his childhood in which he was his own ideal.[16]

As the ideal ego is generated as compensation for the critical faculties of the self, so the poet's creation of the poem becomes a kind of imaginative compensation for the self who sits down to breakfast, fragmented, judged and unabsolved. The poet's self is displaced onto his work—a new self representation to which cathexis is once again possible.

Interestingly, it appears from Yeats's writing that the poem is not only narcissistically cathected for the poet; it is capable of being narcissistically cathected—cathected as a self-representation— by his audience as well. The hearer adores the poet, Yeats says, because the poem may become part of the process of his own identity construction just as it is the poet's, because "nature" (that is, human nature) "has grown intelligible, and by so doing a part of our creative power." So the "intended" poet-self which the poem *becomes* also *becomes* a cathected part of our own listening selves. It is in this way that the solitary imaginative act involved in poetry returns to the social world—not as an object in the world, but as a part of the listener, a new piece of the listener's identity which has been created or realized by the poet's crisis.

This, then, is the use of art for Yeats. Poetry is made out of the forces that also make magic (forces which are real in the domain of the imagination), but it does something even magic cannot do: it creates, at least when it is being written, and probably recurrently whenever the poet experiences audience cathexis on the poem, a sense of coherent self, protected both from its own fragmenting, destabilizing judgment and from intrusions by the imaginations of others. Further, this coherent self, this identity spilling over with meaning and free from pain, is something that can be shared by others, realizing the poet and the hearer at once. Like magic, it is ultimately a shared experience; but it differs from magic in that it is more fully generated by processes of self-construction within the poet.

Magical Bodies in the Work of Dion Fortune

More than Yeats, Fortune thinks of the forces which propel human beings as libidinal forces, and she also tends to think of the frustration or blocking of libidinal forces as causes of illness. She does not situate herself in the discussion on narcissism; however, because of her willingness to embed herself in the terminology of psychoanalysis, and to cross reference between psychological and magical terms, it is not difficult to extend her mapping of the forces and structures she describes onto Freud's.

Fortune also explicitly connects novels with fantasies of wish-fulfillment (understood as an extension of the experience of dreaming). In the introduction to her novel *The Sea Priestess*, she describes the combination of interpretation and wish fulfillment performed in the novel as having the same function as psychotherapy:

People read fiction in order to supplement the diet life provides for them. If life is full and varied, they like novels that analyse and interpret it for them; if life is narrow and unsatisfying, they supply themselves with mass production wish fulfilments from the lending libraries. I have managed to fit my book in between these two stools so neatly that it is hardly fair to say that it falls between them. It is a novel of interpretation and a novel of wish-fulfillment at the same time.

Yet after all, why should not the two be combined? They have to be in psychotherapy, where I learnt my trade. . . I think that if readers in their reading will identify themselves with one or another of the characters according to taste, they will be led to a curious psychological experience — the experience of the therapeutic use of phantasy, an unappreciated aspect of psychotherapy.[17]

Unlike Freud, for whom dreaming is used largely to furnish evidence of a wish likely to be hidden from the dreamer, it is evident here that Fortune describes what might be called active dreaming, the construction of wishes that become experiential through being enacted in processes analogous to dreaming. For Fortune, psychotherapy involves both the active encouragement of such dream processes and the interpretation of their causes and results. There are various ways of going about the process of activating our own dream life, and one of them is novel reading. Another, of course, is magic.

When Fortune describes the construction of a Magical Body, it is clear even from the opening sentence that this act has fundamental similarities with the act of novel reading. Her essay begins by citing a work of fiction: "James Branch Cabell has a story of the dull, ordinary Felix Kennaston who makes for himself an imaginary personality named 'Horvendile' through whom he experiences high adventure."[18] After briefly commenting on the utility of such fantasies in retaining good mental health, noting how much easier they are for children than adults, and linking the production of both magic and fiction to the "same level of the subliminal mind," Fortune goes on:

There is a technique in the repertoire of the adept by means of which he builds himself just such a vehicle of experience as Cabell made his dreary hero create in the imaginary personality of 'Horvendile.' Equipped with such an instrument formed out of such stuff as dreams are made of we can enter the dream world of the astral plane and act out therein a dramatic representation of our subliminal lives.

. . . I had long been familiar with the method of going forth by night in the Horvendile body. . . In my own experience of the operation, the utterance to myself of my magical name led to the picturing of myself in an idealized form, not differing in type, but upon an altogether grander scale, superhuman in fact, but recognizable as myself, as a statue more than life-size may be a good likeness. Once perceived, I could re-picture this idealized version of my body and personality at will, but I could not identify myself with it *unless I uttered my magical name* [original emphasis]. Upon my affirming it as my own identification was immediate.[19]

When Fortune alludes to "such stuff as dreams are made of" she evokes the context of Prospero's famous speech from the last act of *The Tempest*: as the play ends, the magical theatre becomes a metaphor for the human condition, in which life is "rounded by a sleep": we have lived the life of the play within our own lives, which are ultimately not less made of dreamstuff. Fortune's wish fulfillment is a kind of functional conceptual hybrid which combines Prospero's magical dreamstuff with Freud's dreamwork. For Prospero, identification of the magical life of the theatre with real life is a kind of platonic joke: life itself is an illusion, a wish fulfillment operation not fundamentally more real than the theatre. For Freud, on the other hand, dreaming is no joke, because the "wish" involved, though hidden from the dreamer, is a real agent: desires and wishes are *forces* which operate on us, altering our very actions and behaviors in the world even when they are not conscious. For Fortune, a wish can be a real force *and* an illusion *simultaneously*: the point is that the force behind the illusion is manipulable. The wish is real, and thereby affects reality (which reflects the dreamstuff underneath it). The real force of wishing, which is one of the processes of the self, can also generate alternative selves, idealized and superhuman but real on their own plane.

The question is not so much how to generate these idealized selves (which we do all the time), but how, as adults, we may properly realise them: step into and *inhabit* them, on the plane in which they exist as real. For Fortune, the use of a magical name facilitates the identification of self and object, affirming the imaginary double as "self" because the magical name belongs to both. The astral plane is the theatre of these therapeutic doubles, where the ordinary self may be released into a new personality, the self "in an idealized form. . . superhuman in fact," rendered capable of adventures not offered by ordinary life but still necessarily ours, "part of our subliminal lives."

It should already be plain that the magical body has some characteristics in common with Freud's ideal ego; but whereas the ideal ego is generated as a kind of byproduct of an unconscious wish (repressed through a negative self experience), the magical body appears here to be a largely conscious creation (albeit connected to the 'subliminal life'—not fully unconscious nor perhaps fully conscious either).

The generation of magical bodies finds a fuller development in Fortune's novels, in particular *The Sea Priestess*, and *Moon Magic*, the two which concern the character of Lilith LeFay Morgan. Lilith LeFay is depicted as an archetype of the fatal woman, mysterious, attractive to men, and a magical adept, a priestess of many lives. She is described as looking like a woman in her mid to late thirties but (due to the influence of regenerative magical forces) she is spectacularly well preserved, and her real age is revealed as nearer to one hundred and twenty. Besides being older than most, this fatal woman has another unusual quality for the type: instead of destroying the men who fall in love with her (always at the point of meeting her they are sick, repressed, lonely, and near nervous collapse) she heals them. She does this not by satisfying their needs in any ordinary sexual way, but rather by inducing to do magic with her. She uses the reflection their desiring admiration provides to build a magical body, a larger than life image of herself as Priestess of Isis, thus channeling all the stray libidinal forces in the men's lives into a massive cathexis of her own image, bringing down the Goddess who (as it were) eats the surplus libido, and returns them to themselves refreshed and freed of their complexes. Lilith is thus not merely the ideal woman and ideal magician; she is also the ideal psychotherapist.

It is not difficult to see Lilith LeFay as a larger than life superhuman projection of Dion Fortune. In this regard it is perhaps unsurprising that there is an epilogue to *Moon Magic* channeled after Fortune's death by a member of the Society of the Inner Light, in which Lilith LeFay appears again, this time identified straightforwardly as a magical body of Dion Fortune:

I am the same being who dominated Dion Fortune when she wrote *The Sea Priestess* and *Moon Magic*. I am well characterized as 'Morgan' and as 'Lilith Le Fay' in these books and I was known by many names among the ancients but today I am best described a persona or magical body.[20]

It seems likely that Fortune herself had entertained similar ideas, though she is less quick to own them. In the introduction to *Moon Magic*, Fortune writes, "If it be true that what is created in the imagination lives in the inner world, then what have I created in Lilith LeFay? ... .why did she live on after the book about her was finished, and insist on appearing again? Have I furnished myself with a dark familiar?"[21] If Lilith can be channeled independently of Fortune, it would certainly appear that she has gained an autonomous life—a dark familiar indeed.

If Lilith LeFay is identified as a magical body, or autonomous, idealized self-representation of Dion Fortune, it is of interest that she herself experiences herself as divided. Lilith's aspect as priestess of Isis is a constructed "body" too; and early in *Moon Magic*, Lilith speaks of her experiences with this secondary persona in her childhood:

So I came back to the world yet once again as the priestess of the Great Goddess, bringing with me the memory of forgotten arts, one of which is the art of being a woman. I came because I was sent. There was that needed which I had to give.
. . . .I had only my woman's personality with which to work, and I had to create and build it as if it were a work of art, and I worked on myself like a sculptress. It was an odd sensation to feel the two aspects of myself merging, and finally uniting. In the earlier stages I would be either in one consciousness or the other. ... Twice, in crises that might have destroyed the physical personality I was so laboriously building, I united my two selves momentarily, but the child-mind could not stand more than a brief uniting—life was difficult enough as it was.
With adolescence everything closed down. . . .when I stabilised with

175

maturity, it began to open again and I was conscious of an overshadowing. ...I thought of this overshadowing as a spirit control, but gradually I became aware that it was simply my own higher self... My two selves have never been permanently in me, for no human physique would stand that; nor can I invoke my higher self at will, but I know how to make the conditions that cause it to come in. Unfortunately that is a thing in which I always need to have help: I cannot do it single-handed; someone has to see the Goddess in me, and then She manifests...

As I have already said, Wilfred[22] gave me the help I needed in formulating myself to myself.[23]

We may note the difficulty Lilith has in combining the two halves of her self into a whole. As with Yeats' union with Mask or Anti-self in his poetry, Lilith's momentary melding with her alternate personality feels like a "crisis"; and as with Yeats' Masks, too, there seem to be opposing elements in the two selves: they struggle against each other, they cannot comfortably coexist for an extended period, for "no human physique could stand that"; their unity is desirable, but necessarily short lived.

But there are aspects to Lilith's attempts to bring down her magical body which distance this concept from Yeats' Anti-self: while the Mask with which Yeats becomes united in his poetry can be cathected by others after the fact, Lilith's secondary personality, as noted already, *requires* a cathexis by another person in order to make the conditions right for it to appear. She needs to have with her someone (preferably male and in love with her) who can "see the Goddess" in her. In order that she may be able to "formulate herself to herself" she needs a mirror. In *Moon Magic*, this mirror is Rupert Malcolm.

Not coincidentally, the ritual for the bringing down of Isis in needs a literal mirror as well; and there is a mirror over the altar in Lilith's temple which plays an important role in the magical operation. This mirror Lilith identifies for Rupert Malcolm as "the Door Without a Key," or the door to the astral plane. Lilith has earlier identified the "Door Without a Key" as the door to the unconscious:

This we call the Door Without a Key, which is also the Door of Dreams; Freud found it, and he used it for the coming forth by day; but we who are initiates use it for going forth by night. I regret that I must speak in riddles concerning these things, but not otherwise can they be spoken of.[24]

But this riddle is not difficult to resolve; it is as close as Fortune comes to making an explicit distinction between the process of Freudian psychoanalysis and her own form of magical psychotherapy. If Fortune had been able to tease out Lilith's riddle here, she might have said something like this: Freud's therapy is a 'going forth by day' because his method involves laying open to the daylight the unconscious libidinal promptings of the subject through interpretation of dreams, thereby releasing the cathexis on dissociated complexes. Her therapy is a 'going forth by night' because her method involves restructuring the darkness of subliminal mind by entering into it and creating benevolent complexes by channeling a libidinal cathexis ("magnetism" or "vital force") onto a set of desired forms. Both of these processes work as a way of releasing the undesirable blocked libidinal urges, which, for both Freud and Fortune, are understood to cause illness in the subject.

A vivid picture of how the magical process works to release this blockage—like sex, but different—is presented in the ritual descriptions of *Moon Magic*. Here, in the ritual for bringing down Isis, both Lilith and Malcolm, in their ceremonial robes, are in the earthly temple, illumined only by candlelight, looking into the dark mirror above the altar. Lilith is behind Malcolm, with her arms over his shoulders; Malcolm, in a state of extreme tension, is gripping Lilith's hands so hard that he is causing some pain:

We both looked in the mirror. There was the man's haggard face, the eyes almost mad; and above it a woman's face, perfectly calm, floating apparently in space, for my black robe was invisible in the darkness. The silver head-dress caught the light. The black pools of the eyes held no expression. It did not seem like my face even to me.

Then behind me, there began to be a warmth and a power. Isis was formulating.

177

Above my head I saw Hers. I was no longer conscious of the agony in my hands or the strain on my body. All I felt was the power flowing through me in electric heat...

Over the man and myself there formed a cloud, a silvery cloud of palest moon mist, slowly glowing to gold and growing warm as it glowed. It was the aura of Isis emanating from us, from our united magnetism. It is the thing that is behind marriage. It held for a while and then it slowly dissolved. Magnetism had gone off from both of us, and Isis had absorbed it. Malcolm dropped back against my breast, and I thought he had fainted till I heard him give a prolonged sigh... I could feel his hands sweating. Mine were cold as ice, so I knew which way the power had flowed.[25]

Characteristically, the description evokes sex without actually describing sex. The materialization of Isis in the mirror above Lilith's head seems to occur at the moment that would precede a sexual climax, and is followed by the sudden flow of power, "like electric heat," which takes the place of ejaculation. An aura forms around them for a little while, until the residue of magnetism is devoured by Isis (a projection of the whole, fully realized ideal self of Lilith LeFay) leaving no mess. Upon absorbing the "magnetism" which went into her creation, Isis dematerializes, leaving both parties relaxed, experiencing only the residue of their polarity. It seems clear how this process helps to heal Rupert of the libidinal blockage which has given him only half a life prior to this experiment: for him, it is a straightforward channeling of sexual energy into magic. It is less clear at the outset how the operation works for Lilith—whether, that is, she has any libidinal cathexis of her own, or what the health benefits of formulating Isis might be for her. As represented in the novel, Lilith seems to be a fully autonomous being, free of sexual desires and simultaneously free of the neuroses and illnesses that plague ordinary people. Indeed she evidently has no needs of other human beings at all, save one: the need to be mirrored by another person to bring down the goddess, to experience her ideal self as real. Given the essentially Freudian principles underlying the understanding of health and illness in Fortune's work, it may be hypothesized that what keeps Lilith psychologically functional (or perhaps super-functional) is the strong cathexis on her own self representation as a Goddess. The fact is that this self-representation

178

cannot be maintained without the admiring attention of men, so she does have needs; but she plainly has no object cathexes. Her narcissism forms a complete closed circuit.

Moon Magic is the last novel Dion Fortune wrote, and it is generally agreed to be her richest piece of fiction. Much of its richness inheres in the way the novel documents the process of its own construction: all the lovingly detailed acts of mirror magic by which Lilith formulates herself to herself in the novel can be retrofitted onto the process by which Dion Fortune constructs Lilith LeFay. Both moon magic and *Moon Magic* involve quintessentially narcissistic operations.

Erschaffend wurde ich gesund

One of the key insights in Freud's essay "On Narcissism" is the idea that we must love in order not to fall ill. Freud himself makes a connection between the idea of "love" and the act of creation via a poem from Heine. I quote Freud:

> A strong egoism is a protection against falling ill, but in the last resort we must begin to love in order not to fall ill, and we are bound to fall ill if, in consequence of frustration, we are unable to love. This follows somewhat on the lines of Heine's picture of the psychogenesis of the Creation:
> Krankheit ist wohl der letzte Grund
> Des ganzen Schöpferdrangs gewesen;
> Erschaffend konnte ich genesen,
> Erschaffend wurde ich gesund.[26]

I note first that in this passage there seems to be little distinction drawn between the formation of libidinal cathexes, the idea of "love" and the idea of creation (in this case of the universe by God, but the analogy in the verse is obviously also to artistic creation). "To love," in Freud's usage here, would appear equivalent to, "to charge an object (whether internal or external to the self) with a cathexis." Libidinal cathexis associates itself with creativity in the power to cure illness: both involve discharges of psychic energy. Creativity is thus a form of "love" as the term is being used here.

This is one of the key points of congruity between the three authors I have discussed. Freud, Fortune and Yeats all clearly see the creations of an artist as being cathected as a part of the artist's self. It is perhaps a key point binding Yeats and Fortune that they also see these creations as narcissistically cathected by others—that is, these artistic creations are sought out and needed by other people because completing the selves of readers too. They do something similar for both artist and audience, by providing a link to a self-representation which is a "completed idea."—whether an incarnate version of self united with Anti-self (as in Yeats), or a larger than life persona with a range of avenues for libidinal cathexis and catharsis (as in Fortune). In both cases, for the novelist and poet, the works of fiction and poetry offer a crucial form of repair to selves which otherwise are at risk (in Yeats's world) of lapsing into "the pain of self-realisation," a kind of chaotic incoherence, or alternatively (in Fortune's world) of being torn to shreds by drives which have no means of externalization.

Narcissistic cathexis has also been associated with creative activity, not only by Freud himself, of course, but by others following him. In a paper first published in the 1960s, Heinz Kohut combats what he sees as a pervasive tendency to understand narcissistic cathexis as *essentially* inferior to object cathexis. His approach is to evaluate the qualities of empathy, creativity, humor, and wisdom as positive "transformations of narcissism." He notes that creative output is always narcissistically cathected:

The fetishist's attachment to the fetish has the intensity of an addiction, a fact which is a manifestation not of object love but of a fixation on an early object that is experienced as part of the self. Creative artists, and Scientists, may be attached to their work with the intensity of an addiction, and they try to control and shape it with forces and for purposes which belong to a narcissistically experienced world. They are attempting to re-create a perfection which formerly was directly an attribute of their own.[27]

We are able to see an essentially similar, and I believe essentially Freudian theorization of narcissistic cathexis as a generator of creative output in the writings of both Yeats and Fortune. I wonder only about the degree to which creative output should actually be considered a positive "transformation" of narcissism, or in fact its very essence.

Notes

1. "Toward a Functional Definition of Narcissism" (1975) collected in *Essential Papers on Narcissism*, ed. Andrew P. Morrison (New York: NYU Press, 1986), 198.

2. Alex Owen, *The Place of Enchantment: British Occultism and the Culture of the Modern* (Chicago: University of Chicago Press, 2004); see especially chapter 5, 174 ff. Also for a useful analysis of the roots of some of Jung's ideas which are more contiguous with occultism see John Ryan Haule, "From Somnabulism to the Archetypes: The French Roots of Jung's Split with Freud," *The Psychoanalytic Review*, 71.4 (1984), 635-659.

3. "Subliminal Promptings: Psychoanalytic Theory and the Society for Psychical Research" *American Imago*, 58.4 (2001), 767-791)

4. Myers, "The Mechanism of Hysteria", *Proceedings of the Society for Psychical Research* 9 (1893-94), 15, quoted in Keeley, 774-5.

5. It is also in this article that we find the first usage of the distinctively Freudian term "unconscious"; see the OED sv "unconscious".

6. Keeley, 780.

7. "Magic," (1901) in *Essays and Introductions*, (London: MacMillan, 1961), 28.

8. "Magic," 29.

9. "Magic," 40.

10. From "The Death of Synge" (1909) in *The Autobiography of William Butler Yeats* (New York: Collier, 1965), 340.

11. Ibid.

12. See the explanation of the terms "Mask," "Will," "Body of Fate" and "Creative Mind" in *A Vision* (NY: Macmillan, 1937), 73 ff: "It will be enough [for the moment]. . . to describe *Will* and *Mask* as the will and its object, or the Is and the Ought (or that which should be), *Creative Mind* and *Body of Fate* as thought and its object, or the Knower and the Known." Yeats's *Will* is elsewhere referred to in *A Vision* as the "normal ego" and *Mask* as the "object of desire, or idea of the good" (83). It seems clear that "Will" here can be mapped with little distortion onto the Freudian "ego" and "Mask" (a concept also referred to in Yeats's oeuvre as "Image" and "Anti-self") onto Freud's "ideal ego."

13. *Autobiography*, 183.

14. Ibid.

15. From "A General Introduction to My Work" (1937), in *Essays and Introductions* (cited above), 509. "Phantasmagoria" is a term which received greater development in *A Vision* as a part of the stage of "Dreaming Back," one of the six stages which prepares the discarnate soul for its next life; see *A Vision*, "The Completed Symbol," 230 ff.

16. "On Narcissism: An Introduction," 36.

17. Fortune, *The Sea Priestess* (York Beach, ME: Weiser, 1978; first published 1938), 7.

18. From *Applied Magic*, chapter 9, "A Magical Body," in *Dion Fortune's Applied Magic and Aspects of Occultism* (London: Aquarian Press, 1987), 55. Throughout the essay, Fortune uses the term 'Horvendile body' as an alternative for 'magical body.'

19. "A Magical Body," 57.

20. "The Death of Vivien Le Fay Morgan" in *Applied Magic*, 166.

21. *Moon Magic* (York Beach, ME: Weiser, 1978, originally published 1956), 10.

22. Male protagonist of *Sea Priestess*.

23. *Moon Magic*, 54-5

24. *Moon Magic*, 76.

25. *Moon Magic*, 133.

26. "On Narcissism," 28. This edition leaves the poem in German, offering the following in a footnote: "God is imagined as saying: 'Illness was no doubt the final cause of the whole urge to create. By creating, I could recover; by creating, I became healthy.'" *Neue Gedichte*, "Schöpfungslieder VII'.

27. Kohut, "Forms and Transformations of Narcissism, " in *Essential Papers*, cited above, 77.

Esoteric Fiction

Esotericism Without Religion:
Philip Pullman's *His Dark Materials*

Joscelyn Godwin

When, in 1995, Philip Pullman's publishers offered a novel called *Northern Lights* to the market niche of "young adults," he had no great hopes for it.[1] Several years before, he had left the security of teaching to write full-time, and had had moderate success with that dwindling readership; he reckoned that his new book "would be read by about 500 people at the most."[2] But the right people did read and review it, and the next year it was awarded the Carnegie Medal for the best children's book. A sequel, *The Subtle Knife* (1997), was an instant bestseller. Three years later, the trilogy was completed by *The Amber Spyglass*, and Pullman's fans, now exceeding his gloomy estimate by several orders of magnitude, argued over whether or not the final volume was a let-down. It did not matter: the book won the Whitbread Book of the Year award, given for the first time to a so-called children's book—though more than one reader exclaimed: "This is Harry Potter for grown-ups!" Translations into dozens of languages followed. In 2004, London's National Theatre staged *His Dark Materials* (the collective title) in two plays of three hours each, and now the first novel of the trilogy has reached the apogee of fame as a "major motion picture." After years of precarious survival in the home of lost causes, Pullman found himself showered with literary prizes, honorary degrees, and the plaudits of the great and the good.[3]

Not everyone is pleased by his success, for reasons that will become obvious. For those who have not read *His Dark Materials*, the essentials can be summarized quite briefly. The heroine, twelve-year-old Lyra, lives in a parallel world somewhat resembling our own, in which history has taken a different course. In the sixteenth century of Lyra's world, the fanatical reformer John Calvin was elected Pope. After his death, the papacy was replaced with a theocratic "Magisterium" headquartered in Geneva, which succeeded in gaining control over every aspect of life.[4] Science was classed as "experimental theology," and all speculation subjected to rigid censorship. By the present day, when the story happens, technology has advanced to the point of steam trains and majestic zeppelins.[5]

That is the modern history of Lyra's world. The ancient history, scattered in hints throughout *His Dark Materials,* embraces not only hers but all the myriad worlds, and it goes as follows.[6] The universe is uncreated and consists of material particles, the most subtle of which are known in the book as "Dust." At some point, these particles became self-conscious, and matter began to understand itself, and to love itself. As it did so, more Dust was formed, and the first conscious being emerged: an angel, known in the book as "The Authority." When other angels emerged from the evolving substance, the Authority told them that he had created them (which was a lie), and sought to exercise his power over all conscious beings. Later, one came who was wiser than the Authority (elsewhere identified as Sophia or wisdom), but she was banished.[7]

Before our present world was created, some of the angels, followers of wisdom, rebelled against the Authority and were cast down.[8] They continued to work for his downfall and for the opening of the minds he sought to close.[9] Led by Sophia, they gave to the evolving beings in each world a gift that would help them understand themselves and become wise. In some worlds, they gave them a dæmon.[10] In our world, these angels had dealings with humans, and interbred with them.[11] The awakening to fully human consciousness occurred here between 30,000 and 40,000 years ago, as part of the rebel angels' plan against the Authority.[12]

On rare occasions, humans on both sides of the conflict were able to rise to angelic status. Such was Baruch, one of the pair of angels who helps in the assault on the Authority. Another was Enoch, who graduated from the human state 4000 years ago, and was chosen as Regent of the Authority under the name of Metatron.[13] At the time of the story, this Regent, seeing conscious beings becoming dangerously independent, is planning to intervene much more in

186

human affairs and to set up a permanent Inquisition in every world.[14] The Authority, for his part, has gradually withdrawn to his residence in the "Clouded Mountain." When we meet him near the end of the book, he is in the last stages of senility, and dies.[15]

One of the defining characteristics of epic literature is the presence of the divine and its interaction with humans. It figures largely in Homer's *Iliad* and *Odyssey*; Ovid's *Metamorphoses* and Virgil's *Aeneid*; Dante's *Divine Comedy*, Milton's *Paradise Lost* (together with Blake, the primary literary influence on Pullman and the source of the phrase *His Dark Materials*), Goethe's *Faust*, and Wagner's *Ring of the Nibelung*. If these do not always "justify the ways of God[s] to man," at least they represent them, with all their implications. Another characteristic of epic is that it usually contains a cosmogony or creation myth, and a cosmology or explanation of the world-system.

His Dark Materials satisfies epic tradition in these respects, as also in the heroic and tragic nature of its protagonists. This summary also reveals some of the things that irk the defenders of the faith. Pullman's depiction of the Church and its ministers makes them out to be sleazy, repressive, and cruel. The trilogy's dramatic mainspring is the reversal of the outcome of the last War in Heaven—the one described in *Paradise Lost*, in which God's angels conquered Satan's. In the process, Lyra and her boy companion Will Parry travel to the Land of the Dead (another requisite of epic literature) to find a drab Homeric Hades in which the Authority has imprisoned the spirits of all conscious beings. Will and Lyra's task is to let these ghosts out, so that their subtle atoms can return to nature, a process of dissolution experienced as ecstatic release. The children learn the lesson that there is no paradise but the here and now, and no prospect superior to the "republic of heaven" that we may build while we are alive. The promises and threats of the monotheistic religions, in short, are revealed as a pack of lies.

Catholics and Evangelicals alike have savaged *His Dark Materials* on the grounds that it denigrates religion and woos its young readers to atheism.[16] As we know from the examples of Salman Rushdie (author of *The Satanic Verses*) and, more recently, Mel Gibson (director of *The Passion of the Christ*), nothing generates more publicity than upsetting people's religious sensibilities and getting them to protest against one's work. But one has to be careful about whom to annoy. Although Mr. Pullman has rightly said that "every single religion that has a monotheistic god ends up by persecuting other people and killing them because they don't accept him," he has more sense than to attack Islam or Judaism directly.[17] In secular Britain, Christianity is easier game, and less likely to hit back in unpleasant ways.[18] Instead of slinking around in fear of the Ayatollah's assassins, as Mr. Rushdie did for years, Pullman has the Archbishop of Canterbury eating out of his hand.[19] It remains to be seen how this will go down in the USA, if the filmmakers do not shirk Pullman's image of what many Americans still regard as God.

Seen from the other side, it is no wonder that many Christians of another stamp, Archbishop Williams included, feel no animus toward Pullman and his novel. For one thing, they can recognize fiction when they see it. For another, the Calvinist theocracy of Lyra's world is the last brand of Christianity they want to identify with. They share what Pullman describes as his "deep anger and yes, horror at the excesses of cruelty and infamy that've been carried out in the name of a supernatural power."[20] As to whether the books encourage atheism in their young (or even older) readers, that is a matter for reflection rather than hysteria. Dr. Williams says that it is healthy for anyone to ask himself or herself what sort of god they do *not* believe in.[21]

While its cosmogony is atheist, in the sense that the universe is uncreated, and its cosmology materialist, *His Dark Materials* lacks for nothing in wonder and magic. Spurning the drab, denatured universe of the existentialist novelists, Pullman has drawn on another current that has often run in opposition to the churches: the esoteric tradition. Magpie-like, he has picked up fragments from Hermeticism, from Kabbalah and Jewish legend, from Gnosticism, theosophy, and the occult sciences, and interwoven them with current notions of physics. His worlds proliferate with angels, witches, shamans, specters, talking beasts, and especially with dæmons.

Readers and critics agree that one of his happiest inventions is the dæmon: a part of the individual exteriorized in the form of an animal, bird, or insect of the opposite sex, which accompanies every person closely their life long. The dæmon speaks with a human voice, but has the senses and skills of the appropriate animal. It acts as playmate or companion, as an ever-present partner in conversation, and often as a wise counselor. The dæmons of children are unstable, changing from one animal to another according to whim or circumstance, until at puberty they settle into a permanent form. Lyra is distressed when she first comes into the world of her friend Will, which is our world, and sees people without their accompanying dæmons: it seems to her indecent, or tragic, until she persuades herself that people in our world have their dæmons inside themselves. Among the obvious forerunners of this brilliant notion is the *daimon* of Socrates, with its habit of warning him against imprudent actions or dangerous circumstances. Another is Carl Jung's anima or animus as a contra-sexual element in the unconscious, its instinctual wisdom sometimes represented in dreams or visions by an animal or bird. Then there is the idea of finding one's own "animal spirit," which has entered the imagery of the New Age by way of Native American and other shamanic cultures. These parallels show why Pullman's invention rings so true, especially to young readers who yearn for a close and faithful companion, and often find an invisible one, to the annoyance of rational parents and teachers.

Pullman, like any author in touch with the mysterious sources of the creative imagination, is definitely on the irrational side here.[22] He skillfully avoids the reductionism to which the atheist world view is often prone, and the consequent one-dimensionality of the human being. Lyra, already familiar with her dæmon-soul, speculates that humans comprise three things: the body, the dæmon, and the "ghost." Mary Malone, a character from our world, remarks on how Saint Paul talks of body, soul, and spirit, so that Lyra's three-part view of human nature is not so strange to her. As for the ultimate fate of these components, the body eventually decays and its atoms return to nature, as do those of the dæmon, which vanishes into thin air immediately upon death. That leaves the spirit or ghost, which as Lyra says is "the part that can think about the other two."[23] So long as the Authority ruled, the ghosts of all conscious beings have been kept captive in the Land of the Dead. After Lyra and Will have opened a way out, the ghosts, too, return to their natural elements, joyfully recombining with the wind and dew and earth, and perhaps with the very atoms of their own sweethearts and dæmons.[24]

Readers of the late-antique writings ascribed to Hermes Trismegistus will detect an echo of a famous passage describing what happens after death:

First, in releasing the material body you give the body over to alteration, and the form that you used to have vanishes. To the demon you give over your temperament, now inactive. The body's senses rise up and flow back to their particular sources, becoming separate parts and mingling again with the energies. And feeling and longing go on toward irrational nature.[25]

In short, each human element and faculty returns to its appropriate cosmic reservoir. But in Hermetism this is not the end of the human being. The sage continues: "Thence the human being rushes up through the cosmic framework," surrendering its evil tendencies as it passes the sphere of each planet, "and then, stripped of the effects of the cosmic framework, the human enters the region of the Ogdoad [the eight higher powers]; he has his own proper power, and along with the blessed he hymns the Father." And beyond this stage, suggestive of the Christian Paradise, there is still more: "The final good for those who have received knowledge [is] to be made God."

The consensus among esotericists, at least the non-Christian ones, is that few humans attain personal immortality, much less the deification that Hermetism holds out as the highest possibility for man. It supposedly takes a heroic effort of preparation during one's lifetime in order to achieve this in the after-death state; the great majority of humans are simply recycled in soul as well as body. (There is a separate current, more occult than esoteric, that takes quite seriously the idea that human souls, after death, are imprisoned—whether by an Authority, by the Moon, or by their own incapacity—in some intermediate sphere.[26]) In Pullman's worlds, this recycling is welcomed as the normal course of nature. After body, dæmon, and ghost have all dispersed, nothing is left to rush up through the cosmic framework and eventually become a god.

But in *His Dark Materials,* too, there are the exceptional instances of humans like Metatron and Baruch, who have become angels and are virtually immortal. Surprising as it may seem, the eschatology of *His Dark Materials* is quite Hermetic.

An aura of Hermeticism, this time of the Renaissance rather than classical Antiquity, surrounds the alethiometer, a golden compass-like instrument which Lyra learns to use for divination. It seems to have been invented in Prague (the Prague of Lyra's world), about 300 years ago, and its function is to "tell the truth" (Greek *alètheuein*).[27] The device displays thirty symbols on its dial, each of them like a ladder of meanings down which one must search for the right one. Farder Coram, the Gypsy sage, explains to Lyra that the first meaning of the anchor, for example, is hope, the second steadfastness, the third snag or prevention, the fourth the sea, and so on.[28] Under his guidance, Lyra finds that she can work the instrument by setting its three pointers to define a question, then entering a state of suspended awareness. The answer comes in symbolic form, which has to be interpreted either through intuition (as in Lyra's case) or, more laboriously, through consulting treatises.

One thinks immediately—and Pullman confirms the association—of the order of ideas made familiar by Frances A. Yates: the emblem books of the Renaissance; the ranked images employed in the art of memory and in artificial languages like Kircher's Polygraphy; the rotating volvelles in the books of Ramon Lull and other cosmographers.[29] Other associations are with the exquisite clockworks and dials of German workmanship; the questioning of angels by John Dee and Edward Kelley; and the use by occultists of child mediums whose innocence grants them privileged access to wisdom. I note parenthetically that if the alethiometer had been invented in *our* Prague, it would have had to be a century earlier, in the time of Michael Maier, Emperor Rudolf II, and the Rabbi Loew. But in Lyra's world, with a Calvinist theocracy in place by the mid-sixteenth century, there would have been no wars of religion, no Thirty Years War to extinguish the alchemical and Hermetic tendencies of central Europe, and no Scientific Revolution to impose a mechanistic view of nature.

Later we learn that it is Dust that makes the alethiometer work.

Mary Malone discovers that Dust (which as a physicist she calls Shadow-particles, or dark matter) will respond intelligently to a certain state of mind, a state she has cultivated through consulting the Chinese oracle *I Ching*.[30] She uses a similar "trance-like open dreaming" to perceive her own dæmon.[31] These are some of the many instances of altered states of consciousness in *His Dark Materials*. Will Parry also has to control his mind in order to wield the subtle knife that cuts through everything and makes windows between worlds. He first develops this control under excruciating pressure, after the knife has cut off two of his fingers; later, when he lets himself be distracted by thoughts of his mother, the knife breaks. During the reforging of it by the armored bear Iorek Byrnison, Will is ordered to "Hold it still in your mind! You have to forge it too!", which demands another excruciating effort. [32] This resembles the situation of the alchemists, whose work in the chemical laboratory was futile unless accompanied by prayer and mental effort, with due observance of astrological conditions—all in obedience to the law of correspondences.

No less dedication was required of Will's father, John Parry, whose curiosity compelled him to undergo the initiation of a shaman. In a ritual lasting two nights and a day, his skull was perforated by a trepanning drill.[33] As a result, he gained the power to control men, summon up storms, and travel out of the body, even to other worlds. This he did through "the faculty of what you call imagination. But that does not mean *making things up*. It is a form of seeing."[34] John Parry's definition of the imagination is precisely what one meets with in the school of Henry Corbin, the Sorbonne scholar who first brought the theosophy and Neoplatonism of Persia to the attention of the West.[35] For Corbin and his English admirer Kathleen Raine, the imagination is the organ through which one has access to the "imaginal world" that is without a material substratum, but absolutely real. However, for Pullman, as for Raine, a readier source of such ideas lay to hand in William Blake—if a creative genius needs a source for anything so obvious.

As these pieces of evidence add up, it appears that *His Dark Materials* is esoteric through and through. From the academic point of view, it satisfies all four primary requirements through which

Antoine Faivre has defined Western esotericism.[36] There is the *principle of correspondences* in the alethiometer, whose multiple symbols that convey an infallible truth imply that their source, the cosmic Dust, is similarly structured. There is the principle of *living nature* in which everything receives being, consciousness, and even love from the same mysterious Dust. There is the *function of the imagination* and the presence of an imaginal world, which in many of Faivre's examples is coupled with an angelology—also present in the book. There is the *experience of transmutation* on Lyra's part as she meets her own death, her dæmon reaches its fixed form, and she fulfils her destiny as the new Eve. (In fact, the whole trilogy is about Lyra's transmutation.) Faivre defines two further components of esotericism that are often present, but not indispensable as the first four are. One is an *esoteric transmission or tradition*, which is found in the crucial episode of Will's initiation as bearer of the subtle knife. This object was created about 300 years ago by a guild of philosopher-alchemists, the last of whom, Giacomo Paradisi, bestows it on Will, together with instructions as to its use and the rules that must be observed.[37] (479-480) Faivre's final component is the *practice of concordance*, which reconciles the differences between exoterically conflicting religions and philosophies, but this is of little account when all religious beliefs are regarded with indifference.

Other critics have sensed in *His Dark Materials* "some form of à la carte Buddhism"—a religion (or philosophy) that is never mentioned in the book but bears many points in common with it.[38] No single, personal God is responsible for the creation of the Buddhist universe, summarized in the image of the Wheel of Existence to which all beings, except the enlightened ones, are bound. The "long-lived gods" do exist as an order of beings within the Wheel, but they do not deserve human attention, much less worship. Like the Authority, they are prone to inflate their own importance, but unlike him they have no power over us. Both the Buddhist system and that of *His Dark Materials* accord special importance to the human state, though Buddhism specifically excludes the existence of a personal, immortal soul. In Buddhism, it is only from the human state that liberation from the wheel of existence can be achieved; neither the gods, the animals, nor the dwellers in the other sectors of the wheel have the opportunity of this.

For Pullman, the special quality of the human state resides in our physical bodies: in the fact of our incarnation, which is lacking in other orders of beings, even ones that seem superior, such as angels. Like the gods of Buddhism, Pullman's angels live for aeons, but are eventually subject to decay (like the Authority) and death. They envy our physicality and the intensity of experience that is only achieved in the material world.[39] They also need us. In an episode of heartbreaking beauty, Pullman describes how the children, Lyra and Will, have come to the end of their endurance and are in an exhausted sleep, and angels come on pilgrimage to be near them: "She [the witch Serafina Pekkala] understood why these beings would wait for thousands of years and travel vast distances in order to be close to something important, and how they would feel differently for the rest of time, having been briefly in its presence."[40]

Commentators on *His Dark Materials* can hardly miss its strong flavor of Gnosticism. The theogonic episode briefly summarized above, in which the Authority lies to the other angels and is defied by one female spirit, later identified as Wisdom (Sophia), comes straight from the Gnostic myth of the First Father, Yaldabaoth:

When the ruler saw his greatness—and he saw only himself; he did not see another one except water and darkness—then he thought that he alone existed... And he rejoiced in his heart, and he boasted continually, saying to [the gods and their angels]: "I do not need anything." He said, "I am god and no other one exists except me." But when he said these things, he sinned against all the immortal ones, and they protected him. Moreover, when Pistis [=Sophia] saw the impiety of the chief ruler, she was angry. Without being seen, she said, "You err, Samael," i.e. "the blind god."[41]

In Valentinian Gnosticism, the true God is the *deus absconditus*, "inconceivable and invisible, eternal and uncreated, existing in great peace and stillness in unending spaces."[42] Yet in a sense he (or rather It) reaches out to mankind, extending the possibility of *gnosis*, saving knowledge, on which the whole religious philosophy depends (in Christian Gnosticism, Jesus Christ was the representative of this true God). Pullman's trilogy does not attempt to define a "true God"—

which in any case can only be defined by negatives—but it includes the saving gnosis in the form of Dust, which likewise responds to its creatures and promotes conscious life, love, and freedom. In the same Gnostic school, "a deep contempt is now displayed towards the biblical God of creation and his government of the world."[43] *His Dark Materials* names this God unambiguously by the Hebraic terms of "Yahweh, El, Adonai, the King, the Father, the Almighty."[44] But when Lyra and Will actually see him, and watch him die, it is not contempt or triumph they feel, but compassion. At the same time, the value-system of *His Dark Materials* turns this "very powerful and persuasive system of thought" on its head, because as Pullman points out, "The essence of Gnosticism is its rejection of the physical universe and the whole tendency of my thinking and feeling and of the story I wrote is towards the celebration of the physical world."[45]

Although it is bad practice to identify the beliefs of fictional characters with those of their authors, Pullman has been forthcoming enough in interviews and autobiographical writings about the connections between his storytelling and his own thoughts and feelings. More than once, he has stated that he is an atheist. Asked to explain this, he has modified it by saying that he is an atheist in respect to his own experience, having no need or place for the hypothesis of what people call God; but in respect to the whole of reality, since he cannot know everything about it (and nor can anyone else), he is an agnostic.[46] As with any other mature and complex personality, there are different sides to his character, and they all contribute to his writing. There is something in him of the conventional left-wing intellectual, which emerged in his reproach of C.S. Lewis's Narnia books for those cardinal sins of racism and sexism.[47] Yet he shares the moral earnestness that, in Lewis's case, arose out of "mere Christianity." At the dénouement of *The Amber Spyglass,* an angel tells Lyra and Will how to collaborate in the work of Dust: "by helping [everyone else] to learn and understand about themselves and each other and the way everything works, and by showing them how to be kind instead of cruel, and patient instead of hasty, and cheerful instead of surly, and above all how to keep their minds open and free and curious."[48] If I had met this quotation out of context, my best guess would have been that it came from somewhere in the Narnia books.

Pullman is often impatient with current pieties, as when he tells the Archbishop of Canterbury: "I'm temperamentally 'agin' the postmodernist position that there is no truth and it depends on where you are and it's all a result of the capitalist, imperialist hegemony of the bourgeois ... all this sort of stuff." Again, when asked a question about the spiritual education of children, he shows disdain for trendy and cliché-ridden thinking: "I don't use the word 'spiritual' myself, because I don't have a clear sense of what it means. But I think it depends on your view of education: whether you think that the true end and purpose of education is to help children grow up, compete and face the economic challenges of a global environment that we're going to face in the twenty-first century, or whether you think it's to do with helping them see that they are the true heirs and inheritors of the riches—the philosophical, the artistic, the scientific, the literary riches—of the whole world. [...] I know which one I'd go for." As a parson's grandson, he knows how much the Church has contributed to civilization, and deplores the way that the Church of England has discarded the Elizabethan language, the music, and the rituals in which he was raised: "if ever I go into a church and look at the dreadful, barren language that disfigures the forms of service they have now, I am very thankful that I grew up at a time when it was possible for me to go to Matins and sing the Psalms in the old versions."[49] Lyra's world, though gently comical in its old-fashioned ways, is a nostalgic vision of what the world might have been if untouched by modernism, infatuation with technology, and the proletarianization of culture.

The more one learns of Pullman's tastes and moral vision, the less he seems to share with the aggressively secular intellectuals who lord it over the British cultural scene and who, on a superficial understanding of his books and beliefs, acclaim him as one of their own; and the more rooted he seems to be in the traditional values of the humanist—using the term in the historical sense of a student and lover of the *litterae humaniores*. In the quotations gathered above, in his many other pronouncements, in his efforts to save the state educational system, and of course throughout his

196

books, he has always taken the side that seeks to enrich the life of the imagination.

Can a sense of the sacred exist apart from, and even in defiance of, the revealed religions? Without a doubt, all peoples have had this sense, mediated as may be through ritual, philosophy, meditation, aesthetic or erotic experience. The dogmatic atheist alone shuts it out: if he begins to feel it, he immediately checks the feeling and substitutes scientific awe (or existential angst). The sense of the sacred announces the presence of something incomprehensible and greater than ourselves, with qualities akin to benevolence and intelligence. Dust has all these properties. It is not mindless matter or whatever modern physics has reduced matter to, but the source of all the mind, consciousness, and love in the universe. As soon as Lyra hears of it, she is attracted by it, and her quest to find the source of Dust is her spiritual quest.

Unfortunately, it is religious people who have defined all the terms one would like to use in discussing these matters: spiritual, sacred, holy, divine, etc. As soon as one uses them, one seems to be on their ground. This is a problem for those outside religion but with a strong spiritual consciousness: they don't want to sound pious. No wonder Pullman shuns the word "spiritual." In the English intellectual world from which he comes, there is a marked division between the Christians and the non-believers. Christian intellectuals, second to none in their brainpower and erudition, dominate one side of the divide; their allies are the college chaplains of Oxford and Cambridge. Although the two sides treat each other with perfect decorum and often friendship, there is an uneasy feeling that the Christians would like to convert the others, and that they rejoice when someone enters their fold. The non-believers are usually uninterested in conversion, but Pullman is an exception, and it is his potential success in "de-evangelizing" the young that causes consternation.

What does he offer as an alternative? *His Dark Materials* adopts an esoteric world-view, but he can hardly expect people to live by that in the real world; there is no indication in his own interviews and other writings that he practices alchemy, Kabbalah, Buddhism, or whatever Gnostics are supposed to practice. Like William Blake,

197

instead of the Authority, he offers the Imagination.

The creative imagination is independent of belief, for it does not obey the structures and strictures of this world. It has the power to create new worlds for the outer and inner senses, and to transmute the experience of a world which we appear to share with other beings (though we can never be quite sure of that). In recent millennia, one of its sources of energy has been the biblical mythology and its believers. The irony of *His Dark Materials* is that, like *Paradise Lost,* it co-opts the Hebrew myth: within the rules of the story, the Authority is a real being, the angels did rebel against him, Eve was tempted, etc. Outside the story, the author has an agenda, as surely as Milton did, though in the contrary direction. But to those who value the imagination more than the certainties of believers (religious and atheistical alike), it is the stories that count.

Readers of *The Amber Spyglass* will recall the emphatic command to the dead: "Tell them stories!" and its context. Until Lyra's "harrowing of hell," the ghosts of all humanity have been trapped in the Authority's prison. Under the new covenant that Lyra makes with the Harpies who guard the Land of the Dead, the ghosts will henceforth tell their lives' stories, then, if they have told true, will return to the impersonal bosom of nature, their every atom rejoicing in its freedom. There are no posthumous rewards for good conduct, or punishments for evil; the story is literally the meaning of life. In our world, Philip Pullman may be something of a moralist, but in *His Dark Materials,* the ultimate value is aesthetic: the alchemical distillation of experience into art.

Notes

1. A slightly different version of this article was published in *Tyr: Myth, Culture, Tradition,* 3(2007). In the American edition of the trilogy, as in some foreign editions, the first volume of *His Dark Materials* is entitled *The Golden Compass,* to match the titles of the other two volumes; but this does not do justice to the theme and atmosphere that make *Northern Lights* one of the great Arctic novels. The title refers to the journey to the polar

regions that occupies much of the book, and to the Aurora Borealis, which provides a spectacular backdrop to its climax.

2. Quoted from Philip. Pullman, "About the Writing." http://www. philip-pullman.com/about_the_writing.asp.

3. A common sobriquet for the university city of Oxford, Pullman's home.

4. Philip Pullman, *His Dark Materials* (London: Scholastic Press, 2001), 31. Subsequent page references are to this edition.

5. Lyra's world somewhat resembles the theocratic Britain of Kingsley Amis's novel *The Alteration* (1976), in which it is supposed that Martin Luther became Pope. Pullman's little book *Lyra's Oxford* (London: Scholastic, 2004) fills in some further details about Lyra's world and its ways of life.

6. In his conversation with Archbishop Rowan Williams, Pullman says that this creation myth is never fully explicit, but that he discovered it as he was writing it. "The Dark Materials debate: life, God, the universe...," chaired by Robert Butler, *Arts Telegraph,* March 17, 2004. http://www. telegraph.co.uk/arts/main.jhtml?xml=/arts/2004/03/17/bodark17.xml.

7. Pullman, 622.

8. Pullman, 367.

9. Pullman, 983.

10. This is not stated in *His Dark Materials,* but in the BBC's "Interview with Philip Pullman." http://www.bbc.co.uk/religion/programmes/beliefs/scripts/philip_pullman.html.

11. Pullman, 439.

12. Pullman, 530.

13. Pullman, 648. Pullman's theology and angelology are based, often quite faithfully, on apocryphal scriptures such as *I Enoch* and the collection of texts found at Nag Hammadi. See James C. VanderKam, *Enoch, A Man for All Generations* (Columbia: University of South Carolina Press, 1995); J. Edward Wright, *Baruch Ben Neriah: From Biblical Scribe to Apocalyptic Seer* (Columbia, University of South Carolina Press, 2003).

14. Pullman, 647.

15. Pullman, 926.

16. The Catholic writer Leonie Caldecott deplores that "Pullman is effectively removing, among a mass audience of a highly impressionable age, some of the building blocks for future evangelization." L. Caldecott, "The Stuff of Nightmares," *The Catholic Herald,* October 29, 1999. http://www.christendom-awake.org/pages/misc/reflections.htm.

17. "Heat and Dust," interview with Huw Spanner, *Third Way,* 2000. http://www.thirdway.org.uk/past/showpage/asp?page=3949. Pullman described

this interview as "the best I've ever read."

18. Sarah Johnson puts it with brutal bluntness (and a total lack of appreciation of the novelist's art): "What if Pullman had replaced the Magisterium's crosses and churches with crescents and mosques? Not that he would have dared. Like any playground bully, Pullman knows which kids are least likely to kick him back." "A Preachy Rant against the Church," *The Catholic Herald*, January 16, 2004. http://www.christendom-awake.org/pages/misc/reflections.htm.

19. Rowan Williams, "A Near-miraculous Triumph," [review of the dramatization of *His Dark Materials*] *The Guardian*, March 10, 2004. http://www.guardian.co.uk/arts/features/story/0,11710,1165873,00.html. See also "The Dark Materials debate."

20. BBC "Interview with Philip Pullman."

21. Rowan Williams, "A Near-miraculous triumph."

22. "I am the servant of the story—the medium in a spiritualist sense, if you like..." Pullman in "Heat and Dust."

23. Pullman, 733.

24. Pullman, 906.

25. *Corpus Hermeticum*, I, 24 (translated by Brian P. Copenhaver).

26. See Joscelyn Godwin, "The Survival of the Personality According to Modern Esoteric Teachings," in R. Caron, J. Godwin, W. Hanegraaff, & R. VandenBroeck, eds., *Mélanges Antoine Faivre* (Leuven: Peeters, 2001), 403-414. Several of the esotericists mentioned there refuse to make a distinction between spirit and matter, or regard the whole of manifestation as to some degree material.

27. In the developing vocabulary of esoteric studies, "Hermetism" refers to the teachings of Hermes Trismegistus, while the broader term "Hermeticism" refers to later developments along Hermetic principles, especially alchemy.

28. Pullman, 106.

29. "Philip Pullman Webchat," response to question by Graham King. http://www.bbc.co.uk/radio4/arts/hisdarkmaterials/pullman_webchat.shtml.

30. Pullman, 401, 406.

31. Pullman, 1005.

32. Pullman, 750.

33. Pullman, 423.

34. Pullman, 997.

35. For example, in Henry Corbin's *Creative Imagination in the Sufism of Ibn 'Arabi* (Princeton: Princeton University Press, 1969), and more accessibly in his *Spiritual Body and Celestial Earth* (1977).

36. Antoine Faivre, *Access to Western Esotericism* (Albany: SUNY Press, 1994) is one of the many places in which he defines esotericism through these 4+2 components.

37. Pullman, 479-480.

38. Greg Krehbiel, "Philip Pullman's *His Dark Materials*," *Journeyman* I/1 (2001). http://www.crowhill.net/journeyman/Vol1No1/Darkmaterials. html.

39. Pullman, 898.

40. Pullman, 550.

41. "On the Origin of the World" II, 100, 103, in James M. Robinson, ed., *The Nag Hammadi Library in English* (San Francisco: Harper & Row, 1977), 163, 165.

42. Kurt Rudolph, *Gnosis: the Nature and History of an Ancient Religion,* tr. R. McL. Wilson (Edinburgh: T. & T. Clark, 1983), 62.

43. Rudolph, *op. cit.,* 79.

44. Pullman, 622.

45. "Philip Pullman Webchat," reply to question by Russell: "Would you call yourself a Gnostic?"

46. This précis is based on the BBC's"Interview with Philip Pullman" and on "Heat and Dust."

47. Pullman made these remarks at the 2002 book festival in Hay-on-Wye; see *The Guardian,* June 4, 2002.

48. Pullman, 995-996.

49. "Heat and Dust."

"Knowing in Terms of Togetherness":
D. H. Lawrence and Esotericism

Glenn Alexander Magee

Lawrence's New Science

In his late essay "A Propos of *Lady Chatterley's Lover*," D. H. Lawrence distinguishes between two ways of knowing: "knowing in terms of apartness, which is mental, rational, scientific, and knowing in terms of togetherness, which is religious and poetic."[1] By "apartness" he means something close to what scientists and philosophers would call objectivity, but he means more than this. "Knowing in terms of apartness" means trying to know the world as if one were not actually a part of it. It means ignoring the fact that nature is an organic whole that includes the scientist, and that the scientist, as a living thing, is already enmeshed in relationships with other things that may make pure objectivity impossible. It means believing that life and matter can only be studied in an other, and that to study them in oneself is "subjective." In short, "knowing in terms of apartness" is an artificial standpoint which involves the covert assumption that the scientist is an unnatural being.

As others before him had done, Lawrence traces the origins of this "objective" standpoint to monotheism, which seems to always involve setting man up as an outsider in nature, to whom nature has been bequeathed for mastery and analysis. Lawrence writes, "The Christian religion lost, in Protestantism finally, the togetherness with the universe, the togetherness of the body, the sex, the emotions, the passions, with the earth and sun and stars."[2] "Knowing in terms of apartness" involves not only setting ourselves up as apart, but also treating other beings as separate and apart from each other rather than in organic relation. Nature, from this standpoint, is at best a clockwork mechanism built from related but separable parts, not an organic system.

Contrary to appearances, Lawrence is not claiming that science is valueless. Science can help us understand, in purely physical terms how this or that works, but it cannot connect us to nature in any deep, non-intellectual, non-theoretical sense and help us to feel at home in the universe. Nor can it give us any insight into the perennial existential questions that human beings agonize over. It cannot show us *why* we or anything else exists, or give meaning to our existence. "Knowing in terms of togetherness," on the other hand, can give us the clue to understanding the ultimate mysteries of the universe, and actually give meaning to the day-to-day lives of human beings.

"Knowing in terms of togetherness" means, in part, knowing nature by means of our affinity with it; knowing "from within," in other words. Lawrence's alternative to scientific reason does not make the mistake of thinking it can step out of the world and know it, or of thinking that nature is an artifact which can be understood by breaking it down into its "parts," or of thinking that the living can be explained in terms of the dead. Instead "togetherness" involves a type of thinking that emerges from living in intimate connection with the cosmos. It involves inspired, imaginative connections which, through a single phrase or image, can illuminate fundamental truths about our selves and the world. This is the basis, Lawrence believes, of poetry and the visual arts—but also of myth and the pre-modern "occult sciences."

Indeed, Lawrence's "knowing in terms of togetherness" seems to amount to a resurrection of the occult science of correspondences, the basis for which was the Hermetic claim that the macrocosm, the larger universe, is mirrored in the microcosm, the individual, and vice versa. The "science of correspondences" animated Hellenistic Hermeticism, alchemy, the Renaissance magic of Ficino, Pico, Bruno, and Agrippa, and the mysticism of Paracelsus and Boehme. Attacked throughout the modern period by the advocates of "knowing in terms of apartness," it seemed to breathe its last with the Romantic *Naturphilosophie* of Goethe, Schelling, Hegel, and Coleridge.[3] It is therefore surprising to find Lawrence endorsing it in works such as *Apocalypse.*

For Lawrence, imagination is the key to "knowing in terms of togetherness," and the mytho-poetic (and occult) imagination essentially involves the production of correspondences. However, this activity is not under the control of the conscious will. Lawrence believes that certain images or connections spring from the subconscious mind into consciousness due to the organic connection between the body and nature, or microcosm and macrocosm:

There certainly does exist a subtle and complex sympathy, correspondence, between the plasm of the human body, which is identical with the primary human psyche, and the material elements outside. The primary human psyche is a cosmic plasm, which quivers, sense conscious, in contact with the circumambient cosmos. Our plasmic psyche is radio-active, connecting with all things, and having first-knowledge of all things.[4]

Certain stimuli in the environment will cause the imagination to produce images of various kinds, and through these images, and the relations between images, we may obtain profound insight into the cosmos. If the microcosm does indeed mirror the macrocosm it stands to reason that what wells up from the human unconscious in the form of imaginative material may provide us with important clues to the nature of the cosmos itself. However, these clues all come in the form of images, metaphors, and non-rational inspirations of all kinds.

A simple example can get us closer to Lawrence's meaning here. It is not uncommon for someone to develop a stomach ache or indigestion while they sleep, and to dream that something heavy is sitting on their abdomen, or that they are on a ship in stormy, churning waters, or caught in a traffic snarl. In other words, the dream content reflects awareness of the bodily state, only the awareness is translated into symbolic terms. Poetry very often depicts bodily states or functions, or emotional states, in symbolic terms, so that we may say that the poet is a sort of waking dreamer. Dream, poetry, and myth all spring from the same source: the imagination. And the imagination is a faculty that is ultimately under the control of the unconscious mind, spontaneously bringing forth meaningful images that reflect correspondences between one thing and another; correspondences between the human mind or body and the greater world. Just as the sensations in the stomach cause the unconscious to bring forth an image in dream awareness, so all manner of things in the outside world can act upon us and, owing to our sympathy with them, activate our imagination and cause us to recall an image. As Jung and others have noted, some images seem to be universal, which probably means that the human mind is *structured* to respond to the world in terms of those images, and that imagination is one of our basic tools for understanding and dealing with the world.

The images of "knowing in terms of togetherness" reveal universal truths. They are equivalent to what Vico called "imaginative universals." To arrive at these, however, Lawrence writes that "we have to roll away the stone of a scientific cosmos from the tomb-mouth of that imprisoned consciousness."[5] And he tells us we must "put off our personality, even our individuality, and enter the region of the elements."[6] In short, he aims to enter into the realm of the "collective unconscious." Lawrence's imagination, he believes, will guide him to a deeper understanding of elemental relations than science could ever give.

In his practice of "knowing in terms of togetherness"—whether in fiction, poetry, or philosophical essays—Lawrence actively draws images and metaphors from the Bible. As he himself said, "I was brought up on the Bible, and seem to have it in my bones."[7] But Lawrence seeks to go back to older sources: "The religious systems of the pagan world did what Christianity has never tried to do: they gave the true correspondence between the material cosmos and the human soul. The ancient cosmic theories were exact, and apparently perfect. In them science and religion were in accord."[8] And he writes, "Do we imagine that we, poor worms with spectacles and telescopes and thought-forms, are really more conscious, more vitally aware of the universe than the men in the past were, who called the moon Artemis, or Cybele, or Astarte? Do we imagine that we really, livingly know the moon better than they knew her?"[9] Lawrence allows his imagination to be activated by the myths and symbols of the past, but this is not the same thing as slavishly repeating them: "We can never recover an old vision, once it has been supplanted. But what we can do is to discover a new vision in harmony with the memories of old, far-off, far, far-off experience that lie within us."[10]

206

Lawrence's Esotericism and Its Sources

So far I have argued that Lawrence's "knowing in terms of togetherness" is based upon an Hermetic conception of the role of imagination. In addition, when Lawrence expounds the results of "knowing in terms of togetherness" he recapitulates images and patterns of thought characteristic of Hermeticism, especially alchemy. But what were his sources?

In 1917 Lawrence and his wife Frieda were living in Cornwall and were joined there for a time by Philip Heseltine, with whom they had an on-again, off-again friendship. Heseltine, who later composed music under the name Peter Warlock, had an active interest in occultism and probably discussed his interest with Lawrence. He subsequently introduced Lawrence to Meredith Starr, who had settled in Cornwall with his bride Lady Mary, daughter of the Earl of Stamford. Lawrence did not particularly like Starr, whom he thought a bit of a buffoon, but he did find Starr's library of great interest. It was Starr who seems to have introduced Lawrence to the works of Madame Blavatsky, although there is some evidence that Lawrence may have encountered her ideas earlier, though second-hand.[11] According to Frieda, Lawrence subsequently read and "delighted in" all of Blavatsky's works, as well as many by Annie Besant and Rudolf Steiner.[12] It also seems likely that Lawrence read either Eliphas Lévi's *Transcendental Magic* or *A History of Magic*, or both.[13] In a letter from 1918, he describes magic as "very interesting and important" and "not by any means the nonsense Bertie Russell says it is."[14]

In general, Lawrence's correspondence during this period reflects his strong interest in theosophy and occultism. Discovering that his friend the psychoanalyst David Eder was also interested in theosophy, Lawrence wrote to him: "Have you read Blavatsky's *Secret Doctrine*? In many ways a bore, and not quite real. Yet one can glean a marvelous lot from it, enlarge the understanding immensely."[15] In a letter to his friend Nancy Henry, Lawrence encouraged her to read *The Occult Review*, and to visit the occult bookshop owned by the *Review*'s publisher, William Rider.[16] In a letter to another correspondent, Lawrence declared that the idea of a "body of esoteric doctrine, defended from the herd" appealed to him, though he insisted he was not a theosophist.[17]

Whatever his reservations about Blavatsky may have been, Lawrence would declare four years later in *Fantasia of the Unconscious* (in a passage that sounds like it could have been written by any theosophist) that he believed in the existence of a universal esoteric science:

I honestly think that the great pagan world of which Egypt and Greece were the last living terms, the great pagan world which preceded our own era once had, I believe, a vast and perhaps perfect science of its own, a science in terms of life. In our era this science crumbled into magic and charlatanry. But even wisdom crumbles. I believe that this great science previous to ours and quite different in constitution and nature from our science once was universal, established all over the then-existing globe. I believe it was esoteric, invested in a large priesthood. Just as mathematics and mechanics and physics are defined and expounded in the same way in the universities of China or Bolivia or London or Moscow today, so it seems to me, in the great world previous to ours a great science and cosmology were taught esoterically in all the countries of the globe, Asia, Polynesia, America, Atlantis and Europe.[18]

Possibly also due to Blavatsky's influence, Lawrence came to reject evolution, in which he formerly had believed, declaring instead that history exhibited the progressive decay of humankind, concomitant with the loss of this esoteric wisdom.[19]

It is not difficult to make out what Lawrence believed this wisdom to have consisted in. To begin with, it was founded on his mytho-poetic "knowing in terms of togetherness," and the science of correspondences. The chief non-fiction texts in which Lawrence attempts to reconstruct the lost wisdom are his essay "The Two Principles" (likely written 1917-1918), *Psychoanalysis and the Unconscious* and *Fantasia of the Unconscious* (written 1920 and 1921 respectively), and *Apocalypse*, his last work, written in 1929. There are also hints in other, shorter works, notably the aforementioned essay "A Propos of *Lady Chatterley's Lover*." However, that essay, as well as *Apocalypse*, tends in the main to be programmatic: laying out hints about the general nature of the esoteric science and the methodology underlying it. "The Two Principles" and Lawrence's two books on the unconscious actually present what he apparently believes to be a partial reconstruction of the esoteric science.

The two books on the unconscious were strongly influenced by James M. Pryse's theosophical work *The Apocalypse Unsealed*, which may also have been provided to him by Meredith Starr. Pryse (a close friend of Blavatsky and of W.B. Yeats) argued that the Book of Revelation has to be understood not as prophecy but as a manual of spiritual development, and he interpreted the work's "Seven Seals" in terms of the seven *chakras* of Kundalini yoga. In Lawrence's two books on the unconscious (especially the later *Fantasia of the Unconscious*) he adapted what he had gleaned from Pryse (and possibly other sources) into a bafflingly complex account of the distinct "bodily centres" of consciousness, at one point actually employing the term *chakras*. This was, in effect, a careful, highly technical elaboration of his long-held view that there is a bodily way of knowing that is deeper and truer than purely mental or intellectual awareness.

Much of the imagery of "The Two Principles" (which I will discuss at length in the following section) is alchemical. Some of this could have come from Blavatsky, but anyone familiar with esotericism who happens to peruse Lawrence's works will come away with the impression that he quite probably had other sources. Robert E. Montgomery, in *The Visionary D. H. Lawrence,* devotes an entire chapter to parallels between Lawrence's ideas and images and those of Jacob Boehme, but he fails to adduce any evidence to suggest that Lawrence was directly acquainted with Boehme's writings.

Hermetic imagery also finds its way into Lawrence's poetry and prose fiction, some of which I will discuss briefly later on. Indeed, when Lawrence re-wrote *Women in Love* while in Cornwall and under the influence of Meredith Starr (or, at least, Meredith Starr's library) he amplified the revision with an Hermetic subtext. As Mark Kinkead-Weekes notes, "when, in revising the new typescript of *Women in Love* into almost the novel we now have, he gave it an esoteric dimension using 'Starr's destructive electricity,' Pryse's *chakras,* and Blavatsky's ether, he was opening out ... what was already there in the experience of the previous version."[20] Two Lawrence scholars—James C. Cowan and Robert E. Montgomery—have also discussed at length what they believe to be an alchemical subtext to Lawrence's late novel *The Plumed Serpent* (a work which William York Tindall, writing in the 1930s, called Lawrence's "most theosophical").[21]

Another possible "Hermetic" influence was Carl Jung. We know for sure that Lawrence read Jung's *Psychology of the Unconscious* (*Wandlungen und Symbole der Libido*), probably in 1918, and thought highly enough of it to send it to his friend Katherine Mansfield that same year. It remains somewhat unclear how Lawrence evaluated Jung's theories, and his comments on Jung (both in *Fantasia of the Unconscious* and in his letters) suggest that he did not always appreciate the differences between Jung's views and those of Freud. David Eder was highly enthusiastic about Jung's work, however, and had declared his allegiance to Jung when the latter broke with Freud. He may have passed some of his own enthusiasm along to Lawrence, as well as information on Jung's research into esotericism. The chief reason for suspecting a Jungian influence is Lawrence's belief, expressed at length in *Apocalypse*, in universal symbols which are stored in the human subconscious and provide inspiration to artists, mythmakers, and dreamers. However, the idea that there are universal symbols which awaken various innate responses in human beings is a perennial idea, and not original with Jung. It is, in fact, a feature of the Hermetic tradition itself.

As to *Apocalypse*, the origins of this text also give us some insight into Lawrence's Hermetic connections. In 1923, while he was living in Taos, New Mexico, Lawrence received a manuscript on the Book of Revelation by an English esotericist and painter named Frederick Carter.[22] Lawrence responded very positively to Carter's work, which re-awakened his long-standing interest in John the Divine's Apocalypse. That same year Lawrence published, under a pseudonym, a review of John Oman's scholarly study *The Book of Revelation*, which had been brought out by Cambridge University Press. In 1924 on a visit to England Lawrence stayed with Carter for a few days, during which time, according to Carter, they discussed alchemy and Hermetic and astrological symbolism.[23] As a result of that visit, Carter became the inspiration for "Cartwright," an eccentric occultist who appears in Lawrence's novella *St. Mawr*, written later that year.

In 1926 Carter revised and shortened his manuscript and published it, without Lawrence's help, under the significant title *The Dragon of the Alchemists*. (I will have something to say about the symbol of the dragon in the next section.) In 1929, after the Lawrences had returned to Europe, Carter renewed his correspondence with Lawrence, presenting him with material for a new, longer book. Lawrence again responded with enthusiasm, and this time he agreed to write an introduction for the work. Carter then subsequently visited the Lawrences in November of that year, staying with them for nearly two weeks. During that time, Lawrence worked on the introduction, producing about 20,000 words. By January of 1930 he had produced a grand total of about 45,000 words, and was entertaining the idea of publishing what he had done so far as a separate book, and writing a new, shorter introduction for Carter. He did indeed produce that shorter introduction, but Carter chose not to include it when his book was finally published under the title *The Dragon of Revelation* in 1931. Meanwhile, Lawrence's short introduction was published in *The London Mercury* in July 1930, while the original, long version was published as *Apocalypse* in 1931, the year after Lawrence's death. In 1932, Carter published the story of his encounter with Lawrence, and his interpretation of the latter's philosophy, in *D. H. Lawrence and the Body Mystical*.

In sum, the evidence suggests that Lawrence got much of his knowledge of esotericism secondhand—from authors like Blavatsky, Pryse, Besant, Lévi, and Steiner, and from individuals like Heseltine, Starr, and Carter. However, his writings occasionally suggest that he may have had other (perhaps primary) sources. Not only do his allusions to this or that Hermetic idea or image suggest this, but the apparent depth of his insight into Hermetic thought-patterns suggests it as well. In what follows I shall introduce the reader to Lawrence's Hermetic worldview primarily through a discussion of "The Two Principles."

211

Lawrence's Esoteric Cosmology

At the core of Lawrence's metaphysics is the Schopenhauerian claim that the universe is an objectification of a self-propagating, non-rational force.[24] In "The Two Principles," as we shall see, he refers to this force as "the creative reality." However, the terminology he uses is inconsistent. That is because Lawrence prefers to speak in images and is not fundamentally concerned with abstract terms. In more than one late essay he refers to "the Pan mystery."

One image that occurs several times in both his fiction and non-fiction is that of the *dragon*, the most extended treatment of which takes place in *Apocalypse*:

The dragon is one of the oldest symbols of the human consciousness. The dragon and serpent symbol goes so deep in every human consciousness, that a rustle in the grass can stir the toughest 'modern' to depths he has no control over. First and foremost, the dragon is the symbol of the fluid, rapid, startling movement of life within us. That startled life which runs through us like a serpent, or coils within us potent and waiting, like a serpent, this is the dragon. And the same with the cosmos. From earliest times, man has been aware of a "power" or potency within him—and also outside him—which he has no ultimate control over. It is a fluid, rippling potency which can lie quite dormant, sleeping, and yet be ready to leap out unexpectedly.[25]

The dragon is the creative mystery that exists within us and without us, in the cosmos as a whole. It is the infinite life that exists at the beginning of time, and which "specifies itself" as individual creatures, just as Schopenhauer's will specifies itself as me and as the world outside me.[26] A few lines later in *Apocalypse*, he remarks that "Modern philosophers may call it Libido or *Elan vital*, but the words are thin, they carry none of the wild suggestion of the dragon."[27]

Lawrence employs other symbols for the creative mystery. One of the most famous of these is the phoenix, the mythic bird which is born in flame and dies back into flame perpetually, ever being renewed. Lawrence seems to have adopted the phoenix as his personal symbol in April of 1928, shortly after completing *Lady*

Chatterley's Lover. However, the image itself occurs much earlier in his fiction. Tindall notes that Blavatsky discusses the phoenix in *The Secret Doctrine*, describing it as a symbol of "initiation and rebirth."[28] The phallus and the sun are other images Lawrence frequently uses to depict the same idea.

Lawrence's "The Two Principles" is his account of how the creative mystery bodies itself forth as the universe. The essay was originally part of the cycle of essays that was to become *Studies in Classic American Literature*. Lawrence begins by noting that in the novels of Dana and Melville the sea is the great protagonist. The purpose of the essay, ostensibly, is to recover a pre-modern way of approaching such "elemental connections as between the ocean and the human soul." The cosmogonic myth in "The Two Principles" opens as follows:

> Following the obsolete language, we repeat that in the beginning was the creative reality, living and substantial, although apparently void and dark. The living cosmos divided itself, and there was Heaven and Earth: by which we mean, not the sky and the terrestrial globe, for the earth was still void and dark; but *an inexplicable first duality*, a division in the cosmos. Between the two great valves of the primordial universe, moved the 'spirit of God,' one unbroken and indivisible heart of creative being.[29]

This passage is preceded, incidentally, by one in which Lawrence warns us that there never was a literal beginning, and that he offers an account of the beginning merely "to fix a starting-point for thought." In any case, the opening of the myth calls to mind a number of sources, but especially Genesis. This impression is strengthened in the very next paragraph, where he tells us that "the spirit of God moved upon the face of the waters." However, suddenly we veer into what looks remarkably like the thought-world of Jacob Boehme. Lawrence tells us that "the waters" refer to "the mystic Earth," and Heaven is "the dark cosmic fire." From the waters/Earth and Heaven/Fire is born Light. Lawrence's "inexplicable first duality" amounts to a yin-yang dichotomy between a hot-fiery principle, and a cold-wet principle.

According to Lawrence, the waters are then divided "by the firmament." After this familiar, Biblical image, however, we are again in strange territory: "If we conceive of the first division in Chaos, so-called, as being perpendicular, the inexplicable division into the first duality [the waters and fire], then this next division, when the line of the firmament is drawn, we can consider as horizontal: thus we have the ⊕, the elements of the Rosy Cross, and the first enclosed appearance of that tremendous symbol, which has dominated our era, the Cross itself. The universe at the end of the Second Day of Creation is, therefore, as the Rosy Cross, a fourfold division."[30]

The same symbol (⊕) appears in Volume One of Blavatsky's *The Secret Doctrine*, where she describes it as a device employed by some who use it to represent the "pregenetic Kosmos," calling it "the Union of the Rose and Cross."[31] In "The Two Principles" Lawrence employs two other symbols that occur in *The Secret Doctrine*: the Egyptian ankh and the traditional symbol of Aphrodite or of the feminine. Moreover, his text renders these symbols exactly as they are rendered in *The Secret Doctrine*, and he links them with the cross symbol just as Blavatsky does.[32]

To return to Lawrence's cosmogony, the four points of the Rosy Cross give us "the waters above the firmament," "the waters below the firmament," "fire to the left hand of the firmament, and "fire to the right hand of the firmament." Each moves back and forth across the firmament. At the center is the sun: "The sun is the great mystery-centre where the invisible fires and the invisible waters roll together, brought together in the magnificence of the creative spell of opposition, to wrestle and consummate in the formation of the orb of light."[33]

Lawrence offers his "fire" and "water" as two ultimate principles from which all things come — like the fire and ice of Norse mythology, or the Love and Strife of Empedocles's philosophy (which was an important influence on Lawrence). All life, he tells us, exists in a balance of Fire and Water. Individual living things will tend, however, to one or the other. Fire and Water become "purer," Lawrence claims, as they "withdraw" from life. For example, at its extreme the Water principle becomes ice and snow. Attentive readers of Lawrence's fiction will note that he tends to depict his characters as either "watery" or "fiery." Montgomery notes that in *Women in Love* Birkin and Ursula are the fiery pair, contrasted to Gudrun and

Gerald, who are watery. Gerald meets his end in the novel when he commits suicide by wandering off into the snowy Alps and freezing to death. For Lawrence, this act represents Gerald quite literally "returning to his element." Cathcart, the Gerald-like main character of Lawrence's short story "The Man Who Liked Islands" suffers a similar fate.

Every new thing, Lawrence tells us, is born from the marriage of Fire and Water. Further, again following tradition, Lawrence identifies Fire as the masculine principle, Water as the feminine. These two are contained *in potentia* in the living plasm that exists at the beginning of time. Fire and Water are separated out of the plasm, and then come together again an infinite number of times to produce the myriad living things of creation. Lawrence refers to the separation of Fire and Water, however, as death. When Fire and Water come to be out of the plasm, it is the death of the plasm. But whenever Fire and Water come together again to form a new creature, it is as if the plasm is reconstituted through or within that object. Thus, in effect, the cosmos begins—as he also maintains in *Fantasia of the Unconscious*—with the death of life. But this is merely the death of life in its existence as an undifferentiated and infinite force or plasm. It is then "reborn" through the infinity of individual creatures constituted through the marriage of Fire and Water. As to non-living things, these are, Lawrence believes, merely the dead remains of primordial life.

Water, Lawrence informs us, is not H_2O. Hydrogen and oxygen are themselves *produced* when we break down the original alchemical water by introducing fire into it. The hydrogen and oxygen derived from water are called by Lawrence "the alchemistic air."[35] "Earth" is the living plasm in its "dead state," when Fire and Water have been "separated" out of it and no longer exist in organic connection. Thus, at the end of what Lawrence calls the "second day of creation," all the four elements have emerged from the creative reality: fire, water, air and earth. Thus is born the material cosmos.

Ultimately, of course, we must ask *why* the "creative reality" divides itself and then issues a world of living (and non-living) individuals through which it is continually being reborn. Lawrence's answer will leave many unsatisfied. He simply seems to believe that there exists in creation a *nisus* towards individuation. For Lawrence, the *telos* of creation is the proliferation of living individuals in higher and higher forms.

Although this is offered as a basic fact about the universe, Lawrence does attempt to account for the "mechanism" of individuation through his theory of the Holy Ghost. In *Fantasia of the Unconsious* he writes, "Midway between the two cosmic infinites [of Sun and Moon or Fire and Water] lies the third, which is more than infinite. This is the Holy Ghost Life, individual life."[36] Individual life, Lawrence believes, is oneness accomplished out of the twoness of Sun/Moon or Fire/Water, and the Holy Ghost is the ideal quintessence of individual life, drawing the Fire-force and Water-force together to make a new being.

At any rate, from the dualistic theory of fire and water in "The Two Principles" Lawrence then derives the outlines of a psychology, a theory of sex differences, and even a philosophy of world history — all in the same essay!

Sun and Moon

In "The Two Principles" we saw Lawrence refer to Fire and Water as the fundamental duality in existence. In *Fantasia of the Unconscious* he speaks of Sun and Moon:

There are two sheer dynamic principles in our universe, the sun-principle and the moon-principle. And these principles are known to us in immediate contact as fire and water. The sun is not fire. But the principle of fire is the sun-principle. That is, fire is the sudden swoop towards the sun, of matter which is suddenly sun-polarized. Fire is the sudden sun-assertion, the release towards the one pole only. It is the sudden revelation of the cosmic One Polarity, One Identity. But there is another pole. There is the moon. And there is another absolute and visible principle, the principle of water. The moon is not water. But it is the soul of water, the invisible clue to all the waters. So that we begin to realize our visible universe as a vast duality between sun and moon.[37]

However, Sun and Moon do not just "symbolize" Fire and Water. In *Fantasia* Lawrence speaks as if Sun and Moon are the source of the forces he calls Fire and Water, or that the latter somehow emanate from the former. He tells us, for instance, that "The sun is not, in any sense, a material body." On the face of it, this seems an absurd claim. But what Lawrence means is that that the sun is not a material body in the sense of a static *thing* with definite parameters. Instead, it is "an invariable intense pole of cosmic energy"; not a body, but a locus of pure energy. Again, Lawrence is forcing us to think in a new way that is actually a very old way; to return to the pre-modern "physics of the life-world" that we find in Aristotle, Medieval philosophy, and Hermetic and mystical writings.

Lawrence's treatment of the moon is similar, but much less plausible. Surprisingly he claims that it is not dead matter either: "The moon is an immense magnetic centre. It is quite wrong to say she is a dead snowy world with craters and so on. I should say she is composed of some very intense element, like phosphorus or radium, some element or elements which have very powerful chemical and kinetic activity, and magnetic activity, affecting us through space."[38] The moon is the source of the "watery forces," including gravitation, electricity, magnetism, and "radium-energy." The sun is the source of heat and "expansion force.[39] The sun is a "positive infinite," and the moon a "negative infinite."

Unsurprisingly, Lawrence identifies the Sun-principle as masculine, the Moon-principle as feminine. In "A Study of Thomas Hardy," Lawrence tells us that "everything that is, is either male or female or both," and in the language of his later writings this means that everything is sunny or moony or a blend of the two.[40] (A Taoist would inform us that it is more accurate to say that everything is a *mixture* of the two, with each thing tending toward being more one than the other.) In *Women in Love*, one chapter is entitled "Moony," and in it Birkin moons over Ursula, and reflects on the feminine power of the moon. Birkin's mood in this chapter is an expression of the perennial male ambivalence toward the feminine: on the one hand a fascination with it, on the other a resentment of its powerful hold. In his essay on Hardy, Lawrence remarks, further, that the "male will or spirit" is a "Will-to-Motion," and the female a "Will-to-Inertia."[41]

As I have already discussed, in "The Two Principles" Lawrence spins out a strange alchemical myth in which fire and water interact and produce the elements of matter, and thus, ultimately, the entire physical universe. And the *telos* of all of this is the living individual. "We live between the polarized circuit of sun and moon," Lawrence tells us.[42] However, he goes on to write as if, in some way, it is the living individual that actually gives rise to or "feeds" the sun and moon! In the "Foreword" to *Fantasia*, Lawrence suggests that he derived some of these ideas from a reading of James G. Frazer's *Golden Bough*. He quotes Frazier as saying "It must have appeared to the ancient Aryan that the sun was periodically recruited from the fire which resided in the sacred oak."[43] Lawrence then identifies the oak with the Tree of Life, and re-writes Frazier as follows:

"It must have appeared to the ancient Aryan that the sun was periodically recruited from life." —Which is what the early Greek philosophers were always saying. And which still seems to me the real truth, the clue to the cosmos. Instead of life being drawn from the sun, it is the emanation from life itself, that is, from all the living plants and creatures which nourish the sun.[44]

Nevertheless, this is, without, question, the most strange and obscure material in *Fantasia of the Unconscious*, stranger even than Lawrence's kundalini-like theory of "bodily centres."

Lawrence writes:

The sun and the moon are the two eternal death-results of the death of individuals ... We stand upon our own grave, with our death-fire, the sun, on our right hand, and our death-damp, the moon, on our left. And the earth flings us out as wings to the sun and moon: or as the death-germ dividing into two nuclei. So from the earth our radiance is flung to the sun, our marsh-fire to the moon, when we die.[45]

And:

When individual life dies, it flings itself on the right hand to the sun, on the left hand to the moon, in the dual polarity, and sinks to earth. When any man dies, his soul divides in death; as in life, in the first germ, it was

218

united from two germs. It divides into two dark germs, flung asunder: the sun-germ and the moon-germ. Then the material body sinks to earth.[46]

Lawrence makes it clear, however, that what the sun and moon feed on is the *souls* of living things, not their material bodies. This is also, for a number of reasons, a problematic claim. Often, Lawrence's use of the term "soul" seems to suggest the traditional religious meaning of the term. For example, he tells us in *Fantasia* that "I am sorry to say that I believe in the souls of the dead. I am almost ashamed to say that I believe the souls of the dead in some way re-enter and pervade the souls of the living; so that life is always the life of living creatures and death is always our affair."[47] However, in "The Two Principles," Lawrence writes that "There is no utterly immaterial existence, no spirit. The distinction is between living plasm and inanimate matter."[48] That essay pre-dates *Fantasia of the Unconscious*, however. Lawrence's encounter with theosophy is the probable explanation for this apparent shift in his views. The above quote from *Fantasia* seems clearly theosophical (or spiritualist).

Lawrence's description of how souls feed the sun and moon bears a strong resemblance to the ideas of G. I. Gurdjieff (1872?-1949). In his *In Search of the Miraculous*, Gurdjieff's disciple P. D. Ouspensky quotes the master as saying that

Organic life on earth feeds the moon. . . The moon is a huge living being feeding upon all that lives and grows on the earth. . The process of the growth and the warming of the moon is connected with life and death on the earth. Everything living sets free at its death a certain amount of the energy that has "animated" it; this energy, or the "souls" of everything living—plants, animals, people—is attracted to the moon as though by a huge electromagnet, and brings to it the warmth and the life upon which its growth depends, that is, the growth of the ray of creation.[49]

Lawrence's close friend Katherine Mansfield was a follower of Gurdjieff, and died (of tuberculosis) while staying at Gurdjieff's "Institute for the Harmonious Development of Man" at Fontainebleau in January 1923. Although Lawrence's remarks about Gurdjieff in his correspondence are negative in the extreme, it is possible that

Gurdjieff's ideas, communicated via Mansfield, may have exercised some influence on his thinking. Elsewhere in *Fantasia*, for example, Lawrence employs an idiosyncratic distinction between "knowledge" and "being" seemingly identical to that found in Gurdjieff. Lawrence writes,

Knowledge is to consciousness what the signpost is to the traveler: just an indication of the way which has been traveled before. Knowledge is not even in direct proportion to being. There may be great knowledge of chemistry in a man who is a rather poor *being*: and those who *know*, even in wisdom like Solomon, are often at the end of the matter of living, not at the beginning.[50]

Ouspensky quotes Gurdjieff as follows:

"There are," he said, "two lines along which man's development proceeds, the line of *knowledge* and the line of *being*. In right evolution the line of knowledge and the line of being develop simultaneously, parallel to, and helping one another. . People of Western culture put great value on the level of a man's knowledge but they do not value the level of a man's being and are not ashamed of the low level of their own being."[51]

Conclusion

A full discussion of the Hermetic and esoteric elements in Lawrence's writings would require a book unto itself, and the preceding remarks merely scratch the surface. A great deal more, for example, could be said about what may be described as Lawrence's spiritualist views, and how the ghostly visitations in some of his short stories (e.g. "The Borderline") seem to reflect Lawrence's literal belief in spirits.

Further, I have mentioned but cannot go into detail concerning Lawrence's recasting of the chakra system, and his apparent belief in the reality of kundalini energy. This, of course, would take me outside the purview of Western esotericism. However it was Lawrence's belief (and the belief of many others) that the tenets of the yogic metaphysics were universal, but in the West had come to be concealed behind various masks.

Finally, to those who might be interested in exploring Lawrence's works and their esoteric elements further, I will say that it would be a serious mistake to believe that we find Lawrence's "philosophy" in his non-fiction essays, and illustrations of that philosophy in his poetry and fiction. For one thing, Lawrence himself tells us that the poetry and fiction came first and his philosophical ideas actually grew out of those writings, not the other way around. This is exactly what we should expect from Lawrence, given his views on the nature of imagination. Lawrence's poetry and prose fiction are exercises in "knowing in terms of togetherness." With his unfettered imagination, Lawrence brings forth images and symbolic meanings of all sorts which tend, in a peculiar sort of way, to get under the skin of his readers and to make them see the things in a new way. For the scholar of esotericism, Lawrence presents the unique case of a modern author producing a richly varied body of work not only employing references to esoteric sources, but consciously working according to an Hermetic conception of imagination.

Notes

1. Warren Roberts and Harry T. Moore, eds., *Phoenix II: Uncollected Writings of D. H. Lawrence* (New York: Viking Press, 1970), 512.
2. Ibid., 512.
3. For further details see Glenn Alexander Magee, *Hegel and the Hermetic Tradition* (Ithaca: Cornell University Press, 2001).
4. *Phoenix* II, 227 ("The Two Principles").
5. D. H. Lawrence, *Fantasia of the Unconscious*, ed. Bruce Steele (Cambridge: Cambridge University Press, 2004), 175.
6. *Phoenix* II, 227 ("The Two Principles").
7. D. H. Lawrence, *Apocalypse*, ed. Mara Kalnins (Cambridge: Cambridge University Press, 1995), 54.
8. Ibid., 227.
9. Ibid., 53.
10. Ibid., 54.
11. See Mark Kinkead-Weekes, *D. H. Lawrence: Triumph to Exile*, 1912-1922 (Vol. 2 of *The Cambridge Biography of D. H. Lawrence*; Cambridge

University Press, 1996), 387.

12. William York Tindall, *D. H. Lawrence and Susan His Cow* (New York: Columbia University Press, 1939), 133-134. Tindall interviewed Frieda Lawrence.

13. Kinkead-Weekes, 437, 838.

14. James T. Boulton and Andrew Robertson, eds., *The Letters of D. H. Lawrence*, (Cambridge: Cambridge University Press, 1984), II: 239.

15. Ibid, 150.

16. Ibid., 299.

17. Ibid., 143.

18. *Fantasia*, 63.

19. Kinkead-Weekes, 388.

20. Ibid., 389.

21. James C. Cowan, "Alchemy and *The Plumed Serpent*," in *D. H. Lawrence and the Trembling Balance* (University Park: Pennsylvania State University Press, 1990); Robert E. Montgomery, *The Visionary D. H. Lawrence: Beyond Philosophy and Art* (Cambridge: Cambridge University Press, 1994), 194-207; Tindall, op.cit., 144.

22. My account of the Lawrence-Carter relationship owes much to Mara Kalnin's Introduction to the Cambridge edition of D. H. Lawrence's *Apocalypse*, op. cit. See especially pp. 12-17.

23. Frederick Carter, *D. H. Lawrence and the Body Mystical* (London: Archer, 1932), 5; 34.

24. Daniel J. Schneider has some interesting things to say about Lawrence's debts to Schopenhauer in his *The Consciousness of D. H. Lawrence: An Intellectual Biography* (Lawrence, Kansas: University of Kansas Press, 1986), 49-50.

25. *Apocalypse*, 123.

26. One important difference between Lawrence and Schopenhauer is that Schopenhauer sees the will as active in non-living nature, whereas Lawrence's creative mystery expresses itself only in living things. Non-living things are merely, as we have seen, the dead residue of the living.

27. *Apocalypse*, 124.

28. Tindall, 138.

29. *Phoenix II*, 227-28. My italics.

30. Ibid., 228.

31. H. P. Blavatsky, *The Secret Doctrine*, (Pasadena: Theosophical University Press, 1988), I: 19.

32. Ibid., 5.

33. *Phoenix II*, 229.

34. Montgomery, 152-167.

35. *Phoenix* II, 232.

36. *Fantasia*, 173.

37. Ibid, 173.

38. Ibid.,170.

39. Ibid.,176.

40. Edward McDonald, ed., *Phoenix: The Posthumous Papers of D. H. Lawrence* (New York: Viking Press, 1936), "A Study of Thomas Hardy," 446.

41. Ibid., 448.

42. Ibid, 170.

43. Ibid., 64.

44. Ibid., 64.

45. Ibid., 174.

46. Ibid, 177.

47. Ibid., 70.

48. *Phoenix II*, 230 ("The Two Principles").

49. P. D. Ouspensky, *In Search of the Miraculous* (Orlando, Florida: Harcourt Brace Jovanovich, 1949), 85.

50. *Fantasia*, 111. Italics in the original.

51. Ouspensky, 64-65.

Faux Catholic:
A Gothic Subgenre
from Monk Lewis to Dan Brown

Victoria Nelson

"God is dead. Meet the kids."
—Neil Gaiman, *The Anansi Boys*

We've seen it on the big screen any number of times: the possessed woman writhing, screaming, face morphing (courtesy computer-generated imagery) into a hideous leer as despairing relatives edge prudently away from the imminent prospect of projectile vomiting.

Demon possession, open-and-shut case. Who you gonna call?

Not your rabbi, imam, or Methodist minister. No, you want that Roman Catholic priest with his collar, cross, holy water, and Vulgate Bible—all the papist trappings that Protestant Americans shun in real life but absolutely demand for a convincing onscreen exorcism. A mild-mannered Episcopal reverend, a Southern Baptist preacher in a Men's Wearhouse suit reciting the Lord's Prayer in English over that tormented soul? I don't think so. Nothing less, or other, than the sting of holy water, the hiss of the cross against burning flesh will make the demon wail in agony.

And what about that secret office, always housed deep in the bowels of the Vatican, laboring over the centuries to keep the parchment containing secrets threatening to orthodoxy from falling into the wrong hands or stop an incarnation of a rebel angel, even Satan's own child born to a mortal woman, from wreaking havoc on the world? What a letdown, and certainly harder to accept, if the headquarters of this agency so crucial to the salvation of humankind were located down the corridor from the bingo room in the local Lutheran church basement.

225

After the incense clears, this is the central paradox in movies and books like *The Exorcist, Stigmata, The Omen, End of Days*, and countless others: that an exoticized, patently fictional, and some would say anticlerical fantasy about Catholicism strangely empowers and elevates the very denomination it seems to slander.[1] The Catholic League for Religious and Civil Rights decries these movies and novels but fails understandably to appreciate their implicit subtext: first, that this fantasy pop culture religion I like to call faux Catholicism provides the *only* effective defense against the forces of evil as embodied in the Judeo-Christian figure of Satan, and second, that the battle between good and evil is most effectively waged not with the Church's real-life theological doctrine but with its perceived magical talismans—talismans that continue to exert a (shall we say) unholy fascination on Protestants and other non-Catholics. And furthermore, as we will see in the case of Dan Brown, that even an idea heretical to all Christian denominations— that Jesus was only mortal, mated with Mary Magdalene, and had human descendants—is one seen by his readers as well as the author himself to be most effectively combated by the institution of the Catholic Church.

Why the implicit bestowal of greater authority and power by mostly non-Catholic writers and filmmakers on a denomination they don't belong to or believe in? First and most obviously, Roman Catholicism is the only church besides the Orthodox that provides full historical continuity from the beginnings of Christianity and that also, not coincidentally, possesses the most elaborately developed mechanisms for keeping its dogma consistent over the centuries. Other reasons for this ambiguous valorization may be found in the literary source of this fare, the Protestant anticlerical Gothic novels of the eighteenth century that initiated this enduring and endlessly reinvented genre into international popular culture.

I take as my foundational text Matthew Lewis's *The Monk*, published in March 1796 when its author was not quite twenty-one. By the usual standards, *The Monk* belongs to the "middle" period of the original Gothic—with Horace Walpole and his *Castle of Otranto* (1764) marking the genre's beginning, followed by the novels of Anne Radcliffe, most notably *The Mysteries of Udolpho* (1794). It was Lewis more than any previous Gothic writer, however, whose work took England and Europe by storm. Like *The Da Vinci Code* two centuries later, *The Monk* created an international sensation and made its author an overnight celebrity. Like Brown, "Monk" Lewis, as he came to be known, was accused of copying other sources; by its fourth edition *The Monk* had also been expurgated of some of its more scandalous sexual material.[2]

Precociously astute about human nature and the temptations of ambition, Lewis fashioned a narrative whose mad eroticism and pell-mell pace keep *The Monk* a lively read even today. In the course of a long and convoluted plot set mostly in Madrid, two young gentlemen, Lorenzo and Raymond, lose their lady loves to evil clerics—Agnes, Lorenzo's sister and Raymond's lover, and her baby to the wrath of the abbess of the convent where she has been unfairly confined (but from which she, but not the baby, is eventually rescued), and Antonia, whom Lorenzo hopes to marry, to the lust of the ambitious and newly fallen abbot Ambrosio.

We also meet a third young woman, Matilda, who masquerades as a male novice to gain access to Ambrosio and is the first to tempt him down the path of perdition. She tells Ambrosio she has made a pact with the beautiful "fallen angel" Lucifer and eventually the proud abbot does too, so that he may fulfill his lustful desire for the innocent Antonia after murdering her mother lest she expose him. Once Ambrosio has killed Antonia as well to conceal his crime, then made a pact with Lucifer (in his less attractive winged, horned and taloned form) to escape further torture from the Inquisition, Lucifer lets Ambrosio know that Matilda is not human but an agent of Hell, and that Ambrosio's two victims, Antonia and her mother, were his own sister and mother. Then he flies the hapless monk into the sky and drops him thousands of feet onto a rocky precipice where, after six days of eyeball pecking, flesh biting, and blood draining from various natural predators, Ambrosio expires, only to be catapulted into eternal damnation.

Though Lewis serves up the obligatory moldering vaults and gloomy medieval atmosphere of earlier Gothic tales, this faux Catholic story focuses obsessively on the Roman clergy's sexual transgressions, abuses of power, and hypocritical cruelty toward confessed sinners. *The Monk* is all about sexual repression unleashed. Ambrosio's Faustian pact with Satan is voluntary and does not involve "possession" in the modern pop culture understanding of the term. This theme stands in contrast to today's mainstream faux Catholic films and books, which, in an interesting reversal of focus, studiously avoid cleric-lay sexuality in spite of (or perhaps because of) ongoing revelations about sexual abuse of minors by priests and concentrate instead on involuntary possession and heretical doctrine.[3]

Despite its faux Catholic trappings, the original Gothic is generally regarded by its critics as the first Western literary genre operating implicitly in the vacuum left by the departure of religious belief. "Viewing Gothic mystery as a substitute for discredited religious mystery," says Joel Porte after Maurice Lévy, "we may consent to recognize that, despite its wild extravagance and puerile heresies, *le genre noir* represented for its producers and consumers alike a genuine expression of profound religious malaise."[4] Victor Sage has widened the definition of Gothic from the narrow genre featuring "a decorative metaphysical or graveyard feeling" to "a whole complex of popular theological ideals of a predominantly, if not exclusively, Protestant variety."[5] Robert Geary sees the Gothic novel in its beginnings not just as an expression of Protestant anticlericalism or as a simple reaction to eighteenth century rationalism but as part of the process of the secularization of literature in which the supernatural moves out of the traditional religious framework to be cultivated as a sensation in itself.[6] Other commentators have also noted in the Gothic what I have called the transition from "full of awe" to "awful,"[7] the cultivation of feelings of terror or dread as a flawed vehicle to the transcendent—a transcendent shorn of the larger metaphysical context that includes the divine as well as the demonic.

Demonization of the supernatural, along with its exclusion from the everyday world, had already begun in seventeenth century Western Europe with the Protestant Reformation and the scientific revolution. If divine intrusions into our lives such as miracles—so the new thinking went—ended with the age of the patriarchs (around the sixth century C.E.) and if natural wonders such as lightning, earthquakes and floods were not God's punishment but had their causes in the material world, then anything perceived in the material world that could not be explained rationally must belong to the dark side. In *The Monk,* God doesn't manifest in the physical world; only Satan does. By the end of the eighteenth century, this shaky metaphysical split had been abandoned by scientists and theologians but had become entrenched in the Western popular imagination, where it happily took up residence for the next two hundred years.

Over the nineteenth century, the rapidly proliferating Gothic sensibility divided into separate strands emphasizing either anticlericalism, supernaturalism, or romance (the sentiment, not the genre). On the European continent, the anticlerical Gothic carried on in England by works such as Charles Maturin's *Melmoth the Wanderer* (1820) flourished within predominantly Catholic countries. In Eugene Sue's *The Wandering Jew* (1844), in which an evil Jesuit covets the Wandering Jew's fortune (collecting interest all those centuries since the death of Jesus), the clerical transgression is not lust but covetousness.[8] In Italy both Garibaldi in the nineteenth century and Mussolini (in his pre-fascist socialist phase) in the twentieth wrote anticlerical Gothic historical romances.[9] Anti-Catholic exposés masquerading as nonfiction, but cast in Gothic fictional conventions—such as the Montreal prostitute Maria Monk's lurid account called *Awful Disclosures of the Hotel Dieu Nunnery in Montreal* (1836), a bestseller in New York—were popular in nineteenth-century America.[10]

The second Gothic thread, supernaturalism, survived in nineteenth-century post-Romantic ghost and horror stories featuring the menacing spirits of individuals who survived death. In these tales, notably English but also widespread on the Continent (e.g., the French *contes fantastiques* of Charles Nodier, Prosper Mérimée and others), Satan is absent (he will reëmerge, both as a satiric and a serious character in popular literature and film of the twentieth century), as is any openly slanderous depiction of Catholic clerics, though the Church figures in the ruined abbeys of Victorian Protestants like Sheridan le Fanu or the Edwardian M. R. James's ghostly tales with their rigorously historically accurate contexts.[11]

Irish Protestant Bram Stoker's *Dracula* (1897), set in Catholic Eastern Europe, trumped earlier Gothic vampire tales to became the archetype for this "imaginative inversion of the Roman Doctrine of the Eucharist."[12] In America the genealogy of supernaturalism runs from Charles Brockden Brown and Nathaniel Hawthorne through Edgar Allan Poe (in whose stories the apparent presence of the supernatural is almost, but not quite, dispelled by a mad caricature of rationalism) and H. P. Lovecraft. Through the twentieth century, the great tidal bore triggered by dime novels/penny dreadfuls and swelled by pulp fiction, comic books, and movies swallowed all these popular genres and spit them out downriver in a range of new media from animated cartoons to videogaming to virtual reality.

The third strand, the "Gothic romance" written by and for women, still enjoys enormous popularity today. Charlotte Brontë's *Jane Eyre* (1847) remains the founding model for the tale of a young woman, always told from her point of view, who meets an irresistibly charming older man with a very bad reputation to whom, in the secular-psychological shadow of Satanic temptation, she is powerfully attracted against her will. After various plot contortions, the bad man is revealed to be good and she marries him, effectively domesticating the demonic. Through the mid-twentieth century, Gothic romances often presented, just as Poe did, the teasing hint of haunting or the supernatural—the iconic paperback cover illustration typically presented a young woman in distress before a looming mansion under a full moon—but the mystery was always revealed, by story's end, to have a rational explanation. Along with a certain amount of feminist updating that bestows professions and financial independence on its heroines, present-day Gothic romances often forgo the spooky ancestral mansion but have a mystery at their core and remain focused on love relationships successfully consummated in marriage.

Today the dynamic, ever-expanding Gothic (along with its contemporary lifestyle cohort "Goth") includes not only the latest versions of these three strands but a huge array of subgenres, most notably endless permutations of horror stories linked with supernaturalism, including stories of vampires, werewolves, and other denizens of the supernatural dark side first introduced in the nineteenth century. The globalization of popular culture has also blurred the boundaries between Protestant anti-Catholicism and traditions of anticlericalism in predominantly Catholic European countries. Side by side with the anticlerical thrillers of the Spanish writer Arturo Pérez-Reverte[13] stands my favorite example of Protestant anti-Papism from the underbelly of American pop culture, a self-published but fairly widely circulating novel with many sequels called *The Last Days of Christ the Vampire*, in which that secret department deep in the bowels of the Vatican is dedicated to concealing just this central fact about Jesus's true identity. In the context of the shapeshifting, genre-crossing Gothic, Christ as vampire is the essential consequence of the substitution of the demonic for the divine.

New Christian evangelical fiction also draws from the deep well of American popular fiction generally and the Gothic in particular. A case in point is the twelve-volume apocalyptic *Left Behind* series by Tim LaHaye ("renowned prophecy scholar, minister and educator," the cover states), and his cowriter Jerry B. Jenkins. Far from being a literalist version of the Rapture (itself a rather Gothic creation of nineteenth-century American evangelism), the theology of their novels shows the influence of Gothic narrative conventions at every turn. Especially interesting is the authors' depiction of the Antichrist in the figure of Nicolae Carpathia (his surname referencing the fictitious Count Dracula's homeland), an evil Romanian who becomes head of the United Nations and preaches a seditious message of ecumenism and global community. Nicolae dies but, "resurrected and indwelt by the Devil himself," returns to rule the world briefly before the Second Coming and the thousand years of peace on earth occur. The tremendous sales of these books (65 million, another 10 million in children's and graphic novel versions) are another indication that evangelical Christian doctrine itself is being reshaped by the conventions of genre fiction and film—and specifically by the ubiquitous figure of the vampire.[14]

Looming over it all like the proverbial 900-pound gorilla is the Dan Brown phenomenon. Of his two faux Catholic novels, *Angels & Demons* (2000) belongs more closely to the classic Monk Lewis Gothic tradition of the Luciferian rise and fall of a supremely ambitious, power-mad Roman Catholic cleric. This novel also marks the first appearance of the main character Robert Langdon, the Harvard "symbologist" who makes a return appearance in *The Da Vinci Code*.[15]

In *Angels & Demons,* Langdon is flown to a top-secret Swiss research laboratory when one of its chief scientists is murdered. Langdon's task is to decode the word *Illuminati* branded on the dead man's chest, which he authoritatively asserts is the name of a centuries-old but now defunct anti-Catholic secret society of philosophers and scientists, including Galileo, that gradually morphed into "the world's oldest and most powerful satanic cult."[16] Meanwhile, the scientist's adopted daughter Vittoria, herself a scientist, has discovered that a portion of the antimatter her father has succeeded in isolating has disappeared. When the news come that the Vatican is being threatened by an anonymous caller who has stashed the antimatter somewhere in its bowels, Robert and Vittoria rush to Rome on the lab's private jet. The bomb threat has come just as the cardinals, with the death (actually murder) of the previous pope, have convened to elect a new one. But now the four main candidates have disappeared, and one by one their murdered bodies appear in locations across Rome as Robert and Vittoria vainly attempt to decipher the Illuminati-laden historical clues the caller phones in. As the body count climbs, the truth finally emerges: the real terrorist is not the Illuminati but a high Vatican official possessed by a mad desire for power.

In the character of Carlo Ventresca, a.k.a. the *camerlengo* (the cardinal who functions as the pope's private secretary) we clearly see the shadow of Lewis's spectacularly sinful monk Ambrosio. Cardinal Ventreca is described as having "the air of some mythical hero—radiating charisma and authority," but also proves to be the novel's villain.[17] Following the conventions of the modern faux Catholic, Ventresca commits no sexual crimes, but in his murderous quest to become pope he shares the monk Ambrosio's overweening ambition, justifying his assassination of the four cardinals in line for the papacy on the grounds that they were too liberal. When death comes, Ventresca's soul is not carried away by Satan, but there's a whiff of brimstone in the air when he sets himself alight on a high balcony overlooking Vatican Square and burns to death.

Angels & Demons also features a racist, stereotypical portrait of a Middle Eastern "Hassassin," a dark creature with "an appetite for hedonistic pleasure ... bred into him by his ancestors."[18] The Hassassin believes he is taking his orders from an "ancient brotherhood" when all along he has been under the control of the rogue cardinal Carlo Ventresca. Much like the Hassassin, however, readers are more likely to take away the impression they labored under for most of the novel—that the murders were orchestrated either by the so-called Illuminati or by the organized bureaucracy of the Vatican itself—than to remember the last-minute revelation of the true villain.

Brown employs the same time-honored tactic of bait and switch among "Manichaean others" (to use Umberto Eco's useful phrase) in his next novel *The Da Vinci Code* (2003), which belongs to a newer tributary of the faux Catholic Gothic spawned by the 1983 nonfiction book by Michael Baigent, Richard Leigh, and Henry Lincoln titled *Holy Blood, Holy Grail* (first published in the UK as *The Holy Blood, The Holy Grail* in 1982). The first two of these authors unsuccessfully sued Brown for plagiarism, though they did not to my knowledge sue Lewis Perdue, author of the novel *Daughter of God* (2000); Katherine Neville, author of the novel *The Magic Circle* (2002); Stuart Urban, writer-director of the film *Revelation* (2001); or any other of the less spectacularly successful fictions before and after *The Da Vinci Code* that incorporate their pseudohistorical thesis: that Jesus was a mortal man who married Mary Magdalene and whose descendants founded the Merovingian dynasty of France.[19]

The story of *The Da Vinci Code* goes briefly like this: The night before he is to meet with Jacques Saunière, senior curator at the Louvre, Robert Langdon is summoned to the museum by the Paris police. Saunière's murdered body has just been found, ritually posed, in the museum's Grand Gallery, but the curator has managed to leave a string of coded enigmatic clues that hold the secret of his death and much more. Both Langdon and Saunière's granddaughter, cryptologist Sophie Neveu, become suspects as a tangled story unfolds of an ancient society called the Priory of

Sion, of which Saunière was grandmaster, and the great secret the society has guarded against millennia-long assaults by the Catholic church: documents revealing that Jesus was mortal, not divine, that he married Mary Magdalene, who escaped to France with their child, and that the bloodline of Jesus and King David has carried through via the founding dynasty of France, the Merovingians, to the present day. Unraveling two thousand years of suppression of the "sacred feminine" by the patriarchal church, Robert and Sophie leapfrog across England and Scotland seeking the answers to the coded messages left by Sophie's grandfather, Leonardo da Vinci, the Knights Templar and assorted others while being pursued both by law enforcement and the blind albino assassin monk Silas, who seems to be working for his Opus Dei masters but turns out to be, like the prelate who heads Opus Dei himself, the dupe of the wealthy English grail scholar Leigh Teabing. By the novel's end, Sophie herself and her brother are revealed to be the direct descendants of Jesus and Mary Magdalene, and she and Robert enjoy a romantic tryst.

Notable similarities between this novel and *Angels & Demons* include the following: Langdon hooks up professionally and romantically with the granddaughter (*A&D:* adopted daughter) of the murdered wise man, a museum curator (*A&D:* priest-turned-scientist), who is also head of a secret society, and the two must follow a path of coded historical clues across France and England (*A&D:* Rome). In both, four wise men are murdered (here, higher-ups in the Priory of Sion instead of Roman Catholic cardinals) In both, the murders are committed by a simpleminded or crazed assassin and appear to be the work of a secret society (Opus Dei, Illuminati) but turn out to be masterminded by a single person operating entirely on his own (Cardinal Ventresca, Leigh Teabing). But even though, as Robert Langdon declares at the end of *The Da Vinci Code*, the Vatican and Opus Dei are "completely innocent," once again I suspect this last-minute plot reversal may be lost on the vast majority of readers, who take away with them the idea, foregrounded for most of the story, that Opus Dei was really behind it all.

On his website, Brown affirms that he is a Christian and says that his mother was a "sacred musician," but he doesn't specify which denomination.[20] He says that he doesn't read much fiction except the "classics"and the works of Robert Ludlum, whose low-grade, densely plotted thrillers have obviously influenced his work. As displayed in *Angels & Demons* and *The Da Vinci Code,* Brown's knowledge of church history, art history, and Western esoteric societies has the stretched-thin feel of an undergraduate term paper. You don't see a sophisticated understanding here, but rather some earnest and copious notetaking from various secondary sources delivered with the sort of emphatic assurance only a Harvard symbologist can muster. (In *The Da Vinci Code* Robert Langdon's scholarly bibliography for his new book is proudly described as containing no fewer than fifty entries, "many of them academic best-sellers."[21])

The Da Vinci Code contains an echo or two from Pérez-Reverte's novel *The Flanders Panel* (1996), which also featured an Old Master's painting (fifteenth century, Flemish) that conceals a murderer's identity in coded chess-game visual symbols and a hidden written message revealed in ultraviolet light. Among other fictional sources, Brown may have drawn some inspiration from Eco's *Foucault's Pendulum* (1988) without recognizing that this novel was intended to be a parody of occultist conspiracy theory, including that found in *Holy Blood, Holy Grail* (whose main thesis is even rendered as one of *Foucault's Pendulum*'s later chapter headings). There is a resonance between the opening of Eco's novel, in which a ritual murder is about to be enacted in a famous historical space in Paris (the vault of the Conservatoire National des Arts et Métiers, St.-Martin-des-Champs, where the pendulum of Léon Foucault is located), and a murder with ritual overtones in the Louvre, followed by a second murder in the Church of Saint-Sulpice (which contains another artifact of early science, an astronomical sun marker that Brown misidentifies, intentionally or not, as the "Rose Line," a so-called older version of the prime meridian that also supposedly runs through the Rosslyn Chapel in Scotland and the Louvre).

Foucault's Pendulum and *The Da Vinci Code* each proceed — one sophisticated and tongue in cheek, the other in deadly and somewhat plodding earnest—with a manic and completely specious connect-the-dots romp through two thousand years of Western esotericism. Eco, a fervent anti-occultist, conflates too much of the esoteric tradition into one punching bag, but he is dead on in his satiric take on those whose paranoid desire to find connections overwhelms their common sense and ability to deal fairly with the historical record. Taken in the context of *Foucault's Pendulum*, however, the garbled occult history presented in Brown's novel reads like the good semiotician's worst nightmare.

None of this pattern of influences constitutes anything like copying. Like most genre fiction writers, Brown made these elements his own and added some new ones. The case of *Holy Blood, Holy Grail* is a bit different, however. Though it is clear Brown believed he paid his primary source sufficient homage by playfully introducing two of its authors' names in anagrammatic form as the villain "Leigh Teabing" and including an afterword in later printings explicitly citing the book, readers of *Holy Blood, Holy Grail* understand that its authors were correct in asserting that Brown did appropriate, in considerable detail, what they called the "architecture" of their theory about Mary Magdalene and the Merovingian line. The awkward point for a lawsuit is that Brown took their ersatz scholarship at face value as historically true, and a historical fact cannot be plagiarized, only transmitted. But the relationship of *Holy Blood, Holy Grail* to fact was already extremely problematic. In 1993, Pierre Plantard, the supposed direct descendant of the Merovingians (hence of Jesus) prominently featured in *Holy Blood, Holy Grail*, confessed that he had made up the whole genealogy and deposited the "secret documents" himself in the Bibliothèque Nationale.[22]

The authors of *Holy Blood, Holy Grail* may have already had their suspicions about Plantard's veracity when they first wrote their book, which was based on an earlier BBC program. It doesn't seem, though, as if Brown knew of Plantard's confession when he wrote *The Da Vinci Code*—and in any event he gave the Merovingians (and Jesus) a different line of descent with his character Sophie Neveu. Since the litigants (Baigent and Leigh) could not possibly win if their book were judged entirely factual and could equally not confess to a hoax, Baigent tried to backpedal by saying their book presented "evidence, not proof." The judge was having none of this, however, and ruled against them, even to the point of concealing a *Da Vinci Code*-like secret code of his own devising in his written judgment.[23] A subsequent appeal was turned down.

The industry of more than ninety books on the subject of all the things Dan Brown got factually wrong will not be examined here simply because *The Da Vinci Code's* power operates in a realm— that of myth-making and religious speculation— where the factual is irrelevant. The Gothic subgenre spawned by *The Da Vinci Code,* its predecessors, and imitators is unique among contemporary faux Catholic fictions in making the tenets of Christianity an explicit topic and proposing a new religious mystery to take the place of the discredited old one.[24] The stated goal of the murdered curator Jacques Saunière, and of Brown himself, is the restoration of the principle of the "sacred feminine." As Robert Langdon explains to Sophie Neveu, the Priory of Sion "believes that Constantine and his male successors successfully converted the world from matriarchal paganism to patriarchal Christianity by waging a campaign of propaganda that demonized the sacred feminine, obliterating the goddess from modern religion forever."[25] In one of many interviews, Brown elaborated further: "Prior to 2000 years ago, we lived in a world of gods and goddesses. Today we live in a world of God. I simply wrote a story that explores how and why this shift might have occurred, what it says about our past and, more importantly, what it says about our future."[26]

At first glance, it might seem that *The Da Vinci Code* has indeed mainstreamed the notion of the "sacred feminine" out of the margins of New Age pop culture, and at a culturally auspicious moment for doing so. In a context in which the "Goddess Mary" is featured on a *Time* magazine cover with an accompanying article devoted to the new "Protestant Mary,"[27] along with the trickledown effect of popular works on the Gnostic Gospels and newly discovered texts such as the Gospel of Judas that chip away at the façade of the New Testament, "people are looking for a different kind of religious understanding," says Karen King, Harvard professor of ecclesiastical history, of *The Da Vinci Code*. Women, King believes, "find comfort in the idea of a married woman with a baby as an alternate figure to the polarized female models of virgins and prostitutes in Christianity."[28]

The Da Vinci Code, however, presents no real goddess or representation of a divinity. We are told that the Priory of Sion worships Mary Magdalene as "Goddess" and "Divine Mother," but this happens offstage, taking a back seat to the dominant point of Jesus's nondivinity. What's more, if Jesus is a mere mortal, how precisely is Mary Magdalene divine? Whatever her iconic links to goddesses like Isis, Mary Magdalene is portrayed in the novel as a woman who marries, bears a child, and dies; she is given no "ascension to heaven" moment. There is also very little mention of Jesus's mother Mary, who some would argue has served, far more than in any Protestant denomination, as the Catholic Church's own female principle. The story is told from the perspective of the traditional thriller's male protagonist, and the Priory of Sion's hilariously fictitious list of grandmasters taken from *Holy Blood, Holy Grail* (which includes Victor Hugo and Jean Cocteau) has not a single woman in it. The only inadvertent whiff of the goddess in either novel occurs in *Angels & Demons,* when the statuesque scientist Vittoria Vetra provokes outrage by striding through the Vatican in her short shorts.

The Da Vinci Code's greatest attraction for its readers, I believe, is not goddess culture or the sacred feminine, but rather the assertion that Jesus was no divinity but a man like everybody else. For those coming across the Arian heresy for the first time, packaged as "fact" in a very palatable fictional form by an enthusiastic popularizer, it's heady stuff. Yet as recently as twenty years ago, Martin Scorsese's 1988 film adaptation of the Greek writer Nikos Kazantzakis's mid-century novel *Last Temptation of Christ,* which did no more than assert the human side of Jesus and his doubts about his divinity, generated an enormous outcry from Christian groups and was more or less buried by the protest.

Why, then, was *The Da Vinci Code* able to bulldoze the opposition of organized religion at every turn? Not all the reasons for this novel's staggering success, it turns out, had to do with its content. It was a canny top-of-the-line marketing plan, not the book's controversial theological content, that initially put *The Da Vinci Code* within reach of the maximum possible number of readers. Since Gutenberg

238

printed the first Bible, mass printing has altered forever the nature of scripture and transmission of religious doctrine—and so, from the twentieth century on, has the theory and practice of marketing. A notable exception was *The Celestine Prophecy*, a faux Catholic novel-cum-spiritual manifesto presenting a New Age meditative discipline purportedly recorded on "parchments" dating from 600 B.C.E. discovered by Catholic priests in Peru. Initially published by the author, this *Da Vinci Code* of the 1990s eventually sold upwards of 20 million copies.[29]

The Da Vinci Code had been groomed for bestsellerdom long before it ever saw print. Determined to hit it big with this book, Brown put a tremendous amount of work and energy into his initial proposal to the publisher. He was also rightly convinced of the need to compress this rather complicated historical argument and accompanying narrative into very short sound-bite chapters that a much wider audience than habitual book readers would be able to digest easily and understand. Unlike Kazantzaki's deeply literary work, *The Da Vinci Code* is full of zingy one-liners like "The greatest story ever told is the greatest story ever *sold*" and throwaway references to such personages as Walt Disney, who, Brown tells us, "had made it his quiet life's work to pass on the Grail story to future generations."[30] For the 200-page detailed plot synopsis he submitted, Brown received a two-book contract and an advance of $400,000, an amount that basically signals a publisher's commitment to do everything necessary to make a book a bestseller. After the book's success proved even greater than projected, this figure was quickly renegotiated upward. Three months before publication, 10,000 advance reader copies of *The Da Vinci Code* were sent to booksellers (a larger number than the first print run of any of Brown's previous three novels), and the book had a first printing of 230,000.[31]

Yet it is equally clear that neither Brown nor his publisher was at all prepared for the juggernaut that followed. After ten weeks, a million copies were in print. The book sold 6.5 million in the United States in its first year; after the second year, the total was 10 million.[32] As of the end of April 2006, the book had sold over 40 million copies in hardback and over 1 million in the recently released paperback.[33] The release of the movie version the following month spiked those numbers even higher.

In the meantime objections from Christian leaders were immediate and vociferous, though the first official denunciation by the Catholic church did not come until March 2005, two years after publication, when Cardinal Tarcisio Bertone, archbishop of Genoa, spoke out against the book and urged Catholics not to buy or read it.[34] Though Opus Dei refrained from boycotting the movie, bravely declaring it would "generate interest in Christianity," a few weeks before the film version's release, Archbishop Angelo Amato, the second-ranking official in the Vatican's doctrinal office and a close associate of Pope Benedict XVI, called on Roman Catholics to boycott the film, declaring the novel to be "full of calumnies, offenses and historical and theological errors regarding Jesus, the Gospels and the church," according to Reuters. "If such lies and errors had been directed at the Koran or the Holocaust, they would have justly provoked a world uprising," the archbishop said. "Instead, if they are directed against the church and Christians, they remain unpunished."[35]

But nobody listened. Promoted in the United States by no less than ten History Channel programs exploring aspects of the novel with the help of dubious experts (including Baigent and Leigh) and kitschy soft-focus reënactments, the movie opened to record box office profits worldwide, including predominantly Catholic countries. As Thomas Doherty noted in the *Washington Post,* this outcome would have been unthinkable for a previous generation of American Catholics, who formerly exerted a real influence by observing the church's boycott and proscription orders. Hollywood's first Production Code of censorship, written in 1930 by a Catholic publisher and a Jesuit priest, inspired the establishment of the Legion of Decency, the forerunner of today's Catholic League for Religious and Civil Rights. "When the Catholic hierarchy lost the power to energize millions of parishioners for some real Catholic action," Doherty notes, "when American Catholics responded to calls to boycott Hollywood blockbusters with approximately the same obedient deference they accorded the Vatican's advice on birth

240

control, then Catholic dominion over Hollywood lapsed." Today, he concludes, "the only Code that Hollywood adheres to is the kind authored by Dan Brown."[36] Tellingly, after the record opening (only surpassed, ironically, by Mel Gibson's conservative Catholic *The Passion of the Christ* in 2004), the Vatican newspaper *L'Osservatore* dubbed the movie "much ado about nothing" and the uproar around it nothing but a clever marketing strategy designed to promote interest in a dull movie and a dull book.[37]

The multiplatform success of *The Da Vinci Code* occurred in a realm that is simultaneously a fertile field and an intellectual vacuum—that curious ahistorical, apocalyptic world of American pop culture, in which Brown can be called "one of the bestselling authors of all time"[38] just as Elvis is the greatest rock-n-roll star of all time and Hank Aaron/Barry Bonds is the greatest homerun hitter of all time. This shadowy region I call the sub-Zeitgeist is also, depending on one's point of view, either the crucible or the compost heap of new religious movements, where a certain kind of low-level but potent theological rumination is constantly taking place. At least two world religions, Mormonism and Christian Science, were cooked in this cauldron by leaders whose religious manifestos were bestsellers mass printed in the nineteenth century and partially shaped by the conventions of popular literature, both fiction and nonfiction (the romance of gold tablets written in a secret celestial language and the self-improvement tradition begun by Benjamin Franklin, respectively); so was a third, Scientology, in the twentieth. Just as Scientology's deviser L. Ron Hubbard moved seamlessly from writing science fiction novels to founding a science fiction religion, other new religions have blossomed from notions that conflate the fictional extraterrestrial with the formerly celestial.[39] As part of the same trend, magic cults and quasi-religions have sprung up around fantasy and science fiction, including the works of J. R. R. Tolkien, H. P. Lovecraft and the television series *Star Trek*, which brings us back again to the Gothic.[40]

If the absence of the religious transcendent is its defining feature, then *The Da Vinci Code*'s function considered within the Gothic tradition is the unmaking of a godhead rather than the putting forward of a goddess or any other deity in its place. The supernatural

241

is not present as an active agency in any of Brown's four novels, all of which, including his two technothrillers *Digital Fortress* (1998) and *Deception Point* (2001), belong to the conspiracy theory genre. Despite their professed theses, both *Angels & Demons* and *The Da Vinci Code* are profoundly secular books, to which Peter Brooks's comment on the radical Gothic message of *The Monk* and Mary Shelley's *Frankenstein* equally applies: that "the Sacred in its traditional Christian form, even in the more purely ethical version elaborated by Christian humanism, is no longer operative."[41]

Even so, the fact that Gothic fiction of two hundred years ago did not include a married Jesus indicates just how much closer Christianity stood to Western intellectual life then, when heresy was a much more taboo subject than fornicating monks and nuns, than it does today. The Catholic church has reason to be upset about *The Da Vinci Code* because the function it serves in secularizing Jesus is not really to promote a dialogue about Christianity, as both Brown and its apologists have rather ingenuously argued, but rather to help deliver a death blow to the Christian Trinity as it has been understood by all denominations, not just the Catholic church.

On this issue central to all Christianity, we return again to the question: Why construct this fictional heresy around the Catholic Church in particular? As all writers of exorcism movies know, it is easier to tap into a long-established tradition of anticlericalism and show a Christian denomination other than your own engaged in scheming, suppression, and conspiracy across the ages. Clearly, Brown and others take the easy way out. A plot point that would provoke far greater outrage in U.S. audiences, for example, would be to identify close associates of Billy Graham and John Calvin in the historical coverup around Jesus and Mary Magdalene. More than simply deflecting criticism away from Protestant Christianity, however, in Brown's hands the faux Catholic genre still reveals its supremely unconscious deference to the Catholic church as the most enduring and powerful standard-bearer of a Christianity that no longer seems entirely relevant.

Though it is hardly likely to spawn a new sect on its own, the *Da Vinci Code* phenomenon has shown that the traditional belief system of Christianity, not withstanding the evangelicals and religious right,

242

no longer exerts the power over the hearts and minds of the majority that it formerly possessed. Despite all the polls showing that this or that number of Americans regularly attend church, believe in the Rapture and so forth, many Americans who profess to be Christian believers are simply *imaginatively* distant from the precepts of the religion they grew up with. An elderly Midwesterner once told me that he and his wife were raised Methodist but had started attending the Catholic church across the street from their retirement home because the choir was so much better. He considered this a moment. Then, brow furrowed, he leaned forward and whispered: "You know, the Catholics and the Protestants—which came first?" And he still seemed troubled after I told him, as if some larger, more important question behind this one had been left unanswered. As, indeed, it had. I warrant that a considerable number of people in this country fall into this same grey middle area.

Statistics, themselves a kind of peculiarly American secular scripture, always constitute a dubious proof, but sometimes they can accurately reflect certain of these dissonances in belief. One recent poll that records 78 percent of people in the United States as believing in the resurrection of Jesus also shows the rather astounding number of 13 percent now believing that Jesus' death on the cross "was faked" and, as represented in *The Da Vinci Code*, that Jesus was married and had a family. The Canadian pollster himself expressed shock at this result in such a religiously conservative country as the United States.[42] A similar poll in the United Kingdom (commissioned, notably, by Opus Dei), where no fewer than one out of five adults has read *The Da Vinci Code,* revealed that 60 percent of people who had read the book believed Jesus had children by Mary Magdalene, as did 30 percent—a significant figure in itself— of those who had *not* read the book.[43]

In short, the populace has a strong appetite for heresy that *The Da Vinci Code* and other works of popular fiction help to feed. This is no new phenomenon under the American sun, where transcendental movements and Great Awakenings war ceaselessly with pragmatic empiricism for hegemony in the national spirit. The crowd searches, restlessly, for religious ideas that capture its imagination. What

243

the secularization of Jesus (and the eventual elevation of assorted female gods) will mean in terms of the sub-Zeitgeist of popular culture, where fantastic literature and religion building have a long history of cross-fertilizing each other, is that the gradual departure of the Christ figure from the category of the divine leaves room for something else to move in and take its place. We are unlikely to be swept away any time soon by a New Age goddess religion—recall that Balzac's mystical potboiler *Seraphita* took Paris by storm in 1835 yet failed to produce a country of Swedenborgian converts— but we should expect other forms of religious speculation packaged in fictional form (most probably Gothic/thriller/ science fiction/ fantasy) to keep arriving on our doorsteps.

In another ten years *The Da Vinci Code* will have faded from memory as completely as *The Celestine Prophecy* already has, but it counts as one of a number of faint tremors indicating that the ground of orthodoxy is shifting under our feet. Even as the walls of various Christian temples show no signs of being able to bend with the unexpected movement produced by these works, elements of conservative Protestant Christianity are imitating radical non-Christian new religious movements by producing their own popular fiction scripture. At first glance, works like the *Left Behind* series may seem a clever vehicle for marketing traditional Christian tenets to a wide audience. But as Dan Brown discovered the hard way, this trickster genre has a way of breaking free of its practitioners and creating its own compelling reality. Once the vampire is in the door, he doesn't go away—and he changes everything.[44] In Western societies today, and especially in the United States, not places of worship or seminaries but dog-eared paperbacks and the Web are the true early warning signals of religious upheavals to come.

Notes

This text is an expanded version of the original paper and appeared in *boundary 2* (Fall 2007). My thanks to Duke University Press for permission to reprint and to the *boundary 2* reviewers and Robert Geary for valuable comments and corrections.

1. Along with "Action" and "Family," the online DVD rental service Netflix offers a major category of movies called *Satanic Stories*.

2. Lewis F. Peck, "A Note on the Text," in *The Monk*, introduction by John Berryman (New York and London: Grove Press, 1959), 30. Lewis (p. 32) earnestly declares sources for the story of the Bleeding Nun and a few of the ballads, ending plaintively, "I have now made a full avowal of all the plagiarisms of which I am aware myself; but I doubt not, many more may be found, of which I am at present totally unconscious."

3. The discussion of the modern faux Catholic Gothic does not include the films of Luis Buñuel, which carry some strong echoes of their eighteenth-century Protestant counterparts. *The Monk* was translated into French by Antonin Artaud and became an important text for the Surrealists; Buñuel wanted to make a movie of it (and did write a script, with Jean-Claude Carrière, that was made into a movie *Le Moine* [1973] directed by Adonis Kyrou).

4. Joel Porte, "In the Hands of an Angry God: Religious Terror in Gothic Fiction," in *The Gothic Imagination: Essays in Dark Romanticism* (Pullman: Washington State University, 1974), 43.

5. Victor Sage, *Horror Fiction in the Protestant Tradition* (London: Macmillan, 1988), xxi-xxii.

6. Robert F. Geary, *The Supernatural in Gothic Fiction: Horror, Belief, and Literary Change* (Lewiston, NY: Edwin Mellen Press, 1992), 11, 16.

7. Victoria Nelson, *The Secret Life of Puppets* (Cambridge, MA: Harvard University Press, 2002), 9.

8. In a fictional foreshadowing of Pierre Plantard's fraudulent claims of his Merovingian ancestry that form the basis of Brown's principal source *Holy Blood Holy Grail*, Sue styles a French family as the direct descendants of the Wandering Jew's sister Herodias.

9. Garibaldi's *Clelia, or Of Government by Priests* (1867) and Mussolini's *The Cardinal's Mistress* (serialized 1909, published 1929). I am indebted to Massimo Introvigne for directing me to these two works. The complicated nuances of the anticlerical Catholic Gothic are perhaps best embodied in Buñuel's famous declaration: "I remain Catholic and atheist, thank God!" ("Pessimism," in *An Unspeakable Betrayal: Selected Writings of Luis Buñuel*, trans. Garrett White [Berkeley: University of California Press, 2000], 263.)

10. The Know-Nothing sentiment lives on in some corners of the American psyche, as witness this brief excerpt from a lengthy and vituperative reader's comment on Amazon.com:

"Monk was slandered by the Catholic Church: Any born again Christian recognizes that the Catholic Church is full of pagan rituals that are evil and satanic. Read the Bible and the truth will set you free. May God bless Maria Monk for her braveness in telling her story in the face of evil." See http://www.amazon.com/gp/product/155753134Xqid=1147716654/ sr=1-4/ref=sr_1_4/104-4488947-5855938?s=books&v=glance&n=28315 5. Posted 5/12/05. Accessed 5/15/06.

11. After Jane Austen's contemporary satire *Northanger Abbey* (finished by 1803; published posthumously in 1818), the definitive Victorian parody of the by-then dated Gothic conventions remains Arthur Conan Doyle's *The Hound of the Baskervilles,* which presents seemingly supernatural scares (killer ghost animal roaming the lonely moors, etc.) only to expose them as the props of a cunning murderer.

12. Sage, *Horror Fiction,* 51.

13. *The Seville Communion,* for example, features computer hackers sending secret messages to the Pope, arcana of the Swiss Guard, and the negative political currents of Vatican bureaucracy under Pope John Paul, elements that are echoed in Brown's *Angels & Demons*). "'Our Holy Mother the church,'" a young priest says to the main character, a priest with no beliefs whatsoever, "'So Catholic, Apostolic, and Roman that it's ended up betraying its original purpose. In the reformation it lost half of Europe, and in the eighteenth century it excommunicated reason. A hundred years later, it lost the workers, because they realized it was on the side of the oppressors. And now, as this century draws to a close, it's losing the young and the women. Do you know how this will end? With mice running around empty pews.'" Arturo Pérez-Reverte, *The Seville Communion,* trans. Sonia Soto (New York: Harcourt Brace, 1998[originally published 1995]), 133.

14. Tim LaHaye and Jerry B. Jenkins, *The Rise of the Antichrist: Nicolae* (Wheaton, IL: Tyndale House, 1997), 380.

15. Brown coined the term "symbology" to indicate the study of symbols in the same way that some people use "phraseology" when they mean wording or syntax: to sound high-toned. Similarly, in a preamble to *Angels & Demons* (New York: Pocket Books, 2001), he declares that the brotherhood of the Illuminati is "factual."

16 Brown, *Angels & Demons,* 34. Robert Langdon (and Dan Brown) seriously misdescribe the Illuminati, a Bavarian political-esoteric society modeled after the Freemasons founded by Adam Weishaupt that operated between the years 1776 and 1790. See Massimo Introvigne on the CESNUR (Center for the Study of New Religions) website, http://www.cesnur. org/2005/mi_illuminati.htm, for a useful discussion of conspiracy-theory notions about the Illuminati circulating since the mid-nineteenth century.

246

Introvigne pinpoints the trilogy of novels collectively titled *Illuminatus* (1975), by Robert Joseph Shea and Robert Anton Wilson, as the vehicle for the more recent mainstreaming of these notions.

17. *Angels & Demons,* 145.

18. Ibid., 35.

19. Lewis Perdue is engaged in a long-term plagiarism suit against Brown for appropriating material from *The Daughter of God* (Seth Mnookin, "The Da Vinci Clone?" *Vanity Fair,* (July 2006): 100 ff.) The novel's plot points bear little resemblance to the *Holy Blood, Holy Grail* thesis, however.

20. See http://www.danbrown.com/novels/davinci_code/faqs.html

21. Dan Brown, *The Da Vinci Code* (London: BCA, 2003), 163.

22. A good summary of the hoax is found in Laura Miller, "The Last Word: The Da Vinci Con," *The New York Times,* February 22, 2004. Accessed on http://www.cesnur.org 5/25/06. "The only thing more powerful than a worldwide conspiracy," Miller comments, "is our desire to believe in one."

23. Among widespread coverage of the case, see http://www.boston.com/news/local/new_hampshire/articles/2006/04/07/excerpts_from_ruling_on_the_da_vinci_code_lawsuit/. Accessed 11/5/06.

24. One of the new wave after Brown, Kathleen McGowan, author of the initially self-published *The Expected One* (New York: Simon and Schuster, 2006), has declared herself a direct descendant of Jesus and Mary Magdalene based on personal visions and family genealogy research in France. Carol Memmot, "Is This Woman the Living Code?" *USA Today* 7/18/06 http://www.usatoday.com/lifr/books/news/2006-070170magdalene-book_x.htm Accessed 7/18/06.

25. *Da Vinci Code,* 124-125. Theodosius, not Constantine, made Christianity the official imperial religion.

26. Lisa Rogak, *The Man Behind* The Da Vinci Code*: The Unauthorized Biography of Dan Brown* (Kansas City: Andres McMeel, 2005), 110, 138n.

27. David Van Biema, "Hail Mary," *Time,* March 14, 2005, http://www.time.com. Accessed April 25, 2006.

28. "Ruffling Religious Feathers," *Harvard Crimson.* http://www.thecrimson.com/article.aspx?ref=357405. Accessed 4/26/06.

29. See James Redfield, *The Celestine Prophecy: An Adventure* (New York: Warner Books, 1997).

30. *Da Vinci Code,* 267, 262.

31. *Man Behind* The Da Vinci Code, 93-95.

32. Ibid., 98.

33. USAToday.com 4/25/06. Accessed 4/29/06.

34. Tracy Wilkinson, "Vatican Seeks to Discredit 'The Da Vinci Code,'" *Los Angeles Times*, March 17, 2005, http://www.latimes.com. accessed 3/17/2005.

35. Ian Fisher, "Vatican Official Urges Boycott of 'Da Vinci' Film," *New York Times*, April 29, 2006.

36. Thomas Doherty, "The Code Before 'Da Vinci,'" *Washington Post*, May 20, 2006, A3.

37 . "Vatican Newspaper Reviews Da Vinci Code," ReligionNewsBlog. com • Item 14748 • Posted: 2006-05-24 10:58:30, accessed 5/30/06.

38. See the discussion in *Secret Life of Puppets*, 74.

39. See, e.g., James R. Lewis, ed. *The Gods Have Landed: New Religions from Other Worlds*, SUNY Series in Religious Studies (Albany: SUNY Press, 1995), for a look at twentieth-century extraterrestrial religious movements.

40. "Who Likes Lovecraft?," paper presented at the Association for the Study of Esotericism conference, Michigan State University, June 13, 2004.

41. Peter Brooks, "Virtue and Terror: *The Monk*," *English Literary History* 40 (1973): http://www.engl.virginia.edu/enec981/Gro... Accessed 8/31/05.

42. Agence France-Presse, "'Da Vinci Code' Affects Christians in North America," http://www.inq7.net, Accessed 4/30/2006.

43. Paul Majendie, "Reading "Da Vinci Code' Does Alter Beliefs: Survey," Reuters, http://www.today.reuters.com/misc/ 5/16/2006. Accessed 5/16/2006.

44. See Laurence Rickets's *The Vampire Lectures* (Minneapolis and London: University of Minnesota Press, 1999) for an extended social-psychological meditation on this popular culture phenomenon.

Esoteric Photography

Dark Materials:
The Chemical Wedding of
Photography and the Esoteric

Chris Webster

References to the iconography of the magical and strange are widespread in the history of photographic image making. Indeed, even in the pre-history of photography early experimenters with the camera obscura had used this seemingly esoteric reproduction of the living as a tool of entertainment, illusionism and theatricality. For example, the Jesuit priest, Rosicrucian, and alchemist Athanasius Kircher (1601?-88) documented many types of methods for experimenting with camera obscura phenomena, also effectively developing and describing the uses of a magic lantern (projector).

Kircher noted experimentations with projection (he claimed to have been able to project letters up to 500 feet) and:

At night, Kircher projected slogans or figures onto the windows of the houses opposite his own (there were paper windows in Rome then). Kircher thought it important for the conversion of unbelievers to project images of the devil, as a warning to them.[1]

Similarly in Johann Spies's *Volksbuch* (1587), Spies mentions Johann Fausten's (Faust) (1480-1540?) use of a "magical mirror" for the entertainment of his students:

Faust was for some years at Erfurt and lectured at the University. On one occasion when he is lecturing on Homer, the students request him to conjure up the ancient heroes of Greece. He promises to do so at the next lecture, which is consequently fully attended. The heroes duly appear in their armour—Menelaus, Achilles, Hector, Priam, Alexander, Ulysses, Ajax, Agamemnon and others, followed by the one-eyed giant Polyphemus, who

251

looks as though he would like to devour one or two of the students. However, he is also persuaded to retire, but the students do not ask Faust to repeat the experiment.[2]

The development of silver photography itself was presaged in the period up to the invention by presentiments of its arrival that related to the mysteries of alchemy and the occult. In 1727 Johann Heinrich Schulze (1684-1744) professor of anatomy at the University of Altdorf attempted to recreate an experiment first made by the physical alchemist Christoph Adolph Balduin (1623-1682) in 1674. Balduin had dissolved chalk (calcium carbonate) in nitric acid. This then formed another substance (calcium nitrate). The interesting property of this substance for Balduin was that it was deliquescent, that is, it absorbed moisture from the air. Believing he was close to acquiring the Philosopher's Stone, Balduin discovered that the substance glowed in the dark after heating and cooling. As a result he called this substance hermetic phosphorus.[3] His observations were published in his text *Aurum superius et inferius auræ superioris et inferioris hermeticum* (Amsterdam, 1675). However in Schulze's experiment the nitric acid was contaminated with silver. Schulze's dissolved chalk created silver nitrate as well as the anticipated calcium nitrate. The compound turned a deep purple colour on exposure to light. Testing this, he exposed the same compound to heat with no effect and concluded that it was light and not heat which had affected the change. Exploring further, Schulze fixed a stencil to a container of the substance:

I covered the glass with dark material, exposing a little part for the free entry of light. Thus I often wrote names and whole sentences on paper and carefully cut away the inked parts with a sharp knife. I struck the paper thus perforated on the glass with wax. It was not long before the sun's rays, where they hit the glass through the cut-out parts of the paper, wrote each word or sentence on the chalk precipitate so exactly and distinctly that many who were curious about the experiment but ignorant of its nature took occasion to attribute the thing to some sort of trick.[4]

Not to be outdone by Balduin, Schulze named this substance *Scotophorus* (bringer of darkness). Schulze's results would have been perceived as a *prima materia* — the "dark materials" of alchemy where the presence of 'hidden treasure' was suspected.[5]

In addition to symbolic alchemical references that seem to relate uncannily closely to the process of photography with light, silver and dark chambers, there were fantastic stories and illustrations that seem to prophesy the fixed camera image through the mirror of the camera obscura device. For example, the novella *Giphantie,* by Charles-François Tiphaigne de la Roche (1722-1774) was published in 1760 and tells a fantastic tale of a hero stranded in a miraculous land where spirits can coat a canvas with a viscous substance that can capture images on its surface once it is left to fix in a dark room. Even before the "official" announcement in France of the invention of photography in 1839, the mirror image was already associated with the concept of a captured image and once again the process is linked to the strange.

In the traditional history of photography, as propounded by the Gernsheim/Newhall axis,[6] the fact of these alternative histories of photography and the manipulation of the transformative space that the photograph could become was sparsely acknowledged. This predominant canon seemed to deem such content as either unpalatable as an area for serious study or regarded such "histories" as irrelevant or peripheral to their reading of photographic "history." Over the last two decades there has been a revision of this position and even general histories of photography are less hierarchical in relation to the variety of uses of photography. Certainly recent exhibitions have indicated an interest in the more unusual applications of the medium. For example in February 2005 an exhibition was held in Paris at the Maison Europeenne de la Photographie of occult photography, *Le Troisième oeil,*[7] *La photographie et l'occulte* (2005), which plotted "the history of modern spiritualism and psychical research from the massive upsurge in the second half of the nineteenth century almost to the present day."[8]

In the nineteenth century, the photograph seemed to affirm that science could transcend the confines of raw nature and that through man's ingenuity photography would be the medium that allowed nature to record itself unfettered by the imperfect mark making of the human hand. One extreme example of this was the case recorded in *The Photographic Times* of 1863 where a murder victim's iris was photographed, the negative enlarged and when viewed under the magnifying glass the outlines of a human face, the murderer's imprint, could be made out:

So exaggerated then was the efficacy of the all-seeing mechanical eye and so readily was its recorded image acceptable that those present had no difficulty in seeing the details of the face of the murderer. They saw what they wanted to see: long nose, prominent cheekbones, black moustache and other sinister distinguishing features.[9]

From its inception the medium of photography was quickly associated with the genesis of an extension of the self, a fragment of the soul, captured in the silver. Indeed the very process of allowing any image to be produced as likeness was linked to the concept of soul replication. As Sir James Frazer (1854-1941) pointed out in his seminal anthropological work *The Golden Bough* (appearing in twelve volumes between 1890 and 1915) many peoples believed the soul to lie in the shadow or reflection. The nineteenth-century travelling photographer often discovered as a result that photography was considered a dire threat to the lives of those photographed and the photographer's reception was often hostile. For example:

When Dr. Catat and some companions were exploring the Bara country on the west coast of Madagascar, the people suddenly became hostile. The day before the travellers, not without difficulty, had photographed the royal family, and now found themselves accused of taking the souls of the natives for the purpose of selling them when they returned to France.[10]

Nor were such concerns only recorded in relation to the non-western "other." In his portrait of 1840 (Fig. 1) the Danish artist Bertel Thorvaldsen (1770-1844) can be clearly seen to be making the horned symbol with his hand to ward off the evil eye.

Fig. 1. A. C. T. Neubourg, Bertel Thorvaldsen, daguerreotype, 1840. Courtesy of the Thorvaldsen Museum, Copenhagen.

Indeed, by the mid nineteenth-century the strangeness of the photographic space was being described by a group of photographers who saw that the machine itself, the camera, could become chimera, projecting fantastic visions of other worlds that because of its very association with the veracious, with truth, would serve as a problematic guide to a world that contained not only raw empirical nature in all its manifestations but spirits too. That the camera might be able to record beyond the sight of the human eye seemed in itself evident from the product of the machine. Photography arrested time, whilst simultaneously it could be applied to long exposures for example drawing the path of the sun and stars across the heavens. Photography would go on to prove the mechanics of animals in motion and indeed see through the flesh to reveal the map of our bones when Wilhelm Conrad Roentgen (1845-1923) produced his first X-ray photographs at the end of the nineteenth-century (Fig. 2).

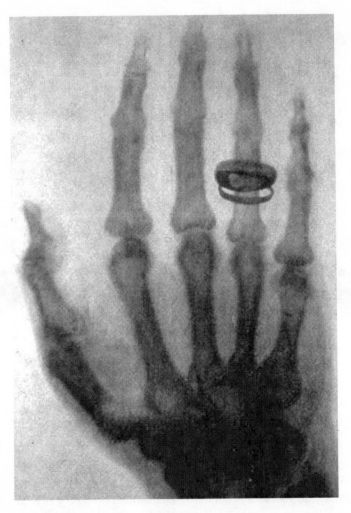

Fig. 2. W. C. Roentgen, X-ray of Albert von Kolliker, X-Ray image, 1896. Courtesy of Radiology Centennial, Inc.

It seems only natural on reflection that the camera image should be used to resolve the form of spirits when considering the history of the development of camera and magic lantern equipment. According to Daniel Schwenter (1585-1636)[11] when he discusses the camera obscura and mirror projection:

One writes a great deal about magicians and witches who pretend to be able to make spectres and ghosts appear; this,

256

however, is mostly a natural occurrence and has its origin in the *Catoptrica* or art of using mirrors: because the majority of these male and female so-called artists use a good mirror in the shape of a cylinder or round column for their fraudulent purposes and hang it in the closet of a dark chamber.[12]

In the case of spirit photography the camera was employed because of its perceived relatedness to the real. The photograph represented authenticity; there upon the plate where nothing had been before was a trace, a certainty of life beyond life. It was this photographic veracity, this machine's verdict, which served to convince that these images were a scientifically recorded truth. According to Rosalind Krauss, "photography was the first available demonstration that light could indeed exert an action ... sufficient to cause changes in material bodies."[13] Although often clumsy, the iconography of spiritualist photographs worked on a level not dissimilar to the interventions developed by early Modernist practitioners of photo-collage. Indeed spirit photography was influential on the Surrealists as an iconography of the bizarre to be celebrated.

But ordinary photographs themselves are the shades of the dead, the actual reflection of the thing photographed captured in silver, recorded as the light was reflected from the skin on the darkening silver. Photographs have an ironic nature in that they serve to confirm mortality rather than ensuring immortality. When discussing Barthes's posthumously published text *Camera Lucida* (1980) John Tagg confirmed the status implied by Barthes:

The camera is an instrument of evidence. Beyond any encoding of the photograph, there is an existential connection between the 'necessarily real thing which has been placed before the lens and the photographic image: every photograph is somehow co-natural with its referent'. What the photograph asserts is the overwhelming truth that 'the thing has been there': this was a reality which once existed, though it is a reality one can no longer touch.[14]

Photographs from the early period of portraiture carry an inherently magical quality about them. The photographer Nadar (1820-1910)[15], for example, when discussing the inventions of the nineteenth-century remarked in his memoirs:

But do not all these miracles pale ... when compared to the most astonishing and disturbing one of all, that one which seems finally to endow man himself with the divine power of creation: the power to give physical form to the insubstantial image that vanishes as soon as it is perceived, leaving no shadow in the mirror, no ripple on the surface of the water?[16]

Photography from its inception was perceived to work "at the very point that divided the visible and invisible worlds. Many occultists could understand it as a tool that was as sensitive to communications from the other world as the physical eye is to this world."[17] As in alchemy, as in Balzac's 'Theory of Spectres'[18], the transformative medium is light. Light is:

the keystone in the Swedenborgian system ... the conduit between the world of sense impression and the world of spirit. It was in terms of a luminous image that the departed chose to put in their spectral appearances at the 19th century séance. And after 1839 it required only a baby step in logic to conceive of recording these apparitions photographically.[19]

Like the dancing phantoms of Kircher's magic lantern projections, light provided the physical key to confronting such mysterious emanations. Although many spirit photographs appear to be crude constructions there is an inherent strangeness to some of these types of images that denotes the nineteenth-century understanding of the ability of the photograph to see where the human eye cannot and more than this to see ghosts as if they are projections or collaged photographs.

Sometimes fuzzy, of varying scale, unmatched lighting between spirit and sitter, variations of technical skill and unconvincing dress, it would seem almost inconceivable to believe that anyone could accept these images as veracious representations of a supernatural origin. But, then, it might seem incredible to us in an age of virtual reality and cinematically projected computer generated imagery that people were terrified by the images produced with the aid of a "magick lanthorn" "a small Optickal Macheen, that shews by a gloomy Light upon a white Wall, Spectres and Monsters so hideous that he who knows not the Secret, believes it to be perform'd by Magic Art."[20]

Throughout the nineteenth-century photography was associated with the occult as the medium's advent so closely coincided with a period where there was a general reaction to the end of metaphysical certainty through the rational arguments of science. In her study of psychical research in England, Janet Oppenheim explored this trend:

Victorians themselves were fully aware that the place of religion in the cultural fabric of their times was scarcely secure. In an effort to counter that insecurity, to calm their fears, and to seek answers where contemporary churches were ambiguous, thousands of British men and women in the Victorian and Edwardian eras turned to Spiritualism and psychical research.[21]

And, according to Carl Jung (1875-1961), the interest in phenomena and new movements such as Spiritualism could "crop up autochthonously ... when a particular view of the world is collapsing, sweeping away all the formulas that purported to offer final answers to the great problems of life."[22]

This "autochthonous" reaction to the arrival of rationalism was particularly marked in the nineteenth-century *fin-de-siecle* especially in Paris where it was claimed that in the late 1890s the city boasted 50,000 practising alchemists.[23] This occult craze was the crucible in which occult ideas and photography became overt. Elizabeth K. Menon has examined images from Paris of this period:

in which prostitutes are depicted as wicked females of subversive nature. In some cases, the portrayals consist of magical or allegorical-alchemical elements which were incorporated into the

259

pictures, in order to enhance the assumed occult nature of these sexually threatening women.[24]

Certainly, as Andreas Fischer argues, there is a greater understanding amongst art historians today of the importance of these images to contribute to a deeper understanding of the period of their nascence and that "Only recently it was recognised that occult and spiritualistic phenomena reflect a broad social movement, which has also inspired many cultural fields, for example literature and the fine arts, especially the beginning of modern art." But Fischer also argues that the popularity of these images "is not only of historical interest, it also underlines the fact that such phenomena are still of great interest to many people today."[25]

By the end of the nineteenth-century, the firmly reëstablished emergence of occult traditions, explorations of the unconscious by the emergent sciences of analytical psychology and psychoanalysis, and the new quantum science, affected and influenced art practice throughout the twentieth-century and into the twenty-first. Experimentations with alchemy and occult symbolism are apparent in the manipulations of August Strindberg's (1849-1912) occult inspired experiments with photography at the end of the nineteenth-century. In 1894 Strindberg had arrived in Paris and had begun his infamous *inferno* period when he would immerse himself in alchemy and the occult.

The photographic experiments that Strindberg produced in this period are beautiful renditions of the light of the moon and night sky produced in an unorthodox manner by simply laying photographic materials in a developing bath in starlight. His *Celestographs* (as he called them) utilised, indeed relied upon, elements of chance and chaos—an approach that refuted the didactic approach embedded in photographic practice as to the 'correct' use of materials and methods. Strindberg believed that the emanations of the stars would directly record on the paper surface.

Fig 3. August Strindberg, celestograph, silver gelatin print, 1894. Courtesy of the Strindbergsmuseet (copyright holder) and the National Library of Sweden (owner of the original work).

These "celestographs" may not be objective replications of the night sky but they are light exposures of "something." Indeed they have the appearance of nebulae. Strindberg's images prophesy the images made through the Hubble Space telescope a century before its launch. Strindberg was pushing the physical chemical processes of photography and although he was working automatically, his use of the medium relates back to the concept of the indexical properties of the photograph in conjunction with its supposed occult abilities

261

to record the "unseeable." Moreover, his combination of occult practice and artistic intent with these photographic materials make him a bridge to the early modernist experiments that would lead to Surrealist hybrids of occult and art theory.

Twentieth-century art movements were deeply influenced by the iconography and esoteric ideas central to occult practices that emerged in the nineteenth-century. French occultist Eliphas Lévi (1810-1875), for example, profoundly influenced André Breton and the development of the Surrealist manifestos. For instance, Lévi wrote "Analogy yields all the forces of nature to the Magus. Analogy is the quintessence of the Philosophical Stone, the secret of perpetual motion, the quadrature of the circle … the science of good and evil." Breton later echoes him:

Poetic analogy has in common with mystical analogy that it transgresses the deductive laws in order to make the mind apprehend the interdependence of two objects of thought situated on different planes, between which the logical functioning of the mind is unlikely to throw a bridge.[26]

It can be argued that in photographic practice in particular, the thread of Surrealism and its occult iconography was continued to the late twentieth-century and beyond by photographers and in reaction to the straight purist aesthetic that predominated Modernist photography especially in an American context.

In a contemporary context artists have continued to reappraise occult symbolism and the referential presence of the photographic form as a means of reconnecting with the strange and with the numinous often absent from an increasingly secularised society. As occult practitioners had historically utilised art as a communication form for the recording and perpetuation of its encoded ideas so too have artists utilised the often adumbrative and mysterious symbols of the occult as analogies for a metaphorical communication. This might not only allow a deeper engagement in the work by the viewer but could also form part of a process of self-expression on the part of the artist that contributed to a process of self-analysis towards individuation.

In 2003 an exhibition entitled *Disembodied Spirits* opened at the Bowdoin College Museum of Art, Maine; the exhibition set out to demonstrate that in contemporary practice many artists are exploring the sublime and the uncanny through imagery that draws upon historical sources, often making direct reference to spirit photography itself. The exhibition explored the relationship between photography and the "indexical imprint of a "that-has-been" emerging from the presence of something that is no longer present." The exhibition curator, Alison Ferris, explained:

The Disembodied Spirit ... suggests that the representations of ghosts can be understood as more and other than novelties and can, in fact, open the way for new understandings of vision and "reality" in our contemporary, digitized, hypermediated world ... The Disembodied Spirit features works by artists such as John Clarence Laughlin, Ralph Eugene Meatyard, Duane Michals, and Francesca Woodman, all of whom depict the ghost in a manner that evokes the same pathos Roland Barthes finds in photography—an indexical imprint of a "that-has-been" emerging from the presence of something that is no longer present. John Baldessari, Joseph Beuys, Bruce Nauman, and Mike Kelley each have created works that directly quote, sometimes ironically, the history of spirit photography. Bill Viola, Tracey Moffatt, and Sally Mann grapple with what modern history has rendered ghostly. They employ or suggest historic photographic and film techniques to intimate that history, like a ghost, haunts our present ... Others, such as Ann Hamilton, Cornelia Parker, and Nancy Burson, use the suggestion or metaphor of spirits to explore how art can breach fantasy and materiality, the psychic and the physical.[27]

In this exhibition, Ferris brought together a disparate group of artists where the link between their practice was the fact that they exploited the photographic referent as indicative of something beyond the frame, as suggestive of *the psychic and the physical*. This is the idea that the indexical nature of the photograph is subverted to create an aura of strangeness as a link to suggesting the sublime, the unconscious, and the otherworldly. It is a discourse that has emerged

263

as a direct result and reaction to, the emergence of new technologies in imaging.

In the one hundred and sixty years since its chemical inception, artists utilising the ghost trace of light in photography have explored the strange characteristics of the medium through the staged photograph. Often such making existed on the fringe of the recognised canon of the history of photography.

The connection between the camera obscura space and the uncanny has been prevalent since the inception of the medium. The earliest experiments used terminology such as miraculous, marvellous and magical. The transmutational state where light, the fleeting trace of life, could be codified into image-icon still has echoes of the marvellous even in the twenty-first century. Kircher's projections of devils with his magic lantern equipment, Fausten's manifestations, and "spirits" walking in the air in public demonstrations of the camera obscura—all form part of a history of associations through to the photographic period with its ghosts, soul stealing and evidential structures. The photographic space is still accredited with the ability to "see" where the human eye cannot and photographic related technologies that "see" wavelengths of light invisible to the human eye serve to confirm the notion that it is still feasible in the dark chamber of the camera obscura to capture a ghost through the lens. Here the physical universe is transmutated like lead into gold to become a reënchanted and numinous space.

Notes

1. Hermann Hecht, *Pre-Cinema History: An Encyclopaedia and Annotated Bibliography of the Moving Image Before 1896* (London: Bowker-Saur, 1993), 15.
2. Hecht, 6.
3. Phosphorus—Greek for "the bringer of light" and "hermetic," after Hermes Trismegistus, the mythical founder of alchemical knowledge from which the term "hermetica" arises.
4. Beaumont Newhall, *The History of Photography: From 1839 to the Present* (London: Secker and Warburg, 1982), 10.
5. According to Mike Ware, Schulze did not experiment further with his Scotophorus as his intention had been to replicate Balduin's phosphorus—darkness itself was not the desired end but rather light, hence his naming of the substance is possibly an ironic appellation. This raises an interesting question centred on the philosophical and psychological understanding of the relationship between the positive of light and the negative of investigating "the dark." Mike Ware, "Luminescence and the invention of photography: 'a vibration in the phosphorus'," *History of Photography* 26(2002): 7.
6. Photo-historians Helmut Gernsheim (1913-1995) and Beaumont Newhall (1908-1993) held the hegemony on Modernist photographic historical writing until the 1960s and their interpretation of photographic history was one that was mostly focussed on a masculine and un-manipulated vision of photographic practice.
7. It was additionally shown at the Metropolitan Museum of Art, New York in 2005.
8. Jeremy Stubbs, "A Recent Paris Exhibition of Occult Photography, plus some related phenomena," http://www.surrealismcentre.ac.uk/publications/papers/journal3/.
9. Joe Nickell, *Camera Clues*, (Lexington: University Press of Kentucky, 1994), 146.
10. James Frazer, *The Golden Bough: A Study in Magic and Religion*, (Ware: Wordsworth Editions Ltd., 1993), 193.
11. The text *Deliciae physico-mathematicae, oder mathematische und physikalische Erquickstunden*, (Nurnberg, 1636), was an important contemporary text on magic highly prized by practising magicians.
12. Hecht, 13.

13. Rosalind Krauss, "Tracing Nadar," *October 5* (1978): 30.

14. John Tagg, *The Burden of Representation*, (London: Macmillan, 1988), 1.

15. After a successful career as a political cartoonist Nadar (Gaspar Félix Tournachon) opened a photography studio in Paris in 1854 and although only practising for six years as a photographer became one of the most prominent nineteenth-century photographic innovators.

16. Krauss, 39.

17. Andreas Fischer, "A Perfect Medium — Photography and the Occult," http://www.collegeofpsychicstudies.co.uk/index.html

18. Honoré de Balzac (1799-1850) believed that the body was made up of layers of ghost-like images and that each instance of being photographed stripped away a layer.

19. Krauss, 37.

20. Hecht, 28.

21. Janet Oppenheim, *The Other World: Spiritualism and Psychical Research in England, 1850-1914*, (Cambridge: Cambridge University Press, 1985), 1.

22. Carl Jung, *The Spirit in Man, Art and Literature*, (London: Routledge & Kegan Paul, 1984), 8.

23. Gary Lachman, "Absinthe and alchemy," http://www.forteantimes.com/articles/180_strindberg1.shtml.

24. "Art and Alchemy," http://www.esoteric.msu.edu/VolumeIV/Art-Alchemy.htm.

25. Andreas Fischer, "A Perfect Medium — Photography and the Occult," http://www.collegeofpsychicstudies.co.uk/index.html

26. Lévi and Breton quoted in Nadia Coucha, *Surrealism and the Occult*, (Oxford: Mandrake, 1991), 59.

27. Alison Ferris, "Disembodied spirits", *Art Journal*, Fall (2003), http://www.findarticles.com/p/articles/mi_m0425/is_3_62/ai_108311208 February, 2005.

A Mirror with a Memory:
Spirit Photography and the Future of Ghosts

Cathy Gutierrez

In 1851, a British photographer living in America had a visitor. An attractive young woman entered his studio, carrying a covered basket. As the photographer went about readying his equipment to take her portrait, he had a grisly surprise waiting for him—the subject of the photograph was not the woman but the contents of the basket, the corpse of her stillborn infant. While this episode was shocking to him, this new form of commemorating the dead soon became one of the mainstays of his livelihood. Of his time in America and the many corpses he photographed, he wrote, "[L]ike a ghoul, I had to convert a receiving vault in a cemetery into a workroom, and, surrounded by ghastly companions, picture and endeavor to make imperishable the spectacle of that which was so fast passing away."[1]

Photographers of the dead were universally charged with making the subject as lifelike as possible. As Nancy West has pointed out in her excellent article "Camera Fiends," post-mortem photography came into full bloom at the precise historical moment of Gothic novels and the profession of undertaking, all Dr. Frankenstein figures specifically hired to "bring the dead back to life."[2] Early nineteenth-century photographs of dead children are visions of peacefulness, with the depiction of the body erasing the line between sleep and death. Contemporaneous accounts called photographs "mirrors with a memory," and these mirrors reflected undisturbed comfort and rest, presumably creating a memory of a contented passage into permanent sleep.

The threshold of death was blurred by these revivifying photos that seemed to portray a preview of the resurrection. With the capacity to concretize the past and make the passing imperishable, the technology of photography was enlisted for specifically religious purposes. Photography was charged with curing the woes of industrialization by bringing those separated by distance together. The photographer Marcus Root argued for a triumvirate of technology encompassing the steam engine, telegraphy, and photography that would be both the means and the end of the eschaton.[3] In the highly mobile world of antebellum America, the ability to eradicate space was quickly paired with the ability to eradicate time, as photographs accumulated the past at an increasingly rapid rate.

The American articulation of Spiritualism, a religious movement begun in 1848, would provide the perfect nexus of technology and kinship to embrace the outer limits of this new art—photographing not just the bodies but the spirits of the dead.[4] Modeling their ideas on the recently developed telegraph, Spiritualists proposed that continuing communication between the living and the dead was not only possible, it was the logical—and empirical—outcome of the technologies of the day. With the telegraph, photography, and later the telephone providing instant and invisible communication across space, Spiritualists simply noted that space went up to heaven as well as across to the territories; with refinements on the Mesmeric trance state, mediums (most often women) became the living instrument of communication between the living and the dead. And like contemporaneous discussions of electricity, Spiritualists held their discovery to be scientifically true even if not yet well understood.

Contact with the dead disclosed that heaven resembled the familiar landscapes of earth, with neighborhoods, churches, schools and social occasions, in essence a sanitized version of the ethos of the time. The dead participated in the fascination with technology as well as the burgeoning populism of the new middle class, and like many contemporaneous religious movements both Spiritualists and the spirits reflected a cultural celebration of the ideals of democracy. Spiritualism proposed that people retained all of their individual characteristics at death and therefore wished to maintain their relationships with those on earth. The spirits of the dead also retained their earthly flaws, and were not made perfect upon entrance to heaven but rather were subject to errors and mistakes in the afterlife.

Photography entered the Spiritualist arena with the force of a modern-day miracle: at last, a new technology would eliminate the margin of error that all-too-human mediums still retained. Just as the medium was understood to be more gifted at inhabiting the space between life and death, so too photography was thought to merely be able to capture realities that were slightly beyond the scope of the human eye. The dead were corporeally present one step further on the light spectrum than humans could see. Photography itself had already been charged with two cultural productions that fit smoothly into the Spiritualist agenda: first, it was already the rage to photograph the recently dead, particularly children. In a related current, these mirrors merely reflected what was present: photographs were an objective account of reality, an untampered with document of phenomena.

These attempts at technological innovation were attempts at creating transparent objectivity, wherein human desire could never be accused of tainting the evidence. When the first spirit photographs appeared they did so against the backdrop of a decade of looking for the perfect machine, and the reception not only of the photographs but of photography itself was overwhelming. In 1861, William H. Mumler accidentally entered history by producing the first photograph of a dead spirit. Spiritualists had been revivifying the dead through mediums in trance states, wherein the dead would speak through the instrument of another's living body. This process was understood by believers to be utterly empirical and scientific — the electromagnetic field of a conscious mind merely changed form at the moment of death, and certain individuals were simply more capable of staying in communication after the transformation from the mortal sphere to the spiritual one.

The implications of spirit photography for trance mediums — the majority of whom were women — were complex. On the one hand, photography literally served as an alternate "medium," one that was controlled by men. By creating static portraits of the dead, women were silenced both in life and in death: the male-dominated commercial field of photography served a similar function to that of the female-dominated field of mediumship, and photographs of both genders did not allow the dead the voice that they had in trance speaking. However, photographs of both corpses and spirits were immensely popular forms of enshrining memory, and the preservation of memory fell firmly within the domestic sphere during the Victorian period.

Moreover, the majority of spirits photographed were women. Wives and daughters reappeared with their usually male relatives who had gone for a photographic sitting, thus reassuring the living of the continued bonds of the family past the time of death.[5] Spirit photography often served to reinscribe the importance of the domestic sphere and women's continued fidelity to family. Women occasionally communicated about their own spirit photographs from beyond the grave, explaining the scientific process to their relatives. In one example, a wife explains the process to her husband: "Our thoughts produce our garments, the cut and coloring of the same, and the chemists, using their own magnetic power over the etherealised matter mould it so, and give to it an appearance such as we were in earth life."[6] Women were thus in the peculiar situation of explaining scientific principles to men. However, spirit photography grew outside of the domestic bounds of home and family, taking on an existence of its own that quickly called into question some of the underlying assumptions about Spiritualism and the place of objectivity machines in its schema.

By Mumler's own admission in his 1875 memoir, the entire enterprise had begun as a joke: he had taken what he believed to be a badly developed photograph which he then showed to a Spiritualist customer in order to rib him. To Mumler's horror, he found himself and the photograph plastered on the front page of Spiritualist newspapers in Boston and New York later that week.[7] Mumler was subsequently converted to Spiritualism and came to recognize the joke as ultimately being on him for his prior disbelief. He became a devotee of the cause, specializing in spirit photography for the rest of his career. Spirit photographs, however, were not guaranteed in either form or content. Unlike most trance mediums, "Mumler presented himself as a medium who was in the service of the spirits, not one who could call them up at will."[8] Spirits could decline altogether to be photographed or else a stranger may well appear in one's spirit sitting.

Mumler was not only the first spirit photographer but he was also the first to be taken to court on charges of fraud. In 1869, the mayor of New York requested Mumler's arrest for perpetuating fraud with supposed spirit photographs. The prosecution pulled out the big guns for its case, calling in P. T. Barnum, among others, to demonstrate how spirit photographs could be faked with wet-plate photography. The Honorable Justice Dowling was presented with nine different ways a photograph could be manipulated to make a ghostly figure appear, some of them as simple as having an assistant tiptoe behind the sitter for a fraction of the long exposure time. Double exposures and double-plate negatives gave the would-be charlatan his choice of method in ghost photography. After three weeks of trial, Mr. Mumler was set free; in his closing argument, Mumler's attorney compared him to Galileo, fighting an uphill battle in the name of science against the blind rigidity of his peers.[9]

Given that Spiritualism captured the attention of about half the country's population, the living's need for the dead is self-evident. In the context of the highest infant mortality rates of the century and then in its second boom during the Civil War, Spiritualism was clearly a crutch for the grieving and an amateur but effective form of psychotherapy. Thus it is not particularly surprising that Spiritualism latched onto photography as the technology that could mediate the ephemeral threshold of death. If spirit photography were limited to capturing the posthumous images of one's loved ones, it would be a logical extension of the movement's claims to empiricism and the continued existence of the dead. However, what is striking about the writings on early spirit photography is not the comforting continuation of domestic relationships, but rather a bizarre deviation from that template.

The movement's very successes invited discord and disbelief into its realm. In his superb new book, *Wonder Shows*, Fred Nadis argues that nineteenth-century stage magic, the precursor to today's view of magic as entertaining trickery, began specifically to debunk Spiritualists and Mesmerists. By reproducing the same techniques and effects as those employed in séances, this new wave of crusaders sought to at least blur the boundary of objective and observable truth. Nadis writes, "Such popularizers frequently relied on the device of debunking superstition or 'correcting error' as a prelude to their own explanations of scientific phenomena. In their rationalist

271

stage performances, the magicians demanded the audience decode their acts and search for the physical explanation … Popular science magazines also recognized the affinity between science and stage magic and also published explanations of the stage illusion of magicians and Spiritualists."[10]

A very similar situation in the realm of photography, however, was less clear about the divisions of the heavenly and the humbug. As Clement Cheroux has noted, "There are many other cases in the history of photography in which the same photographic form signifies both a thing and its opposite, and it is no surprise that superimposition should simultaneously have produced an iconography of belief and another of entertainment."[11] Like magic, spirit photography suggested two mutually exclusive interpretations of the evidence, that it either proved or disproved Spiritualist claims. Spiritualists not only rallied against this alternative interpretation, they denied its existence altogether.

Six years after Mumler's acquittal for photographic fraud in New York, a similar case was taken against Edouard Buguet of Paris. Monsieur Buguet had been producing spirit photographs for two years when he came under surveillance in his Montmartre studio. Unlike Mumler, how, Buguet immediately admitted fraud, demonstrated how he manipulated the spirit photos, and not only retracted his claims to mediumship but promptly repositioned himself as an exposer of frauds. Perhaps startlingly, however, the artist's own admission of guilt did nothing to dissuade many of the veracity of his former ghosts. Cheroux argues, "For although the evidence for deception had been produced during the hearing, and Buguet had admitted fraud without the slightest equivocation, some of his clients persisted in recognizing the faces of their loved ones in his images. Bending over backwards to maintain their belief, convinced that behind the trial lay a settling of political scores, a new Inquisition or Galileo affair, the spiritualists refused to accept that they had been duped, much less to abandon their faith."[12]

Whereas the intent of the stage magician who flouted deception and secrecy as the currency of mediumship, the intent of photographers meant little to nothing in assessing the final worth of spirit photographs. While American believers enjoyed less cognitive dissonance with Mumler maintaining his naïve innocence throughout, by the 1870's the public had to be aware of the myriad possibilities of manipulating photographs to produce ghostly images. Buguet in fact continued his photographic career by producing "anti-spirit" photographs, which his calling card referred to as "complete illusion." While he would continue as a trickster, never again would he be accused of fraud.

The most famous and most representative Spiritualist photographer and advocate was probably James Coates. Coates was writing in the early eighteen-seventies and his magnum opus, *Photographing the Invisible*, remained in print over forty years later. In this work, Coates marshals the existence of unidentified ghosts as proof of the objective truth of spirit photography. If you do not know the ghost in your own picture, then you are certainly not manufacturing a false memory to suit your own needs. He writes: "I aver ... that many of the so-called, unrecognized spirit photographs have been identified subsequently by persons related to *the departed*, but neither knew the operator-medium; the sitter; nor the occasion when the same was taken; showing in many cases— at least—that the psychic 'extra' was not that of a thought-form within the subconscious of the medium, or the picture of a departed produced by the desire of the sitter, but rather a portrait produced— by Invisible operators—as best they could, either hoping for or actually anticipating recognition ultimately."[13]

Most remarkable in Coates's portrayal of unidentified spirits is how the ghosts are characterized. We are told repeatedly in contemporaneous sources that it takes extraordinary effort for a spirit to materialize for a photograph. (One such report cites this fact as a reason for the exorbitant cost of spirit photographs, claiming that the dead wouldn't exert that amount of effort for an inexpensive and therefore undervalued picture.)[14] Up until this point, the dead had held an extraordinarily privileged position in Spiritualist thought— they were generally beneficent enough to talk to the living, taking time out of their busy schedules in heaven to give advice and solace to mortals.

At just about the same time, a new column started cropping up in Spiritualist newspapers, one that I think of as the "dead personals." Boston's long-lived and highly circulated weekly, *The Banner of Light*, featured messages that its staff mediums had received from unidentified spirits. The coverage for these stray messages was a full five columns of around eighteen inches, and the names of the spirits were indexed alphabetically at the beginning for ease of perusal. The banner of each column issued a standard request: "The communications from the following spirits will be published in regular course. Will those who read one from a spirit they recognize, write us whether true or false?" The lost souls, as it were, communicate their full names, where they were born, raised, and lived, frequently how they died, and occasionally the names of friends and relatives they would like to get in touch via a medium.

The problem of recognition is overt in these pleas from the dead. In 1859 a Charlotte Brown communicated from beyond the grave, "I told old Mrs. Cady, the woman who was with me when I died, that I would certainly come back to her. I do not care to come to anyone else … I have acquaintances and perhaps some friends living in Lowell, Saco, and some in Boston, but they would hardly care to hear from me, for they think I did not do well. I am sorry, very sorry, that I lived as too many lived and died as too many die. I wish to tell that dear old woman that her kind words are not lost and I shall repay her for them."[15]

What we see here is a remarkable reversal of prior articulations of the spirit world; between the dead jumping into random photographs hoping one day to be recognized and the communications from pitiable spirits, for the first time, the dead are needy. The power dynamic is reversed, and the dead require a continued relationship with the living. I wish to posit that this reversal is largely predicated on the advent of photography. Unlike spirit communications via living mediums, the representation of the dead in photographs provided a static and permanent record of death onto which the living could project their own needs. By silencing the dead, photography made death the perfect palimpsest, so that the past could be rewritten in the image of the living. The mirror with a memory that was held up to Spiritualists, in the last analysis, reflected not the ostensible subject of photographs, spirits, but rather the very alive believers who desperately needed the dead and thus attributed that neediness to the dead themselves. The dual motion of projection displaced grief and anxiety that the living experienced onto the departed, captured, imperishable, in the act of searching for recognition.

The double helix of neediness inhabited the space of death, creating a discourse of dependence that elevated the status of the living world in relation to the status of heaven. Spiritualists' understanding of photography as a medium created a metanarrative about the process of projection. Photographs of the dead simultaneously asserted and erased the living's need for continued relation with the dead, in a single deft motion of articulating the need and attributing it to the dead themselves. I would now like to turn to the Spiritualists' need *of* technology, and argue that a similar motion of articulating and displacing that need occurred in writings about photography.

Ghost photographs, then, are perhaps best understood not as documentation of a prior image but rather as a Rorschach test of subjects in the present. This clawing neediness is attested to in several accounts of the moment of recognition. An assertion of doubt is given and then withdrawn: "My wife obtained a tolerably clear photograph of (it is supposed) my father, and although it is certainly very like, there are one or two discrepancies ... I must say, I consider spirit photography to be the most interesting and most truthful manifestations we have yet been blessed with."[16] Or alternately, "My wife, several friends, and myself, recognized the photograph. The likeness is unmistakeable; but there is a bloated appearance ... a bulbiness about the features which my mother never had, nor is it in any photograph portrait taken of her from life."[17]

Memory itself came to be redrawn. Images of the past had to conform to the photographs of the present, and the need to see the dead erased history. At the precise moment when memory was at its most subjective, it had to undergo the same procedure that the mirror of neediness reflected: it had to be understood as being at its most objective. To accomplish this, believers would concede that their own memories were less reliable than the photographs. The human margin of error conceded disputes about the past to the objective technology of photography.

As Walter Benjamin, Susan Sontag, and others have noted,

photography introduced a new form of alienation into man's thinking about himself. A photograph moves the subject outside of herself, where her image objectively exists but only at the expense of her consciousness radiating it. The objectification of photography further allows for the image to be reproduced, commodified, and circulated in the market economy. In short, the self-alienation produced by photography makes the subject less real rather than more.[18]

What is curious here is that none of the academic discussions about the objectifying nature of photography apply to spirit photography—the dead are not undergoing objectification, but rather, subjectification.[19] They come into existence *as dead* through photographs, and if need be, the past will be rewritten to make that fact objectively true. Paradoxically, the notion of progress rested on reinscribing history, in which the past was pulled into the present. History quite literally haunted Spiritualists, suggesting that the era's telos of time, its very love affair with the idea of history itself, was destined to collapse under its own weight, dying a natural death at the moment it brought the dead back to life.

The subordination of the subjective to the objective resulted in the fetishization of objectivity itself. In contemporaneous depictions of photographers and their cameras, the human body was frequently portrayed as a spindly tripod with stereoscopic eyes serving as lenses. In their excellent *Instruments and the Imagination*, Thomas Hankins and Robert Silverman describe how the camera literally begins taking on a life of its own: "The appearance of a photographer at work encouraged the connection between man and camera and the anthropomorphic description of the photographic instrument. With the artist's head beneath the camera's hood, the human and the machine seem fused. Optically, both survey the same scene, sharing the camera's lens ... In this portrayal of the roles of man and machine, the camera was alive, while the human photographer was reduced to subservience."[20] The camera is not the perfect eye, but rather the eye is the imperfect camera.

Unlike uncontested unmasking of the Spiritualist agenda by stage magic, Spiritualists would not allow photography to be moved out of the arena of the objective. Claims of science or even pseudo-science could be battled on their own terms, and if stage magicians

276

could reproduce table-tipping that did not eliminate the possibilities that spirits could as well. As the eminent French Spiritualist Allen Kardec once observed, "fake diamonds take nothing of the value of real diamonds, artificial flowers do not prevent there being natural flowers."[21] This epistemological buffer could not be extended into the real of art: the realm of imagination proved much more threatening than competing claims of scientific legitimacy, and the Spiritualists galvanized against the suggestion of artifice in photography in a manner they had never approached with the admitted deception of magicians. By fetishizing the observable as necessarily objective, Spiritualists thus protected their own projections against charges of artifice. The image invites an inversion of the normal course of things. By reanimating the dead, spirit photography created a cultural negative, in which the mirror with a memory reflected not the past but the present's desperate need of it.

Spirit photography posited seriously for the first time the prospect that the dead were not residing strictly in some alternate afterlife but were in fact hovering between us. The world became peopled with invisible beings, modern day daemons, *genii*, and ghosts. Photographs of the dead severed the simplicity of a straight-forward march of time: the dead coexisted with the living on an invisible horizon that was ever-present, where the ghosts of the past commingled with the ghosts of the future.

Notes

1. Cited in Nancy M. West, "Camera Fiends: Early Photography, Death, and the Supernatural," *Centennial Review* 40 (1996)1: 171-172.
2. Ibid., 172.
3. See Robert S. Cox, "The Transportation of American Spirits: Gender, Spirit Photography, and American Culture, 1861-1880," *The Ephemera Journal* 7 (1994), 94.
4. All thoughtful commentators on Spiritualism question the precise "creation" of this movement since phenomenologically similar events had been happening in Europe and America since time immemorial. However,

I maintain the use of the traditional dating because it serves handily as a reference when people could self-identify as believers, which I think is particularly important given the often shocking nature of political and theological claims the Spiritualists made. For a discussion of Spiritualism as the "exoteric" branch of the occult "church" in America, see Godwin, *The Theosophical Enlightenment*, Chapter Ten, especially 188. Godwin seems to give some credence to the later claims by more hard-line occultists that Spiritualism was seeded or perhaps even masterminded by occult adepts to prepare society for future hermetic truths. See Godwin, 197-200.

5. Robert S. Cox, "Transportation of American Spirits: Gender, Spirit Photography, and American Culture, 1861-1880," *The Ephemera Journal*, 7 (1994): 98-99.

6. James Coates, *Photographing the Invisible: Practical Studies in Spirit Photography, Spirit Portraiture, and other Rare but Allied Phenomena* (New York: Arno Press. 1973) xv-xvi. Reprint of the 1911 edition, 200.

7. See William H. Mumler, *The Personal Experiences of William H. Mumler in Spirit Photography* (Boston: Colby and Rich, 1875), 4-6.

8. Crista Cloutier, "Mumler's Ghosts," *The Perfect Medium: Photography and the Occult*, Clement Cheroux and Andreas Fischer, eds. (New Haven: Yale University Press, 2004), 20.

9. The *Times* reprinted a full transcript of the closing arguments. See the *New York Times*, May 4, 1869.

10 Fred Nadis, *Wonder Shows: Performing Science, Magic, and Religion in America* (New Brunswick: Rutgers University Press, 2005), 118.

11. Clement Cheroux, "Ghost Dialectics: Spirit Photography in Entertainment and Belief," *The Perfect Medium: Photography and the Occult*, Clement Cheroux and Andreas Fischer, eds. (New Haven: Yale University Press, 2004), 46.

12. Ibid., 51.

13. Coates, xv-xvi.

14. See *The New York Times* April 13, 1869.

15. *The Banner of Light*, August 20, 1859.

16. M. A. Oxun (Moses Stainton), "Researches in Spiritualism," *Human Nature: A Monthly Journal of Zoistic Science* 149.

17. Ibid., 151.

18. See Walter Benjamin, *Illuminations* (New York: Schocken, 1968), 230-231. For a discussion of photographic representation in colonial contexts, see Michael Taussig, *Shamanism, Colonialism, and the Wildman: Studies in Healing and Terror* (Chicago: University of Chicago Press, 1991).

19. I am indebted to my friend and colleague Geoffrey McVey for not only this excellent observation but also this felicitous phrasing.

20. Thomas L. Hankins and Robert J. Silverman, *Instruments and the Imagination* (Princeton: Princeton University Press, 1995), 161.

21. Cheroux, op. cit., 53.

Esoteric Gardens

Enlightenment and Freemasonry
in Eighteenth-century Venice:
The Hermeticism of Querini's Garden at Altichiero

Patrizia Granziera

The garden and villa of the Venetian senator Angelo Querini was located on the banks of the Brenta River, near the town of Padua. Unfortunately, very little is left of this historical garden. A detailed description of this garden was written in 1787 by Countess Justine Wynne Rosenberg, an educated woman who was well known among the Venetian intellectual elite and a good friend of Angelo Querini. With the help of this eighteenth-century description, we will try to reconstruct this "philosophical" garden, and explain how it might have been used as an initiatory space.

Angelo Querini (1721-1796) belonged to a small élite of enlightened cosmopolitan intellectuals with strong links to Freemasonry who were criticizing the government of Venice, which at that time was in a state of decadence. They were trying to spread the ideals of the English enlightenment in the Veneto region. In Italy, it was Venice that had the closest contacts with English society. This allowed a continuous exchange of political ideas between England and Venice.

An important member of this enlightened circle was Scipione Maffei, one of the first Freemasons in the Veneto. He belonged to the lodge in Verona, probably founded by Thomas Howard, Duke of Norfolk and Grand Master of the London Grand Lodge, who was in the Veneto in 1729.[1] Maffei was also a good friend of Querini and according to Countess Rosenberg he helped him to identify the authenticity of ancient altarpiece he bought for his garden.[2]

Maffei was instrumental in forming the tastes of the Franciscan father Carlo Lodoli (1690-1761). A famous teacher of philosophy in Venice, Lodoli also taught in a school for the sons of the nobility: his pupils included Andrea and Bernardo Memmo, Girolamo Ascanio

Giustinian and Angelo Querini. His teachings concerned the nature of society and the meaning of authority. He wanted his pupils to apply the critical method to Venetian State documents, and he came into conflict with the State Inquisitors.[3] Lodoli's above-mentioned disciples, Bernardo and Lorenzo Memmo, Querini and Giustinian eventually became Freemasons and belonged to the same Venetian Lodge called de la Fidelité (of the chapter of St. John) as their names appear in a lodge list of 1785.[4] This lodge was founded in 1780, after the first English lodge, called Union, was closed.

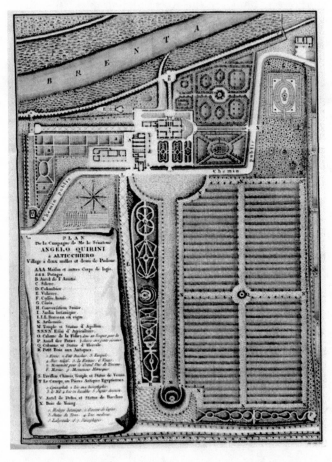

Fig. 1. Map of Querini's garden, Justine Wynne Rosenberg, Altichiero, Padova, 1787, Pl. I.

Angelo Querini, following the teachings of his master Lodoli, was the protagonist of a famous debate against the State Inquisitors. Elected "Avogador del comun" in 1758, he became the leader of a group of patricians who criticized the empowerment of two organs of the Venetian government: the Council of Ten and the State Inquisitors. He affirmed that the "Avogadori," whose task was to check on the execution of laws, had lost their original power, and that the State Inquisitors had slowly acquired more authority on matters that before were only considered the task of the "Avogadori." The "Avogadori" were the direct representatives of the common people. In a way, their function was similar to that of the Roman plebeian tribune. Querini wanted their power to be reaffirmed. This political controversy between liberal and conservative groups ended with the victory of the more conservative party guided by Duke Marco Foscarini. For his accusations, Querini was arrested in 1761 and exiled to Verona. After two years of banishment, he succeeded in coming back to Venice and continued to work in public administration. However, he decided to maintain a low profile in Venetian politics and preferred to express his innovative political ideals in private among friends. A typical "connoisseur" and educated man of his time, Querini in 1777 traveled around Switzerland and visited famous scientists and scholars such as Voltaire, for whom he felt a great admiration.[5] When he came back from this journey, he dedicated his life to the study of archeology, history and natural science and retired to his Villa at Altichiero near Padua where he laid out a garden.

Querini was then a Freemason and an "enlightened" nobleman. Many aristocrats and intellectuals of the eighteenth century Europe were Freemasons. The period of the European Enlightenment coincides with the diffusion of Freemasonry in England and Europe. It is in fact at this point in its history that Freemasonry develops as a focus for intellectuals, politicians, the gentry, artists and architects, thus fostering a continuous exchange of ideas, aesthetic values and beliefs between English and European intellectuals. Freemasons believed in virtue, progress, equality, and they contributed to the preparation of the soil for the late eighteenth century democratic revolutions. These Enlightenment ideals, which they helped propagate through their international links, were also reflected—by means of iconography and design — in the architecture and landscape gardens of the time.[6] From England, these ideals spread to Europe and to Venice.

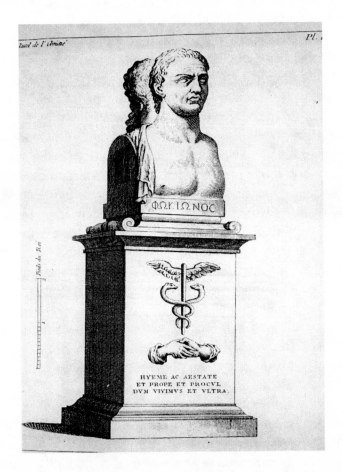

Fig. 2. Altar of Friendship, Justine Wynne Rosenberg, Altichiero, Padova, 1787, Pl.II.

Altichiero's garden is probably one of the best, if not unique examples of this kind of "philosophical" and Masonic garden in the Veneto region. Unfortunately, the only document we possess for the reconstruction of Altichiero's garden and architecture is a description written in 1787 by Countess Rosenberg. We will follow her intinerary throughout the garden. (Fig. 1)

The Countess started the visit of Altichiero from the back door of the Villa, which faced the Brenta river. On the jamb of this door there was a bust of Jupiter, and on the balustrade there were two sphinxes which posed their paws on two coat of arms carrying two inscriptions: one from Hippocrates, the ancient Greek physician, father of medicine and one from the wise Jewish King Solomon.[7] King Solomon was an important figure in Freemasonic history. For Freemasons, the Solomonic Temple was the only building on Earth which was erected as a result of God's direct intervention in accordance with His rules. The reconstruction of the Solomonic Temple in Freemasonic thought represented the intention to imitate the rules of a divine architecture, to apply the natural laws of proportion and balance, and to search for an individual and common purification. The Temple became a moral edifice as an example of what was noble, splendid and true in the first ages of the world.[8] This was, then, the first reference to Freemasonry in the garden.

From this back door of the Villa, a garden path led to the altar of friendship composed of a stone pedestal with two colossal busts of Phocion and Epicurus. On one side of the pedestal there was an inscription dedicated to Girolamo Ascanio Giustinian, senator of the Venetian republic, a Freemason and closed friend of Querini. On the other side there was a Latin inscription saying: HYEME / AC AESTATE/ET PROPE/ ET PROCUL/DUM VIVIMOS/ ET ULTRA (In Winter and in Summer, always till we live and beyond). The pedestal also featured a brotherly shake of hands and a caduceus. (Fig. 2) The caduceus was an ancient astrological symbol of commerce and is associated with the Greek god Hermes, the messenger for the gods, conductor of the dead, and protector of merchants. Hermes was an important figure for Freemasons, as he was identified with Hermes Trismegistus (Hermes the thrice-greatest), the herald and keeper of mysteries and also the god of trial and initiation. Hermes Trismegistus was credited with numerous writings, reputed to be of immense antiquity. The Hermetic books, first printed in the late fifteenth century, were supposed to contain the Egyptian mysteries, which were believed to be a key to a complete knowledge of the Universe and of man.

Fig. 3. Ceres, Justine Wynne Rosemberg, Altichiero, Padova, 1787, Pl. III.

The Hermetic movement influenced the development of Freemasonry and became part of the first system of lodges, which emerged in Scotland, adding to the already Masonic lore the myth of the secret order of invisible brethren who were dedicated to the search of ultimate truths and to the understanding of the mysterious universe.[9] Thus, this altar was a clear reference to Masonic brotherhood and Hermeticism.

It was on top of this friendship altar that Querini chose to place the busts of two famous Athenian characters: Phocion and Epicurus. Phocion was a famous Athenian statesman whose advice was frequently ignored by the Athenian Assembly, in the same way Querini's reforms were ignored and rejected by the Venetian government.[10] The philosopher Epicurus was one of the first Greeks to break from the god-fearing and god-worshipping tradition common at the time.[11] His ideas could be linked to Freemasonry, as this semi-secret society placed itself beyond any particular religion. Freemasonry was not based on a revealed religion: Freemasons as individuals could profess any creed. As Freemasons, they professed a rational religion of nature, a "Religion in which all Men agree," that is, a universal religion. At the core of this natural religion was the idea of a Supreme Principle Creator and an understanding of the moral law.[12] Epicurus not only held a rational view of religion, but also showed little interest in participating in the politics of the day. He advocated instead seclusion. The most well-known Epicurean verse, which epitomizes his philosophy, is *lathe biōsas,* meaning "live secretly," i.e. live without pursuing glory or wealth, but anonymously, enjoying little things like food, the company of friends, etc. Epicurus formed The Garden, a school named for the garden he owned that served as the school's meeting place.[13] Querini followed his example when he decided to retire from politics and lay out the garden of Altichiero, where he could meet up with his enlightened, Masonic circle of friends.

Leaving the altar of friendship, and following the garden path described by the Countess, we reach near the bank of the river a statue of Ceres (Fig. 3). Countess Rosenberg reports that it was placed here in 1770 to honor the foundation of the Agriculture Academy in Venice. Among the Romans, Ceres was the goddess of agriculture; among the Greeks she was worshiped under the name of Demeter, as the symbol of the prolific earth. To her is attributed the institution of the Eleusinian Mysteries in Greece, the most popular of all the ancient initiations. The Greco-Roman Eleusinian and Isaic mystery cults required initiates to await enlightenment, while being kept isolated in darkness, and there were rules concerning silence, patience, and fortitude.[14] These mysteries became part of Freemasonic rituals, as they suggested a Masonic initiation.[15]

In the drawing provided by Rosenberg, Ceres is sitting on a globe showing the three astrological signs of Libra, Scorpio and Sagittarius, which represent the three elements air, water and fire. During some Masonic rites the candidate had to pass the trial by air, water and fire before reaching enlightenment.[16] Ceres is also holding a cornucopia, symbol of abundance and adopted in Freemasonic symbolism as the jewel of the Stewards of a Lodge.[17] Finally the goddess is sitting near a column with an owl on top. Owls were emblematic of night and death. So to a Freemasonic eye, this statue stood for trials of initiation. However to a non-Freemasonic eye, like that of our Countess, it only indicated agriculture. After having described the monuments at the back of the Villa, Countess Rosenberg reaches the façade of the villa and reports that it was covered with two acacias while the portico was decorated with rose bushes. Acacia (Mimosa Nilotica or Acacia Vera) is a symbol of immortality, innocence, and of initiation in Freemasonic thought and the rose associated with Isis and Horus/Harpocrates was considered a flower of silence and secrecy.[18] As an emblem of Isis and later of Venus, roses were used in Isaic rites. Lucius, the protagonist of Apuleius's work *The Golden Ass,* eats roses during his initiation and the flower of Isis was the unfading rose.[19]

A bit farther away from the parterre in front of the house, there was a botanical garden with an altar dedicated to Tranquility, and a statue of the *Genius loci.* In Roman mythology, a *Genius loci* was the protective spirit of a place. It was often depicted as a snake.[20] The serpent had a prominent place in all the ancient initiations and religions. Among the Egyptians, it was the symbol of Divine Wisdom when extended at length, and the serpent with his tail in his mouth was an emblem of eternity. A serpent was also a symbol of healing. Sometimes the serpent was represented with Harpocrates, the Egyptian god of silence.[21] In classical times, his statue was often placed at the entrance of temples and places where the mysteries were celebrated, as an indication of the silence and secrecy that should there be observed. So the *Genius loci* under the form of a serpent could also be a reference to Freemasonic silence and initiation at Altichiero's gardens.

From the façade of the Villa, walking down a long avenue and following a spiral path, one would reach the Temple of Apollo. Apollo is the Sun God and in Freemasonic thought symbolizes rationality, strength, stability. The Sun is a male symbol and it is always present in the Lodge together with the Moon, which symbolizes intuition and sensitiveness. Not far from Apollo statue there was in fact a statue of Artemis/Diana, a goddess identified with the moon.[22] Apollo as the sun god also symbolized enlightenment, and the spiral path that the visitor had to follow to reach this statue could be a reference to the path towards enlightenment.

To the right of the hill where the Apollo Temple was placed, a big portion of soil was dedicated to agricultural experiments. As a man of the enlightenment, Querini was interested in new agricultural experimentations based on diversification and rotation of crops. In the center of this big portion of the garden there was a statue of Hercules placed on top of a column. Hercules represents strength. Strength, Wisdom and Beauty are words with powerful Masonic connotations.[23] In Altichiero, strength is represented by this statue of Hercules, Beauty by a temple dedicated to Venus and Wisdom by another temple dedicated to Athena Pallas (Minerva for the Romans), which was added after Rosenberg's description. We know of its existence because Querini expressed the wish to be buried inside this temple.[24] A marble bas-relief inserted on the plinth of the Hercules column portrays an angry Timon of Athens in the act of destroying the altar of friendship, while Mercury interceded for him with Jupiter watching the scene.[25] According to Rosenberg, it was a gift to Angelo Querini from his friend Gaspare Gozzi. Timon was a wealthy lord of Athens who overextended his munificence by showering patronage on parasitic writers and artists, and delivering his dubious friends from their financial straits. When Timon's creditors made their demands for immediate payment, Timon found himself abandoned by his former friends.[26] The reference here could be autobiographical and linked to Querini's political battles. A similar reference to his political career could be the altar dedicated to the three furies: Ignorance, Envy and Calumny, which was placed in a little wood at the end of the garden.

From here the Countess continued her stroll through the garden along the avenue that leads to the house, where there were a number of little *bosquets* named the "Museum" because of the antiquities scattered around this area. Starting from the end, there was a statue of a small Bacchus, a bust of Euripides, and a statue of Fortune. A bit farther away, in the following clearing, was a monument dedicated to the grand duke of Tuscany, Leopold II. It was placed here after his visit to Altichiero in 1785.[27] On top of it was a sphinx and on the side of the monument a bas-relief with Apollo, Pegasus and the spring of Hippocrene (Fig. 4). The inscription said: AD IRRIGANDUM SEMINA VIRTUTIS (sow the seeds of virtue). In Greek mythology, Hippocrene was the name of a fountain on Mt. Helicon. It was sacred to the Muses and was formed by the hooves of Pegasus. Its name literally translates as "Horse's Fountain," and the water was supposed to bring forth poetic inspiration when imbibed. Here the reference to virtue and cultural enlightenment applies to the craft, as Freemasonry was at the heart of much that was enlightened, forward-looking, and promised a regeneration of society. The sphinx, guardian of the Mysteries, is associated with Egyptian mysteries and thus Masonic initiation.

A bit further away, at the center of a *bosquet,* was a colossal statue of the Roman Republican consul Gaius Marius (157 B.C.E.-86 B.C.E.) a Roman general and politician elected Consul an unprecedented seven times during his career. During his tenure on the tribunal, Marius was something of a populist. He was also noted for his dramatic reforms of Roman armies, authorizing recruitment of unlanded citizens, before excluded from military service. This helped the poor plebian class for which the military service became a new possible source of income.[28] Clearly the statue of Marius reflected Querini's political orientations.

Not far from this statue there were some Etruscan monuments with an urn containing the bones of Lucius Cornelius Scipio, collected from Querini in 1782. At the sides there were two phallic symbols (Fig. 5). The worship of the phallus is said to have originated in Egypt. Osiris, the sun god was killed by Typhon/Seth, and cut up into pieces. When Isis, his wife and the moon and earth goddess, heard this, she searched and found all the parts of his body except his phallus. She buried all the parts and built a column [obelisk] as a symbol of his erected phallus, the missing part, and worshipped it.

Fig. 4. Monument dedicated to the Grand Duke of Tuscany (Leopold II of Asburg and Lorraine 1747-1792), Justine Wynne Rosenberg, Altichiero, Padova, 1787, Pl. IX.

In Egypt, obelisks were originally erected in honor of the sun god and they were an ancient phallic symbol of the male and solar energy. The obelisks in Freemasonic symbolism were associated with the sun and were symbols of continuity, power, stability, resurrection and immortality. In Continental Freemasonry, the monument in the Master's Degree is often made in the form of an obelisk, with the letters M. B. inscribed upon it.[29]

291

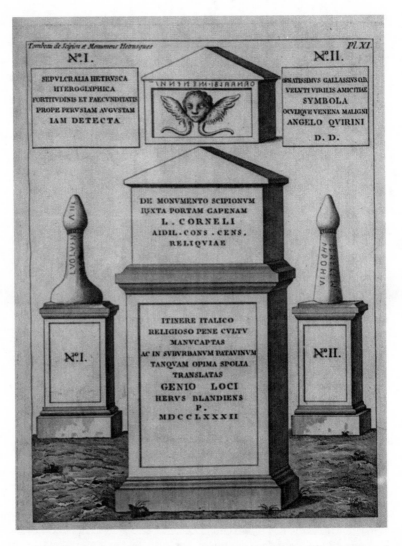

Fig. 5. Urn with bones of Lucius Cornelius Scipio, Justine Wynne Rosenberg, Altichiero, Padova, 1787, Pl. XI.

At the center of this area called the Museum there was also a temple of Venus, which looked like a Chinese pagoda. One had to follow a spiral path in order to reach the temple. Inside there were busts of Scipio, Plato, Silla, and Demostenes and on the wall was reported an inscription from Bacon's work *De Veritate*. Venus was the goddess of beauty, and beauty was symbolically one of the three supports of a Lodge. It was normally represented by the

Corinthian column, because Corinthian is the most beautiful of the ancient orders of architecture.[30] The construction of a Chinese type of building was also a sign of Querini's enlightened mind as a wide-ranging eclecticism was associated with a broadening of the mind and a liberalization of ideas: it indicated universality and freedom from bigotry.

Leaving the hill where the temple to Venus was placed, one would enter a space called the Canopy, which contained some Egyptian antiquities. Canopus (or Canobus) was an Ancient Egyptian coastal town, located in the Nile Delta near of modern-day Alexandria. In this part of the garden, the link with Freemasonry is also reinforced by the presence of Egyptian statues and inscriptions. It was generally believed that the prototypes of initiatory architecture were Egyptian, as Egypt was the home of Hermetic magic developed by the Egyptian priests who venerated Hermes Trismegistus, the first Magus. The first piece of this Egyptian collection was a statue of Anubis. This Egyptian deity was an equivalent to the Greek Hermes, having the head of a jackal, with pointed ears and snout, which the Greeks frequently changed to those of a dog. His duty was to accompany the souls of the deceased to Hades or Amenthes, and assist Horus in weighing their actions under the inspection of Osiris.[31] Part of the collection featured also two Isaic tablets and the emblem of the Nile, a sculpture with the body of a woman and the head of a lion carrying an ankh or key (as Rosenberg says) on its paw (Fig. 6). This idol was collected with the Isiac tablets near Memphis. The Isaic tablets were regarded as containing all secrets of initiation.[32] The ankh, an Egyptian hieroglyphic character, was associated with eternal life and it became a powerful hermetic symbol.[33] The statue of the Nile, was in fact a representation of the Egyptian goddess Sekmet. The Goddess Sekhmet was associated with war and battle. Her name literally means "the Powerful One," and she was the punisher of the damned, those who revolted against moral law in the underworld.[34] Opposite to Sekmet's statue was a statue of Isis (Fig. 7). The piece came from the Adrian's villa. Isis, sister and the wife of Osiris, was worshiped by the Egyptians as the great goddess of nature. In the eighteenth century, largely under the influence of Terrasson's novel *Séthos* from 1731, it was believed that her mysteries constituted one

Fig. 6. Emblem of the Nile (Sekmet), Justine Wynne Rosenberg, Altichiero, Padova, 1787, Pl. XIX.

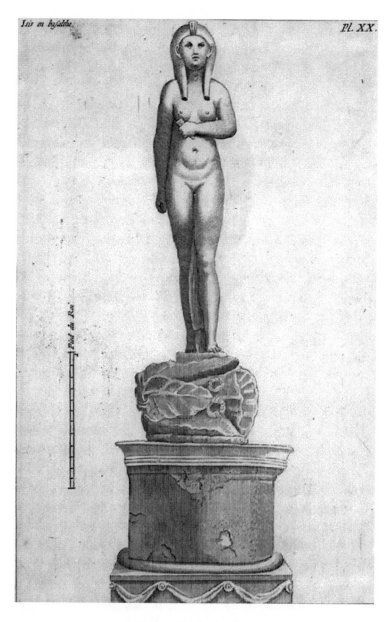

Fig. 7. Isis, Justine Wynne Rosenberg, Altichiero, Padova, 1787, Pl. XX.

of the degrees of the ancient Egyptian initiation. The last piece of this Canopy was a head of Jupiter Ammon. Jupiter Ammon so called by the Greeks, was Amun, the supreme God among the Egyptians of Thebes.[35]

Together with the Canopy, another interesting part of the garden was the so-called "Young's woods" situated to the right of the house. At the entrance there was an wrought-iron gate and two statues of the pre-Socratic Greek philosophers, Heraclitus and Democritus. Inside this space, which looked like real woods with trees and bushes, there were scattered around broken columns, sarcophaguses, and other antiquities. Among some of these ruins and leaning on a column was a statue of Saturn, the god of time, holding a clepsydra and a scepter. A bit farther away was a broken column, which was recuperated by Querini from the ruins of Baiamonte Tiepolo's house in Venice. Tiepolo was the leader of a political battle against the Doge Gradenigo, who in 1297 promulgated some rules that limited the democracy of the Venetian Republic. The Duke banned him from the city and had his house demolished. Later, a column of infamy was placed on the same spot.[36] This is the broken column that Querini collected and made a symbol of fight for democracy. The column inscription, which said MONUMENTUM ANTIQUAE DEMOCRATIE (Monument to ancient democracy), was a clear reference to Querini's political views. In addition, the broken column has a Masonic meaning: it symbolizes the destruction of the Solomonic Temple and the effort that every brother has to make in order to build a new ideal temple.

Another interesting piece of these woods was a botanical clock with a Janus statue, holding a lance used as gnomon to measure the hours on small columns placed around in ellipsis. In Roman mythology, Janus was the god of gates, doors, doorways, beginnings, and endings. He was usually depicted with two faces looking in opposite directions and was frequently used to symbolize change or transition, such as the progression of past to future, of one condition to another, of one vision to another.[37] Being a god of transition explains his placement in these woods where Freemasonic initiation could have taken place. Near this botanical clock, on a higher spot that one could reach after climbing seven steps, was a statue of Cybele, the Phyrgian Earth mother, that Rosenberg calls "Egyptian

Isis." Her head was crowned with a tower. She was holding the sun and moon in her hands and had the three elements inscribed on her belt. Near her statue on the ground was an enigmatic inscription reported by the Countess.[38] Here the first Masonic reference is given by the seven steps that the visitor had to climb in order to reach the statue of Cybele. Seven is an important number in Masonic symbolism. Seven are the steps to enter the temple.[39] The symbolic value of the number seven also derives from the seven liberal arts and sciences, which, according to the old Legend of the Craft, were the foundation of Freemasonry.[40] In addition, Cybele was considered a life-death-rebirth deity. She was associated with the Mystery religion concerning her son, Attis, who was castrated and resurrected.[41] Ceremonies instituted in Phrygia in honor of Attis, the lover and son of Cybele were but a modification of the Eleusinian and Isaic mysteries. Thus, like Isis and Ceres this goddess was associated with initiation rites.

Following the path towards the river there was a Labyrinth. At the entrance there were two busts of Fortune and Repentance, the latter represented by Marsya. The interior was divided into four parterres with flowers and four busts representing the four seasons. At the center was a statue of Diogenes. Nearby an inscription said: NATURA VICTOR HUMANAE (nature defeats humanity). On the pillars at the exit of the Labyrinth there were two statues of Hercules and Paris, indicating that death doesn't make a distinction between the strong and the weak (at least according to the Countess's interpretation). To the west of the labyrinth there were two sarcophaguses, one with representations of Theseus's history and a sphinx, and another with a statue of St. John the Baptist.

The statue of St. John is a reference to the lodge Querini belonged to. This lodge, "La Fidelité," belonged to the Chapter of St. John. Both St. John the Baptist and St. John the Evangelist were venerated as patron saints of the Masonic Craft.[42] In the eighteenth century in all continental lodges, the prologue of St. John's Gospel was recited to open the lodge meetings.[43] Most probably this is the part of the garden that could have been used as an initiatory path by Querini and his circle of friends. Cybele, Janus, the statue of Time, sarcophaguses, the broken column, Young woods and the

297

Labyrinth were all symbols of death and transition. The woods were a memorial to Edward Young (1683-1765) the poet and author of *Night Thoughts*. Young was a melancholy poet who dwelt on the macabre and on death.

The tombs and sarcophaguses may be read by Freemasons as a reference to the Hiramic legend. According to this legend, Hiram, the builder of the Solomonic temple, was murdered by three masonic workers who wanted him to reveal the Master's Word, and they buried him clandestinely. Hiram was reburied in the Temple and Solomon punished his murderers. The initiate to the third degree of Freemasonry embodies Hiram, and the raising of his body from the first grave signifies the rebirth to a new enlightened life. The labyrinth of Altichiero's garden could have been as an initiatory path, as the idea of labyrinth is associated with that of the initiatory cave used in the ancient Mystery cults to evoke the descent into the land of death, and rebirth as new individuals. Besides, in the Masonic temple perambulation, the candidate should follow the sun path starting from the *winter* solstice corresponding to the South under the astrological sign of Capricon to the *spring* equinox in the East under Aries in order to reach the *summer* Solstice to the North under Cancer where the ascending movement of the sun ends and the descending movement starts continuing to the autumn Equinox in the West under Libra.[44] The perambulation starts from the South towards the East and symbolizes the ascending movement of the sun, the path from darkness to light. It forms a square inside the Temple, which evokes the seasons: Winter, Spring, Summer, Autumn. According to Rosenberg, Altichiero's labyrinthine path led through four parterres representing the four seasons, and only after passing through those and other tortuous paths would one reach the center, where there was a statue of Diogenes holding a lantern.

Diogenes (412 B.C.E.- 399 B.C.E.), the Cynic Greek philosopher who avoided earthly pleasures, and criticized the artificiality of much human conduct, became for eighteenth century intellectuals a symbol of reason against prejudices, liberty, and antidogmatism. According to D'Alambert, the French philosopher, Diogenes was a true life model representing the power of free criticism and the equality of natural status.[45] His placement at the center of the Labyrinth could represent the candidate's overcoming of errors throughout his life and his final awakening as the honest man Diogenes was looking for with his lantern. At the same time Diogenes was an example of free thinking and liberal enlightened ideas.

The Countess's itinerary through the garden ends in Young's woods. The allegorical compositions and numerous inscriptions that Rosenberg describes demonstrate a specific plan carried out by Querini in the garden of Altichiero. Everything had a meaning and was created to convey a message. The garden, his life's work, was the image of Angelo Querini, of his classical and modern culture, of his archaeological interests, of his political battles and enlightenment ideas and of his Masonic creed. It was a multifaceted portrait of the owner whose presence was revealed at each step. At the same time, the mythological deities and archaeological finds from Egypt, Greece and Rome, and the Labyrinth, together with the so-called "Young's woods," conveyed also another message to the Querini's Venetian brothers who were able to read Altichiero's hermetic symbolism. To them, this garden represented an initiatory space where they could meet and express in secrecy their *avant garde* enlightement ideals.

Notes

1. C. Francovich, *Storia della Massoneria in Italia dalle origini alla Rivoluzione Francese*, (Firenze: La Nuova Italia, 1974), 41. Maffei, like Poleni, Algarotti and other exponents of the Venetian enlightenment was also critical of the decadent government of Venice and he proposed the reformation of the Republic in his work *Suggerimento per la perpetua preservazione della Repubblica Veneta atteso il presente Stato d'Italia e d'Europa* (which was published for the first time only in 1797). A. Scolari, "Il consiglio politico di Scipione Maffei, contributo alla storia delle dottrine politiche in Italia nel secolo XVIII," in *Atti e Memorie dell'Accademia d'Agricoltura, Scienze, Lettere di Verona*, V(1931)ix: 37-87.
2. Justine Wynne Rosenberg, *Altichiero*, Padova, 1787, 47.
3. G.F. Torcellan, *Una figura della Venezia settecentesca: Andrea Memmo. Ricerche sulla crisi dell'aristocrazia veneziana*, (Roma: Istituto per la

Collaborazione Culturale, 1963), 30-35.

4. Renata Targhetta, *La massoneria veneta dalle origini alla chiusura delle logge 1729-1785,* (Udine: Istituto di Storia, 1988), 150-151.

5. Paolo Preto, *Girolamo Festari, Medicina, Lumi e Geologia nella Valdagno del 700,* (Valdagno: Comune di Valdagno, 1995), 31-36.

6. Patrizia Granziera, *The Ideology of the English Landscape Garden 1720-1750,* PhD thesis, University of Warwick, 1997.

7. The two Latin inscriptions said : DESPERATIS HYPPOCRATES VETAT ADHIBERE MEDICINAM (to the desperate, Hippocrates prohibits maedicaments) and LAETARI ET FACERE BENE (to be happy and to do good).

8. According to the legend, after the flood Pythagoras found the two pillars on which the secrets of geometry were inscribed and he, together with the great geometer Hermes Trismegistus, told these secrets to the Greeks. These pillars, among others, were set up by Solomon to build his temple. The left-hand column was called Joachim and it was associated with establishment and legality; the right-hand column of the Temple was called Boaz and symbolized strength. Jones Knoop, *The Genesis of Freemasonry,* (Manchester: Manchester University Press, 1949), 67-69.

9. David Stevenson, *The Origins of Freemasonry. Scotland's Century 1590-1710,* (Cambridge: Cambridge University Press, 1988), 97-105.

10. In politics, he is known chiefly as the consistent opponent of the anti-Macedonian party, headed by Demosthenes, Lycurgus and Hypereides, whose fervent eloquence he endeavoured to damp by recounting the plain facts of Athens's military and financial weakness and her need of peace. Phocion's criticisms were often unpopular with the Athenian Assembly. Claude Orrieux, Pauline Schmitt Pantel, *Storia Greca,* (Bologna: Il Mulino, 1995), 377-385.

11. *The Internet Encyclopedia of Philosophy,* http://www.iep.utm.edu/

12. David Stevenson, op. cit., 117-124.

13. *The Internet Encyclopedia of Philosophy,* http://www.iep.utm.edu

14. E. O. James, *The Cult of the Mother Goddess,* (London: Thames and Hudson, 1959), 153.

15. James Stevens Curl, *Art and Architecture of Freemasonry,* (London: B.T. Batsford, 1991), 35.

16. Ibid., 158.

17. http://www.phoenixmasonry.org/mackeys_encyclopedia/h.htm

18. A. E. Waite, *A New Encyclopedia of Freemasonry (Ars Magna Latomorum) and of Cognate Instituted Mysteries, Their Rites, Literature and History,* (London: 1921), 1-3.

19. James Stevens Curl, op. cit., 142.

20. Anna Ferrari, *Dizionario di Mitologia Greca e Latina*, (Novara: Istituto Geografico De Agostini, 2006), 589.

21. A. E. Waite, op. cit., 10.

22. Eugenio Bonvicini, *Massoneria Moderna: Storia, Ordinamenti, Esoterismo, Simbologia*, (Foggia: Bastogi Editore, 1994), 221.

23. These three concepts were evoked before starting a lodge meeting, when three candles were lit and the following words were pronounced: That Wisdom might enlighten our work, Strength make it steady, and Beauty irradiate it. Eugenio Bonvicini, op. cit., 222. The three orders of architecture and the three cardinal points were also associated to these three concepts: the Doric order stood for Strength (West) Ionic for Wisdom (East) and Corinthian for Beauty (South). A. E. Waite, op. cit., 43.

24. Bruno Brunelli Bonetti, *Un Riformatore Mancato, Angelo Querini* in *Archivio Veneto*, V (1950-51), 46-49,

25. On the plinth some Latin inscriptions reported the following dialogue;. Timon: O JUPITER SODALITIE.....JURAMENTI PRAESES UBI ARDENS CANDENS TERRIFICUM FULMEN (Oh Jupiter of the brotherhood, guardian of oath, where the lightning is burning, shining, terrifying) Mercury: TIMONEM PROBITAS EVERTIT ET HUMANITAS (honesty and humanity demolished Timon).

26. Rolf Soellner, *Timon of Athens: Shakespeare's Pessimistic Tragedy*, (Columbus: Ohio State University Press, 1979).

27. Leopold II of Asburg and Lorraine (1747-1792) was Grand duke of Tuscany from 1765 to 1790. He was the ninth son of Francis duke of Lorraine, husband of the emperess Maria Theresia, who became Freemason in 1731. Renata Targhetta, op. cit., 27.

28. Augusto Fraschetti, *Storia di Roma*, (Catania: Edizioni Prisma, 2003), 141-144.

29. See http://www.phoenixmasonry.org/mackeys_encyclopedia/o.htm

30. A. E. Waite., op. cit., 43.

31. Anna Ferrari, op. cit., 100.

32. A. E. Waite., op. cit., 10.

33. Clement Salaman and Dorine Van Oyen and Wharton, William D. Jean-Pierre Mahé, (translation) *The Way of Hermes: New Translations of The Corpus Hermeticum and The Definitions of Hermes Trismegistus to Asclepius*, (Rochester: Inner Traditions, 2000), 19.

34. Lorna Oakes and Lucia Gahlin, *Ancient Egypt*, (New York: Barnes and Noble, 2003), 294.

35. Anna Ferrari, op. cit., 73, 564.

36. Gerardo Ortalli and Giovanni Scarabello, *Breve Storia di Venezia*, (Pisa: Pacini Editore, 2001), 49-52.

37. Anna Ferrari, op. cit., 592-594.

38. A Latin inscription on a memorial tablet near Cybele's statue said: D. M. AELIA LAELIA CRISPIS/ NEC VIR NEC MVLIER NEC ANDROGYNA/NEC PVELLA NEC IVVENIS NEC ANUS /NEC CASTA NEC MERETX NEC PUDICA/SED OMNIA/ SVBILATA/NEQUE FAME NEQUE FERRO NEQUE VENENO/SED OMNIBVS/NEC COELO NEC AQUIS NEC TERRIS /SED VBIQVE IACET/ LVCIVS AGATHO PRISCIVS/NEC MARITVS NEC AMATOR/NEC NECESSARIVS/ NEQUE MOERENS NEQUE GAVDENS NEQVE FLENS HANC /NEC MOLEM NEC PYRAMIDEM NEC SEPVLCRVM/SED OMNIA/S cit. ET NES cit.CVI POSVERIT / (Elia Lelia Crespi, neither man nor woman, neither androgynous nor maiden, neither young nor old, neither chaste nor prostitute, but all of them; neither instigated from hunger nor from sword or from poison but from all of them; she lies neither in heaven nor in the waters, nor on earth, but everywhere, Lucio Agato Prisco, neither husband nor lover, nor relative, neither afflicted nor joyous, nor crying, this [tomb] neither mausoleum, nor pyramid, nor sepulcher but all of them. [Lucio] does not know for sure to whom he dedicated it.)

39. James Stevens Curl, op. cit., 75.

40. Eugenio Bonvicini, op. cit., 242.

41. Lynn E., Roller, *In Search of God the Mother: The Cult of Anatolian Cybele*, (Berkeley: University of California Press, 1999), 230-231.

42. James Stevens Curl, op. cit., 30.

43. Eugenio Bonvicini, op. cit., 229.

44. Eugenio Bonvicini, op. cit., 237.

45. Anna lo Bianco, "L'antico come citazione filologica e movente etico di Ghezzi pittore" in *Piranesi e la Cultura Antiquaria*, Universitá degli Studi di Roma, Istituto di Storia dell'Arte, Atti del Convengo 14-17 Novembre 1979, Anna lo Bianco, ed., (Roma: Multigrafica Editrice, 1985), 195-202.

Advent Garden and the Waldorf Imagination: Esotericism, Ritual, and Childhood

Sarah W. Whedon

Six-year-old Maya and her classmates stood at the edge of the darkened room awaiting their turns, each clutching an apple carved to hold an unlit candle. [1] It was a cool evening in the late fall of 1983 and the Waldorf School of the Finger Lakes was holding a celebration that was becoming established tradition for the school and would continue for years to come, the Advent Garden. One at a time the children quietly walked the path of the Advent Garden that parents and teachers had carefully assembled for them. The floor of the room had been marked by a great spiral built of evergreen boughs. At the center of the spiral the adults had placed a stump and on the stump one large candle burned. When it came Maya's turn she carefully walked along the spiral, carrying her apple and candle, and lit her own small candle at this large central flame while parents and classmates watched. Then Maya knew she was permitted to place her candle anywhere along the spiral as she made her way back out. As she set it down her little candle revealed a colorful gnome that had been hidden in the shadows of the evergreens. Maya then continued along the path, back out to the end of the spiral, and the next child took his turn.

Participants understood this ostensibly simple ritual had multiple layers of meaning. It connected the Waldorf School of the Finger Lakes to the history and European origins of Waldorf education; it marked a moment in the annual cycle of natural seasons; it taught a spiritual lesson about divine truth; it provided aesthetic pleasure for the children themselves; and finally it displayed the children for their parents in a positive light and by extension told their parents about themselves as parents. These multiple layers of meaning were made possible by the social context for the enactment of esoteric ideas, where participants had varied levels of knowledge of and commitment to Anthroposophy, as well as by an esoteric anthropology of the child that positions children's subjectivities differently from adults. Thus the meaning for this ritual cannot simply be determined by an external reading of its symbols. Rather putting a reading of the participants' own interpretations into conversation with an external perspective reveals the multiplicity of meaning. The Advent Garden is a particularly interesting ritual for such analysis because those meanings reflect salient themes across American Waldorf education.

Attending to ritual is one method of responding to the charge Arthur Versluis makes that in esoteric studies, "the gist of investigation...seems to be going...toward the complete divorce of the text from the lived experience and even the denial of the lived experience." Study of the Advent Garden as practiced in Waldorf schools is not best conducted in terms of the mysticism or esoteric consciousness to which Versluis draws our attention, because the children who walk the Advent spiral are not intentionally cultivating any such experience. However, it does take seriously "the practitioner's experience." [2]

Before proceeding to analyzing the meanings of the Advent Garden we need to briefly put this ritual in its context. Little scholarly attention has been directed at either Anthroposophy or Waldorf Education. Scholars of religion and esotericism occasionally discuss Rudolf Steiner and Anthroposophy. However, they rarely give the topics sustained attention, often mentioning them primarily to place them within the historical stream of the Theosophical Society or western esotericism more broadly.[3] Meanwhile Waldorf education has been studied primarily by education scholars.[4] Thus scholars of esotericism are missing an opportunity to examine a strong esoteric movement that through practical applications such as Waldorf education takes up a significant and fascinating place in American culture.

Waldorf education was but one of many practical applications, such as agriculture and finance, on which Rudolf Steiner (1861-1925) lectured at the request of students of Anthroposophy, his system of spiritual teachings. Anthroposophy is a Western esoteric system that emphasizes knowledge of the human and each person's capacity to develop spiritual sensory apparatus within a complex historical cosmology involving "Christocentric evolutionism."[5] The system has been described by insiders in various ways, including as occult and esoteric, but perhaps most often (at least in the American context) as a "spiritual science," such that anyone can take up the same methods of spiritual research to verify the knowledge. Henry Barnes, long-time Waldorf educator and former general secretary of the Anthroposophical Society in America, articulates this point when he says, "Anthroposophy ... is not a mystical path, but one of discovery and of objective reflection built upon the foundations of a *scientific* method of knowing."[6]

Anthroposophy as a knowledge system and as an organization emerged out of an esoteric milieu. Steiner worked with the Theosophical Society before forming the Anthroposophical Society and Anthroposophy exhibits the six components that Antoine Faivre asserts are characteristic of the mode of thought that is esotericism. These are correspondences (that microcosm mirrors marcocosm, "as above so below"), living nature (that within a complex, multilayered cosmos, the book of nature is a particular source for wisdom), imagination and mediations (that there is an internal process by means of which the individual comes to achieve wisdom, sometimes through the help of unseen beings), experience of transmutation (that the individual who follows this path will ultimately be dramatically changed), the praxis of concordance (that the elements of one tradition can be found in another), and transmission (that wisdom is passed on from teacher to student).[7] We shall see many of these components present in the Advent Garden.

Waldorf education is an alternative pedagogical system primarily for elementary education, but also extended to early childhood and high school years, which was originally developed in Stuttgart, Germany, in 1918, under Steiner's direction. Waldorf schools exhibit a number of identifying features. Ideally, teachers remain with a class from first through eighth grade, providing steady guidance through these formative years. Pedagogy is based on a view of human development involving the integration of hands, hearts, and heads, which Waldorf educators believe develop consecutively. The arts are integrated into the curriculum, which emphasizes literature and history where a cultures' narratives are chosen based on a correspondence between human development and world history. For example, third graders are taught Old Testament stories, because of an understanding that these stories are most appropriate for their developmental stage. The curriculum emphasizes rhythm and pattern where days begin with ritualized greetings, recitation of morning verse, and other songs or games, followed by a ninety minute "main lesson." Other parts of the day may include mathematics, foreign languages, or eurythmy (a dance form developed by Steiner). [8]

The relationship between Anthroposophy and Waldorf education is a complex and often uneasy one. While the pedagogy is rooted in an Anthroposophical anthropology and cosmology, it is expected that students are never directly taught Anthroposophy, and adults within the schools have varying levels of knowledge of and commitment to Anthroposophy. Therefore the culture of Waldorf schools presents a complex process of the enactment of esotericism. The following analysis of the Waldorf ritual of Advent Garden is based primarily on archival and oral history evidence from the Waldorf School of the Finger Lakes, which opened its doors in Ithaca, New York in 1982 and had to close in 1999. Although there is diversity within the approximately one hundred and fifty schools currently recognized by the Association of Waldorf Schools of North America, this school was in many ways typical, and the analysis is informed by my larger research project, which includes other American Waldorf schools. Advent Garden, sometimes called Winter Garden, is celebrated in Waldorf schools across the country, usually by young children through about second grade, as just one of several annual school festivals of European origin, such as May Day and Michaelmas.

Advent Garden emerges in part from a Christian liturgical calendar in which Advent is a period of preparation for Christmas when the birth of Jesus Christ is commemorated, beginning on the fourth Sunday preceding that holiday. [9] Many Christian churches and families celebrate Advent with candle-lighting rituals and evergreens. [10] This emphasis on light in preparation for the Christmas season is mirrored in the Waldorf ritual with the candles in the spiral

306

of evergreens. Although not all Waldorf families are Christian, many are, and these symbols are visible in American public spaces at Christmas time, thus naturalizing the choice to celebrate Advent Garden. Let us turn, then, to the meanings that are made in the specific ritual of the Advent Garden: connection to history and community, celebration of natural cycles, honoring the divine, aesthetic pleasure for children, and the display of children for adults.

Waldorf History/Community

The first of the layers of meaning that I have identified in the Advent Garden is that its celebration connects a school community to an historical lineage of Waldorf education, as well as an international community, in ways that reflect esotericism's concern for the transmission process. Waldorf educators typically justify their pedagogical choices using a combination of Steiner's teachings and traditions established beginning with the first Waldorf school in Stuttgart, Germany. Using Steiner's writings and lectures as prooftexts is common practice for establishing the authority and authenticity of practical choices.

At the Waldorf School of the Finger Lakes it was common for a November school newsletter to describe and analyze the upcoming celebration of the Advent Garden, or else occasionally a December or January newsletter would recount the event just past. A November 1988 newsletter noted, "The Advent Garden is truly a high point in our yearly School celebrations. The idea of the Garden was first conceived by the teacher of the 'special' class at the first Waldorf school. He wanted to give these children a 'physical' experience of the changing seasons and how that reflects in the human soul."[11] It may in fact be the case that this story is a conflation of more than one historical development that created the Advent Garden.[12] It is unclear at what point exactly the Advent Garden tradition was brought from Stuttgart to the United States. Certainly it was already in use by the time the Waldorf School of the Finger Lakes opened its doors in 1982. Steiner himself did not provide instructions for the celebration of festivals in the schools.[13] However, he did give a number of lectures on festivals, and Waldorf educators do sometimes rely on these to extrapolate for the school context.[14] Regardless of its pedigree, the Advent Garden ritual has been commonly celebrated by American Waldorf schools, and through it celebrants connect themselves to an historically and geographically dispersed Waldorf community and tradition. They also connect themselves to origins in the first Waldorf school at Stuttgart and in Steiner's teachings, thus conferring authenticity on their practices. This authority of the original is the reason newsletters like this one reference the history.

Natural Cycle

To do things in keeping with a Waldorf tradition is not, however, sufficient reason. The most common and most direct reason given for the celebration of the Advent Garden is embedded in observation of the seasonal rhythms of the year. Rhythms and cycles form an important part of Waldorf pedagogy, from the orderly patterns of a school day to cycles of development across the life course. In a lecture on Christmas, Steiner made it clear that even overtly Christian holidays were to be understood as having their origins and deeper meanings in the natural calendar cycle. In his words, "It was as tokens of this 'feeling at one' with Nature and the universe that the great Festivals were inaugurated."[15] Thus, from an Anthroposophical perspective the festivals serve to bring humans into closer and thus more appropriate relationship with nature. This is especially important when Anthroposophists working within the framework of a grand sacred history understand that they are living in "the fifth post-Atlantean epoch" when humans are alienated from nature and spirit.[16] This sort of sacralization of the natural fits also into an American history of nature religion in which out of three central concerns for religion—"God, humanity, and nature"—it is nature that is emphasized, although of course, we shall see that from other perspectives God and humanity each figure prominently in the Advent Garden.[17]

In 1997 in a letter to the second-grade parents of the Waldorf School of the Finger Lakes the teacher provided a typical description of the Advent Garden as it related to the natural seasons. She wrote, "This spiral of evergreens becomes a magical path for the children to walk, one at a time, so that they can physically have the experience of how the world grows dark and nature's activity contracts as winter sets in."[18] Thus the light and darkness of the Advent Garden reflect the patterns of light and darkness of the natural winter season. The teacher's interpretation of the significance of encountering the darkness of the season aligns with Steiner's emphasis on natural cycles. This "magical path" reflects a romanticized and tamed view of nature, which is beautiful and something with which humans can and should harmonize. Here nature is more akin to a gentle and innocent child than to a blizzard. Thus childhood and the natural are constructed in relationship to one another.

This teacher's description further suggests that it is through the embodied experience of the ritual that the children will internalize the knowledge. This is a reflection of the Waldorfian perspective on the child as composed of the component parts of body, heart, and mind (or doing, feeling, and thinking), which speak to one another. The child will learn through the body and transmit this into the heart without having to activate the conscious, linear thinking mind. This is significant because Waldorf educators seek to protect children from having to engage rational, intellectual processes before they are developmentally ready.

Divine/Spiritual

At a deeper level, some teachers also understand the light and darkness of the seasons, which are reflected in the light and darkness of the festival, to be symbolic of personal spiritual light and darkness connected to the Christ figure. A 1984 Waldorf School of the Finger Lakes newsletter stated,

As one walks the spiral path, one can experience the cosmic course of the seasons. In Summer one is completely outside, out in the sunlight, out in nature. But as one spirals in from Summer to Autumn and Winter one finds oneself completely within oneself. Is that also cold darkness? No! Now, one can find a light which shines from within. The light of Love, of the inner man, was given at Christmas time. In the garden it is given to each child.[19]

The Christmas story of the birth of Christ is abstracted here to refer to the mystery of the "Love" or "the inner man," which an Anthroposophically grounded reader would understand as the Cosmic Christ or Christ impulse.

This teacher's explanation in the newsletter expresses virtually the same idea that Steiner expressed when he said of the Christmas season: "Now, when the light of the outer sun is faintest and its warmth feeblest, now is the time when the soul withdraws into the darkness but can find within itself the inner, spiritual Light."[20] Steiner, too, ties this moment in the seasonal cycle to a mythico-historical moment of the Christmas story, and he sees that story as a later manifestation of an older mystery religion: "This sacred moment when the outer light was weakest, when the outer sun was shining with least strength. On that day the pupils were called together and the inner Light revealed itself to them."[21] So celebration and alignment with the natural world become not only good on their own terms, but vessels for accessing deeper spiritual truths of the divine within, and "light" refers simultaneously to the sun, the candle, the child, and the Christ. The ritual of the Advent Garden provides a means of accessing the esoteric mystery of the Christ.

Child's Experience

Scholarship on children's own representations and interpretations of religions indicates that we can expect children to have ideas and experiences that differ from those of adults who may participate in the same religious activities.[22] One of the reasons for multiple layers of meanings to the Advent Garden ritual is that the Waldorf anthropology of the child indicates that the child is insufficiently developed to understand adult explanations of reasons for particular activities. In a popular book on celebrating the festivals, Christine Fynes-Clinton articulates this perspective with respect to festivals when she says, "Great works of art need no explanation; they enrich our lives without extra words. It's the same with the festivals. If children ask "Why?" an uncomplicated answer such as "Because it's just the day for it!" is usually the best one."[23] The intentional choice to keep the adult interpretations hidden from children's knowledge necessitates that children cannot simply parrot what the adults say even if they would want to do so. Indeed, children's experiences of the Advent Garden appear to have been little influenced by any of the meanings thus far discussed. Instead they focus on an immediate aesthetic experience. It is often the case that, whereas Waldorf parents or teachers can describe pedagogical reasons behind activities in the schools, students and former students are more likely to speak of pleasure, or sometimes its twin, displeasure.

When I asked Maya, a former Waldorf School of the Finger Lakes student, who is now in her twenties and working as a teacher's assistant at a Waldorf preschool, if she had memories of Advent Garden, she said, "That was probably one of the most magical things that happened all year."[24] Her language here is similar to that of the teacher who wrote about a "magical path" through cycles of light and darkness. It may be colored by her adult pedagogical training, but she was also able to remember the experience from the perspective of her childhood. She described the experience in terms of mystery, wonder, and embodied aesthetics: "you had your apple with a candle in it and it was all dark. . . this angel or this person dressed in white led you to the center of this *spiral* ... and you had to look really carefully cause there were all these things hidden in it ... a gnome peeking out or a crystal or a shell." She enjoyed the experience of looking and of revelation of the visual: "the awe, you know, how beautiful."[25]

Angela, another former Waldorf student now in college, also remembered the pleasure of Advent Garden as we sat talking together with her mother on their family's front porch:

> That was always something we really looked forward to, and they kept us out of the room where they set everything up and they would usher us in. It was always very dark except for the candles that we would light. It was very solemn, but very deep experience, I guess, which I didn't really focus on when I was little, I just did it. But I could feel the mood change when you were supposed to walk and light a candle. It was just very interesting.[26]

She describes the experience in terms of sight and inner feeling. Again this is an embodied aesthetics. By claiming not to have focused on the depth of meaning to the ritual, Angela signals her

311

awareness from the standpoint of now being a college student that a child's perspective on the event was different from an adult's. Her emphasis is on the doing, on the solemnity and the mood, less than on any meaning of the ritual that might be associated with history, nature, or Christ.

Her mother, Louise, who participated in the same interview immediately chimed in, "It was perfect. I mean as a parent to watch that. We were astounded the first time we saw the Advent Garden. That was just an amazing experience." She went on to compare this event to the May Pole ritual at May Day celebrations in the spring. Both events provided her as a parent with an experience of pleasure in the presentation of her child.

Adult's Experience of Child

Parents, too, received aesthetic pleasure from their own participation as spectators at the Advent Garden, although this was pleasure inflected with different meaning. One Waldorf School of the Finger Lakes newsletter invited parents to attend, promising that, "It is usually a meaningful experience, somehow telling us something about the child."[27] Since the newsletter does not provide us with an indication of what will be learned about the child, it leaves open ambiguous space for parents to develop their own interpretations. These might include the pleasure of seeing one's child behave well and contribute to something that is visually beautiful. It also allows for a displacement of the adult's interest in the natural, the spiritual, or the esoteric as displayed through the child. In other words, it is only the adults who may have a conscious understanding of intentional Waldorfian and Anthroposophical meanings for the Advent Garden, but they enact these meanings through the children. It is not the adults who walk the Advent spiral.[28] This reflects Robert A. Orsi's observation, extrapolated from a study of Catholic childhoods, that

children's bodies, rationalities, imaginations, and desires have all been privileged media for giving substance to religious meaning, for making the sacred present and material not only *for* children but *through* them too for adults in relation to them. The child addressed in religious settings and the religious world that is represented to this child are constituted in relation to each other. This is the dialectic of what is usually misnamed "children's religion."[29]

In other words, what is meaningful can be articulated through children to children themselves, but also to the adults in relationship to them. While the central performance of the Advent Garden involves primarily children's bodies, the performance functions to serve adults at least as much as it does children, and it is only adults who may view it through a consciously esoteric lens.

In a popular book providing instructions for festival celebrations, we see the adult gaze fixed upon the child's gaze. It describes witnessing an Advent garden, setting the scene with music playing and the evergreens laid out in the spiral on the floor. The children approach one at a time, receive a candle and an apple, and move to the center of the spiral. "Here they took a light for their own candle and then proceeded outwards—very carefully, eyes fixed on the candle flame—until they found a gold star on which to place their candle and apple."[30] This is the only segment of their description in which something of the children's attitude or behavior is conveyed. There is a combination of reverence conveyed through the child, who is careful with the candle, and amused, even loving condescension toward the child who struggles to successfully navigate the open flame on an unfamiliar path in front of many watching adults. This romanticized appreciation for the child matches what historians have observed about modern adults' appreciation for a sentimental and innocent child.[31] It also creates a childhood that can be linked to the romanticized nature of the Advent season of darkness.

Conclusions
Thus, depending on age and social position within the school, which are linked to degree of access, knowledge, and reliance on Steiner's teachings, the Advent Garden ritual could be interpreted as a Waldorf tradition, a seasonal celebration, a rite connected to salvific themes, an embodied mystery, or a visually-based projection onto children. Examination of the Advent Garden ritual highlights these themes of innocence, naturalness, and esotericism that are

present throughout American Waldorf schools.

It should be noted that what has been described here are general patterns within the Waldorf School of the Finger Lakes, reflecting patterns that I have observed across American Waldorf schools, and that even with the social groups that constituted the school there was not consensus as to the meaning and value of the ritual. Chris, who was a parent and administrator at the Waldorf School of the Finger Lakes for many years, was concerned about how celebration of the festivals would be perceived by outsiders. He told me that "the festivals were fun and they added—they brought that dimension into the school in a very nice way...but it was always a little bit of a question, more about how other people perceived it or would perceive it...is it a religious school or is it not. With Waldorf there isn't an easy answer...people in our society have trouble with ambiguity."[32]

This very ambiguity may contribute to the endurance of the Advent Garden. In fact, the ritual has been adopted by others, and Advent Garden spirals are sometimes walked in Unitarian Universalist congregations. The esoteric ideas about Christmas time as expressed by Steiner in his lectures were combined with his teachings on child development and education to create embodied ritual practice. However, later the experience becomes available to multiple interpretations depending on participants' esoteric or pedagogical knowledge as well as on their physical position within the ritual enactment. Examination of ritual practice demonstrates that, as Versluis has argued, not "everything is merely text." There is, indeed, more than the text to be studied.[33] The Advent Garden ritual cannot be fully understood without reference to Steiner's texts (in this case mostly lectures), but the process of this interpretation and enactment reveals richer understanding of human experience than is available in the text alone. If we were to read only the works of Rudolf Steiner, we would not learn how children, parents, teachers, and texts worked together in the negotiation of meaning and experience. Extensive as Steiner's works are, neither would we even gain a bird's eye observation of the objective content of the Advent Garden, of Maya and her classmates each taking their turn to walk the spiral.

Notes

1. I presented an earlier version of this paper at the 2006 Association for the Study of Esotericism Conference, Esotericism, Art, and the Imagination, at University of California, Davis, June 2006. I am grateful to Christina Cabeen, Michael Cohn, and Kim Ryser for their feedback and suggestions. I have assigned pseudonyms for interviewees who are not public figures.

2. Arthur Versluis, "Mysticism and the Study of Esotericism: Methods in the Study of Esotericism, Part II" *Esoterica* V (2003): 28-40, 38.

3. See, for example, Daniel van Egmond, "Western Esoteric Schools in the Late Nineteenth and Early Twentieth Centuries," in Roelof van den Broek and Wouter J. Hanegraaff, eds., *Gnosis and Hermeticism: From Antiquity to Modern Times*, (Albany: State University of New York Press, 1998), 311-46; Bruce F. Campbell, *Ancient Wisdom Revived: A History of the Theosophical Movement* (Berkeley: University of California Press, 1980); Joscelyn Godwin, *The Theosophical Enlightenment* (Albany: State University of New York Press, 1994).

4. See for example Stephen Keith Sagarin, *Promise and Compromise: A History of Waldorf Schools in the United States, 1928-1998.* Dissertation (Columbia University, 2004). Also there is a brief discussion in Mitchell L. Stevens, *Kingdom of Children: Culture and Controversy in the Homeschooling Movement* (Princeton and Oxford: Princeton University Press, 2001).

5. Antoine Faivre, *Access to Western Esotericism* (Albany: State University of New York Press, 1994), 90.

6. Henry C. Barnes, *A Life for the Spirit: Rudolf Steiner in the Crosscurrents of Our Time* (Hudson, New York: Anthroposophic Press, 1997), 4.

7. Antoine Faivre, *Access to Western Esotericism* (Albany: State University of New York Press, 1994), 10-15.

8. Ronald E. Koetzsch, "Waldorf Education: Schooling the Head, Hands, and Heart" revised pamphlet published by the Association of Waldorf Schools of North America, 2004, originally published in *East West Journal* 1989 and reprinted in *Utne Reader* 1990.

9. John Rankin, "Christian Festivals" in Alan Brown, ed. *Festivals in World Religions* (London

and New York: Longman Group Limited, 1986, 74-103), 82.

10. Rankin, 83.

11. The Waldorf School of the Finger Lakes, Parent Newsletter, November 14, 1988. Waldorf School of the Finger Lakes records, #6419. Division of Rare and Manuscript Collections, Cornell University Library.

12. A longer version of the narrative is that as early as 1919 in Stuttgart one teacher had children walking a spiral for several pedagogical-therapeutic purposes, but that it was not until 1926 that this was combined with local folk winter holiday customs to create what would become the traditional winter ritual with spiral evergreens, candles, and apples. "Bits and Pieces"2(11), November 20, 2002, Monterey Bay Charter School. www. slv.k12.ca.us/CHARTER/ TITLE9/Bits_Pieces/11_20_02.pdf Access May 15, 2006. Waldorfians searching for a longer history sometimes associate the Advent spiral with labyrinths, but I have not seen historical evidence to make the connection.

13. Interview with Stephen Sagarin April 12, 2005. Sagarin is a longtime Waldorf teacher and former student and has written a dissertation on Waldorf education in America.

14. For example the Open Waldorf webpage on Advent Spiral interprets the Advent Garden in terms of Steiner's lecture "The Birth of Light." http://www.openwaldorf.com/adventspiral.html accessed May 22, 2006.

15. "The Christmas Festival . . ." December 24, 1905, in *The Festivals and Their Meaning: I Christmas* London: Rudolf Steiner Press, 1955, 1967n. p. web address

16. Lawrence Rinder, "Rudolf Steiner's Blackboard Drawings: An Aesthetic Perspective," http://www.bampfa.berkeley.edu/exhibits/steiner/ steineressay.html access May 7, 2006.

17. Catherine L. Albanese, *Nature Religion in America: From the Algonkian Indians to the New Age* (Chicago: University of Chicago Press, 1990), 7.

18. Joan Moora, November 23, 1997 letter to the second grade parents, Waldorf School of the Finger Waldorf School of the Finger Lakes records, #6419. Division of Rare and Manuscript Collections, Cornell University Library.

19. Joan Moora, "Advent Garden," Waldorf School of the Finger Lakes Parent News Letter, December-January 1983-84, Waldorf School of the Finger Lakes records, #6419. Division of Rare and Manuscript Collections, Cornell University Library.

20. Rudolf Steiner, "The Birth of the Sun-Spirit as the Spirit of the Earth. The Thirteen Holy Nights" in *The Festivals and Their Meaning: I Christmas* London: Rudolf Steiner Press, 1955, 1967. n.p. http://wn.rsarchive.org/ Lectures/Christmas/ChrMas_index.html Accessed May 31, 2006.

21. Rudolf Steiner, "Signs and Symbols of the Christmas Festival" December 17, 1906, in *The Festivals and Their Meaning: I Christmas* London: Rudolf Steiner Press, 1955, 1967n.p. http://wn.rsarchive.org/Lectures/Christmas/ChrMas_index.html accessed May 31, 2006.

22. See Susan Ridgley Bales When I Was a Child: Children's Interpretations of First Communion (The University of North Carolina Press, 2006) or Cindy Dell Clark, *Flights of Fancy, Leaps of Faith: Children's Myths in Contemporary America* (Chicago: The University of Chicago Press, 1995).

23. Ann Druitt, Christine Fynes-Clinton, and Marije Rowling. *All Year Round* (Gloucester: Hawthorn Press, no date), 272.

24. Interview December 16, 2005.

25. Interview September 3, 2005.

26. Joan Moora, Letter to second grade parents, November 23, 1997, Waldorf School of the Finger Lakes, Waldorf School of the Finger Lakes records, #6419. Division of Rare and Manuscript Collections, Cornell University Library.

27. However, in some cases adults envious of their children will arrange to walk the spiral on a separate occasion.

28. Robert A. Orsi, "Material Children: Making God's Presence Real for Catholic Boys and Girls and for the Adults in Relation to Them," in *Between Heaven and Earth: The Religious Worlds People Make and the Scholars Who Study Them* (Princeton: Princeton University Press, 2005), 77.

29. Ann Druitt, Christine Fynes-Clinton, and Marije Rowling. *All Year Round.* (Gloucester: Hawthorn Press, n. d.), 108.

30. See, for example, Gary Cross, *Kids Stuff: Toys and the Changing World of American Childhood* (Cambridge: Harvard University Press, 1999), James R. Kincaid, *Erotic Innocence: The Culture of Child Molesting* (Durham: Duke University Press, 1998), and Viviana A. Zelizer, *Pricing the Priceless Child: The Changing Social Value of Children* (New York: Basic Books, Inc., 1981).

31. Interview September 2, 2005.

32. Arthur Versluis, "Mysticism and the Study of Esotericism: Methods in the Study of Esotericism, Part II" *Esoterica* V (2003): 1-26, 31.

About the Editors

Arthur Versluis is Professor in the College of Arts & Letters at Michigan State University. He is author of numerous books, including *Magic and Mysticism, The New Inquisitions, Restoring Paradise, The Esoteric Origins of the American Renaissance, Wisdom's Children,* and *American Transcendentalism and Asian Religions.* He has published articles on topics ranging from comparative federalism to Christian esotericism. He is editor of the journal *Esoterica,* founding co-editor of *JSR: Journal for the Study of Radicalism,* and founding president of the Association for the Study of Esotericism.

Lee Irwin is Professor and Chair of the Religious Studies Department at the College of Charleston in South Carolina. He has studied world religions intensively, with an emphasis on Native American religions, Western esotericism, transpersonal psychology, and contemporary spirituality—particularly in the area of dreams and visions. Among his many published works are: *The Dream Seekers: Native American Visionary Traditions of the Great Plains, Visionary Worlds, The Making and Unmaking of Reality, Awakening to Spirit: On Life, Illumination, and Being,* and *Alchemy of Soul: The Art of Spiritual Transformation.*

John Richards is Professor of Sociology and Philosophy at West Virginia State University, as well as Associate Professor of Humanities at Marshall University Graduate College. His areas of interest include Appalachian and European folk magic, and New Religious Movements.

Melinda Weinstein is Associate Professor of Humanities at Lawrence Technological University and a frequent contributor to the journal *Esoterica.*

Index

Carter, Frederick, 210
Cassirer, Ernst, viii
Casaubon, Isaac, 83
Catholicism, 225-248
Cinema, Esoteric, 23-45
City Dionysia, 11 ff.
Coates, James, 273
Collins, Cecil, xiv, xv, 113-122
Constantine of Pisa, 73-74
Corbin, Henry, viii, 192
Corpus Hermeticum, 27, 83
Costantini, Giovanna, 91-112
Crowley, Aleister, 60, 62
Cumberland, George, 125 ff.
Dali,Salvador, vii
Daly, Mary, 51
Dante, 187
Dark City, 28
Dead Man, 35-42
Dee, John, 191
Dionysus, 5-22
Donnie Darko, 28
Dostoevsky, Fyodor, 151
Doyle, Arthur Conan, 246
Duchamp, Marcel, 94-97, 103
Dworkin, Andrea, 51
Eco, Umberto, 233, 235
Egypt, ancient, 293 ff.
Ehrenreich, Barbara, 51
Eliade, Mircea, 5, 20
Ernst, Max, 91
Esotericism, study of, vii ff.
Euripides, xiv, 5-22
Faivre, Antoine, ix-x, 113
Fanger, Claire, 161-182
Federov, Nikolai, 147-148
Feminism, 51 ff.
Ficino, Marsilio, 83, 92, 204
The Fifth Element, 27
Film, see *Cinema*
Fortune, Dion, 161-182

322

Printed in the United States
122688LV00005B/58/P